The Art of Empowering Others

The life and times of
Gayle Abas Woolson
Knight of Bahá'u'lláh

*She swept through like a conquering queen
but worked like an unpaid serf.*
Elena Marsella, 1949

The Art of Empowering Others

The life and times of
Gayle Abas Woolson
Knight of Bahá'u'lláh

by

Juliet Gentzkow

George Ronald
Oxford

George Ronald, *Publisher*
Oxford
www.grbooks.com

*A catalogue record for this book is available
from the British Library*

ISBN 978–0–85398–633–1

Cover design: Steiner Graphics

For Julien and Colette
and for all of the children of the world

Contents

List of Illustrations

Preface and Acknowledgements

During the final decades of the 1900s, Gayle Woolson was a constant presence both at the Bahá'í House of Worship in Wilmette, Illinois and in the Greater Chicago area. Dressed in formal attire, she could often be seen accompanying groups of children she had trained in public speaking, as they recited their speeches both in the Bahá'í community and at civic organizations. One saw her at small gatherings, showing slides of Latin America in both Spanish and English. She attended most pioneer institutes and summer schools. When I moved to the Wilmette area in 1994, I saw her in these contexts and became aware of her long history of distinguished service. However, it was in her very last years that I became more intimately acquainted with the remarkable depth and consistency of her spiritual nature. She had asked that Ellen Parmelee and I serve respectively as her Power of Attorney for finances and for health care. This resulted in close accompaniment during her final six years in this world.

As executors of her will, it also fell to us to ensure that her belongings were distributed according to her wishes. Her library and papers were bequeathed to the local

Spiritual Assembly where she was domiciled. In going through the boxes containing these and other designated gifts, we discovered that every handwritten note and typed document held historical significance. Wherever possible, Gayle had ensured that facts were verified with primary sources and/or first-hand accounts, and references made to historical reports. Someone asked Gayle, in her later years, if she would write a book or memoirs about her life. She replied that the story was now in fragments which, as we reviewed them, called out to be shared, rather than relegated to shelves seen only by a few. This volume attempts to give context to those fragments, while preserving the first-hand accounts of Gayle and her contemporaries, that their own voices may testify to how dedication to the Bahá'í Faith shaped and transformed their lives and those of communities that emerged through their service.

Many people have generously contributed to the completion of this narrative. I am grateful to Matthew Gentzkow, my son, and his family for the mysterious way in which their needs and generosity created the time and space for the writing to take place. Ellen Parmelee has lovingly accompanied the project from beginning to end. Phil Christensen's gift of an upgrade to Microsoft Office came with encouragement to begin writing the manuscript. Trudy Osvoll, Gayle's niece, kindly shared information about Gayle's family of origin. Eve Shertler, Gayle's co-worker and roommate of several years, has a photographic memory for information that proved indispensable to the narrative. Marlene Koswan offered her home as a haven during many weeks of research. Marlene, Anne Jalali, Lorelei McClure, and Martha Schweitz all gave many hours to reviewing the manuscript, offering valuable critique. Fereydoun Jalali offered expertise in organizing and enhancing time-worn photographs. Anne Perry and Marlene Macke of the Write Life Retreat at Desert Rose provided a creative space in which writers could concentrate and also consult about their work. Lewis Walker, Roger Dahl and Ed Sevcik offered generous assistance from the United States National Bahá'í Archives. Lewis Walker, a long-time trusted friend of Gayle's, generously shared a fount of accurate information about her life and papers. The Spiritual Assemblies of Wilmette, Illinois, of Cedar Rapids, Iowa (Bruce Koerber) and of St Paul (David Sterling) generously provided access to their archives over several years. Steve Townsend's editing of the *Evanston Eagle* preserved both articles about Gayle and those which she wrote about early believers in Evanston. Maureen Haghighi encouraged perseverance with the project. Tarasieh Werle Vahdat of Quito shared documents, photographs, and introductions to friends who had known Gayle during her service in Ecuador. Their remembrances are included in the narrative. Bridgette Schneider photographed Gayle's childhood home in St Paul and the house where she lived when married. Kambiz and Fereshteh Rahmani shared memories from Gayle's teaching trip to Spain through to her last moments. Violette Eghrari shared reflections on the Children's Program. (Other reflections on this Program included in the text are those that

Gayle herself had collected.) Ms Bobby Dotson, Gayle's friend at ManorCare, graciously gave her permission for her name to be used in this book. Thus, the narrative has drawn the participation of many.

While much more could be written of her life, this account is focused primarily on Gayle's international service. Her life after her return to the United States in 1975 is described only in broad strokes. During these latter years, her active service continued. Her spiral calendars continue to note daily meetings, letters written and received, children and family members called, and programmes attended. Her papers document hundreds of people touched in personal ways by her life, and who touched her in important ways, whose names do not appear here. (You know who you are and what you mean to her!) Out of respect, certain descriptions do not identify individuals by name, only to avoid giving a sense of inclusion of some and the exclusion of others. To Gayle, each soul was personally significant and had a precious destiny to fulfil. This story is offered in the hope that her voice and spirit may continue to inspire others, as they did during her life in this world.

Deepest gratitude is offered to the George Ronald team and particularly to May Hofman, whose experienced editing was shared with wisdom, patience, and love, in the spirit of a mentor and friend.

Prelude

'Future generations will extol your labours,
follow in your footsteps,
and derive inspiration from your pioneer activities.'[1]
Written by Shoghi Effendi to Gayle Woolson
in Costa Rica, 1942

As Gayle Woolson came to the close of her life on the eve of her 98th birthday, her pioneering activities lay in the past; her labours had come to a close; even her footsteps were now few. Yet something would remain to extol, to follow, and from which to derive inspiration.

Those who came to visit during her last two weeks wondered at the serenity and trust with which she embraced her imminent passing. It seemed there was wisdom not only in the direction of her footsteps but in how the steps themselves had been taken. She herself has said that she found in the following words of Bahá'u'lláh 'the perfect code of life':

Live then the days of thy life,
that are less than a fleeting moment,
with thy mind stainless, thy heart unsullied,
thy thoughts pure, and thy nature sanctified,
so that, free and content, thou mayest put away this

mortal frame,
and repair unto the mystic paradise
and abide in the eternal kingdom for evermore.[2]

Visitors sitting with her faced a table near the end of her bed on which a softly fluted vase held white and lavender flowers. A guest book gathered notes and signatures of those who came, and some well-worn prayer books offered themselves for use. Beside them was a small framed black-and-white photograph depicting her family standing in formal dress: her maternal grandparents, parents, and five of her eight siblings were there. In the picture Gayle, as a child of about eight, sits beside her grandmother on a bench. She is dressed in an immaculate white frock, a starched bow in her hair. With her hands firmly planted on both knees, she seems barely able to contain herself, ready to spring from the seat of childhood into adventures she could not then imagine but that would take almost a century to unfold. The inspiration that guided and sustained her footsteps, her labours, and her pioneering activities is what this story hopes to explore, turning, whenever possible, to her own words and remembrance.

1

Coming to America and Making a Discovery

The little girl in the photograph with the immaculate frock and the big white bow in her hair was named Alice in 1913 when she was born.[1] (How she came to be known as Gayle is a story that comes later.) Alice wasn't an Arabic name, like those of her parents, Hassen and Middíyyih Abas. It was thought of as American, like her two-year-old brother's name – Morris (nicknamed Murrie). The year she was born, Alice was the 11th most popular name for girls in America. To her Syrian parents, the children's names spoke of putting down roots in a new country where they planned to remain and prosper, where they had been naturalized and therefore aspired to belong. They were names other children would be able to pronounce in school, that wouldn't speak loudly of being different. 'Alice Abas' – the names sounded like they belonged together, especially if 'Abas' had the stress at the beginning rather than the end. 'Alice' meant 'nobility' and carried the sense of dignity and integrity her parents wanted her to feel as she grew up.

The year Alice was born, the newspapers had been full of dramatic news, some exciting, some tragic. The Panama Canal had opened, linking the Atlantic and

Pacific Oceans. However, only a simple ceremony had marked the occasion, as the rumblings of international war drowned out stories of promise and hope. Grand Central Station opened in New York City, the largest hub amidst a network of railroads linking more and more parts of the country. It was the railroads that had brought immigrant families like Alice's west, and would now bring millions in a migration from south to north, following the same pathways as others had trodden years before on the underground railway.

In March 1913, newspapers displayed a dramatic photograph of a young activist, Inez Milholland. Donning a white cape, and having mounted an equally white horse, she led thousands of women in a suffrage parade moving towards the White House on the eve of President Wilson's inauguration. The main organizers, Alice Paul and Lucy Burns, were there. Women from countries where they had won the vote were near the front, then colour-coded groups from each profession. In their first public act were all the founding members of Howard University's newly-formed Delta Sigma Theta, with Sorors Ida B. Wells-Barnett, the famous human rights journalist, and Mary Church Terrell among them. Helen Keller, herself an icon of transcendence, walked the whole distance, despite her loss of sight and hearing. Each of the five to eight thousand women had her own unique history, talents, and field of service. They had one thing in common. All had stepped beyond their traditional, historically limited roles to embrace a wider vision, to claim what they envisioned as their full humanity. What were the winds of change that moved them? How would Alice, born into a time of such transformation, ultimately step forth from her own beginnings to find and fashion her destiny?

By 1913, Alice's parents were already far from their original homes and culture. They had joined a flow of millions of immigrants sailing from Europe and the Middle East to America's east coast, and from Asia to her west coast, drawn by visions of a better future, borne since the 1890s by a burgeoning steamship industry. Migrants were the industry's main support, while a smaller number of wealthy travellers peopled the first-class cabins and upper decks.

Alice's father, Hassen Abas, had been born in Karbet-Roha, Syria around 10 February 1874. Hassen's father died when he was five. His mother, of the Kadrie family, later married a gentleman of the same extended clan. At sixteen, as summer changed to fall, Hassen set off alone to make the long sea voyage to the United States, seeking wider horizons and greater opportunity. New York City was his port of entry and became his first home.

Several years later, Hassen went west to Crookston, Minnesota, a trading and commercial centre of about 7,500 that had grown up at the confluence of several railroads. The area was a traditional hunting ground of the Lakota people, but they had been pushed westward as settlers from Europe and the Middle East gradually took over more and more land.

Since the 1890s, a number of Syrian/Lebanese immigrants had come to Minnesota as farmers, labourers, peddlers and merchants. Those who, like Hassen Abas, set up dry goods stores offered a home base for peddlers, who would buy supplies and then go door to door selling their wares. Because the peddlers carried items not easily available, they often prospered. This work gave immigrants quick entrance into communities, doing a job that did not require fluent English but allowed them to learn and practise it as they worked. Hassen was successful in his business venture. On 26 September 1906, in Crookston, he proudly became naturalized as an American citizen.

He continued to have business connections in New York City, where, in about 1910, he met Kamel and Khalud Hider and their daughter, Middíyyih, originally from Homs, Syria. The family had embarked on their own ocean voyage to America when Middíyyih was eleven. She was now 19 and Hassen 36. The couple, enamoured of each other, decided to marry. Middíyyih's parents became an integral and permanent part of the household. Hassen and his father-in-law established what would become a life-long business relationship that came to include a wide network of family and friends in New York, Minnesota and North Dakota.

The whole family moved together to Crookston, Minnesota, where Murrie and Alice were born. Middíyyih and her mother nurtured the quickly growing household with a spirit of loving-kindness and managerial skill. The family spoke both Arabic and English at home. Of Islamic descent, they read the Qur'án and 'practiced the virtues of right living'. However, they were 'not ingrained with any particular religion'.[2] Alice later recalled her father's eloquence, especially in his native tongue. A gentle man, he was well respected; friends often came to him for advice. Her grandfather, also of high regard, reached out to others in a spirit of service. The family offered their warm, traditional hospitality to all who came to the door. Alice's mother gave birth to a new child about every two years: when Murrie was four and Alice two years old, their brother Julian was born, followed by Haseeb in 1917, Dahela in 1919, and Edward in 1922. The older children were in school and Edward still under a year when the whole family moved to St Paul, Minnesota. They set up a new home and a dry goods store there, as they had in Crookston.

Alice's life in St Paul was busy. As the eldest daughter, though only nine years old, she helped her mother and grandmother care for her younger brothers and, later, three sisters. She and her siblings had to adjust to a new neighbourhood and to new schools. Over the next few years, Alice became a serious student and worked in the family store, while still helping at home.[3]

In 1926, when Alice was 13, another Syrian family came to St Paul: Melvin (Mel) and Sarah Kadrie and their eight children. Shortly after their arrival, their ninth child was born. The Kadrie and Abas families were distantly related through Alice's paternal grandmother, also a Kadrie.[4] Ali (Alex) Kadrie, a cousin of Melvin's, also happened to be living in St Paul. These two families, including the children, would find their lives becoming interwoven beyond the ties of blood. All this began to happen because of a discovery Alex made while peddling his wares.

Alex Kadrie sold various items door to door, including prayer rugs. One day, he came into the home of Dr and Mrs Clement Woolson at 870 Laurel Avenue in St Paul.[5] 'As he came in to demonstrate to Mrs. Woolson his wares, he noticed an Arabic symbol hanging above the fireplace.'[6] He could read it. Intrigued that an American would have an Arabic hanging, he inquired about it and was invited to Friday night meetings, where he might learn more about the new religion it symbolized.[7] Alex told Mel and Sarah what he had found, and they all began to learn more at local public meetings given by Dr Woolson.

Mel was Lebanese, from a Muslim family, and was a direct descendant of the Prophet Muhammad. When he married Sarah, it was the first time in 1,000 years that a Kadrie had married outside of the family. For Sarah, raised strictly Catholic, marrying outside the Church was taboo. She was of Ojibwe, French and English heritage and had grown up on the White Earth Indian Reservation. Following her mother's death, she was enrolled as a boarding student at the St Benedictine Mission School, one of the notorious boarding schools that destroyed the culture, language and sense of identity of generations of indigenous children. Students were primarily trained for domestic work and often given out to families to do menial labour. The *History of the Kadrie Family* states that the experience was 'brutal'. Providentially, Sarah found employment at the dry goods store Mel had opened in Callaway, Minnesota, at the edge of the Reservation.[8] As Mel and Sarah came to know each other, they became close and decided to marry. Following this, they spent time in Canada, a year in Lebanon, and more time in Canada, before finally arriving in St Paul.[9] They had married for love and appreciation of each other's character, stepping outside the exclusive circles of their own traditions. In Lebanon, Sarah found it impossible to live with the limitations placed on women, especially after growing up with the oppression of her own indigenous community in America. Both Mel and Sarah were therefore intrigued to learn of a Faith that taught the equality of women and men and the oneness of humankind.

At the meetings, Dr Woolson was saying that a new Teacher had come into the world, whose title was Bahá'u'lláh. Throughout history, such Teachers had inspired the birth and growth of new civilizations. Many of their names were now lost to history; some remained in the collective memory and experience. Bahá'u'lláh taught that all humanity is one family, that prejudice of all kinds must melt away before this reality. He said the essential spiritual teachings of all religions are similar, but that the Founder of each major religion ordained social teachings attuned to the needs of the time.[10] Alex, Mel and Sarah Kadrie felt as if they were watching a window open on a vast, sunlit vista they had yearned for but never seen.

Inspired by the new teachings, Alex Kadrie shared what he had learned with other Syrians, including Hassen Abas. Of her family's first experience with Dr Woolson, Gayle (Alice) later wrote:

One memorable summer evening in about 1930, my father and grandfather, with a friend of the family, Mr.

Alex (Ali) Kadrie, attended a Bahá'í talk given by Dr. Clement Woolson who was conducting regular meetings in St. Paul. They heard the Bahá'í Message for the first time . . . A new spirit of transformation came into our home through their delight, enthusiasm and excitement . . .[11]

2

A Spiritual Change in the Family

In 1930, as the Great Depression deepened and spread, Alice continued to observe the transformation, as a 'significant spiritual change started to take place in the family'.[1] Following their first attendance at a Friday night public meeting at which Dr Woolson spoke, Alice had noted the excitement with which her father and grandfather conversed. She states that they had accepted the Bahá'í message instantly.[2] They encouraged the 'older children' to attend the meetings, saying that the young people had a very important role to play in building a new, spiritual, worldwide civilization. In a talk given in Cedar Rapids in 1998, Gayle (as Alice was then known) said, 'I was one of the last to go to a meeting . . . I did not quite grasp the immensity of it. It was too much for my thinking.' She did not go back for a while.

> One night I awakened in the middle of the night. I unconsciously propped myself up on my elbows (I must have been sleeping on my stomach) and I looked out in the hall . . . Two wide rays of violet light were coming through the roof to the floor. Violet rays, two, coming down. I opened my eyes and pinched myself.

I had never heard of a vision. The light stayed there. I kept looking, trying to figure out what it was. Finally, I decided this was a sign from God that I should go back to the Bahá'í meetings. I went back to sleep.

As Gayle related the story decades later, she laughed. 'Now I wouldn't go back to sleep. I would stay . . . I wouldn't give up.' She said that she did go back to the meetings and 'understood what it was all about. I felt like I was at home . . . a feeling of being at home . . . this was my place.'[3]

One might wonder how the family had energy to be open to anything beyond the immediate: the urgent needs of family and business were great. Perhaps the receptivity came from being immigrants uprooted from their past and open to discovery in a new land. Perhaps there was a hospitality given to new ideas that mirrored that given to people. Often the family dinner table would host up to twenty at a time, the meal often supplemented with homegrown vegetables from Mrs Hider's large garden in the back yard. Alice, then in high school, still loved to be near her grandmother, whose love for children, like her mother's, had a gentle firmness, high expectation, and unending loving-kindness.[4] Especially during this time, those gathered for meals would share new ideas and discoveries, as they found their way in a new land.

By 1930, the home on Fuller Avenue was bustling with life more than ever. Each of the now eight children had differing needs. Morris was 19 years old, probably just out of high school. Alice was 17, still helping part time at the dry goods store and almost ready to graduate. Julian was also in high school, Dahela and Edward probably in middle school. The youngest still needed full-time care: Victoria was five, Loroli three, and Gerald one year of age. Alice still felt the absence of her other brother, Haseeb, who had died suddenly from an automobile accident when she was ten and he six years old. The younger children only knew him through photographs and stories. Her memory of him in the family was like a place where a branch has come off a tree, leaving a scar in the pattern of the trunk and bark. The space where the branch used to be remains, empty of form but filled with poignant remembrance.

While the Bahá'í teachings were gradually penetrating the Abas family home, a pattern of community functioning was beginning to take shape in St Paul. In 1931, the first local administrative body, or Local Spiritual Assembly, was elected in the home of Clement and Leona Woolson. Eventually, these institutions would be established in every incorporated city of the United States. In 1931, there were fifty-five Local Spiritual Assemblies in the United States and Canada and sixty in other countries (not including Persia, which was organized into seventeen administrative divisions).[5]

Nascent as these Spiritual Assemblies were in 1930, they were called for by Bahá'u'lláh and designed to evolve over time into a pattern for world society that would be unified in principles, yet would foster creative expression and cultural diversity. Alice's father and grandfather became actively involved in the community's development, which included organizing the Nineteen Day

Feasts and Holy Day[6] observances; scheduling study classes that were enriched by a library of Bahá'í books; and holding public meetings, each comprised of a public lecture with musical introduction. There were several kinds of classes. Bahá'í books, such as *Bahá'í Scriptures*, *The Hidden Words*, *The Seven Valleys*, *The Book of Certitude*, and *The Dawn-Breakers* were studied as they became available. Clement Woolson gave a weekly class on the symbolism of numbers in scripture, as he was well versed in Biblical prophecy. On 22 January 1932, Alice's father, grandfather, and Alex Kadrie were present and 'translated portions of an Arabic bible [sic.] which they had brought with them', and 'in comparing the Arabic bible with the English bible they were found to be the same.'[7] The community studied Esperanto,[8] seen as a step towards establishing a universal auxiliary language such as that called for by Bahá'u'lláh. Little by little, Hassen Abas engaged the family's participation. On 24 April Middíyih Abas and two of her sons attended a meeting nineteen miles away in Hudson, Wisconsin. Following this, the Abas and Kadrie families gradually began to bring their older children to attend the weekly Friday meetings where Clement Woolson and others spoke.

With increasing numbers of people attending and the need for a more public presence, the St Paul Assembly decided to rent a space for their meetings. In 1932, they signed a contract for a room in the Midland Trust Building at Sixth and Wabash Streets. It was quite a commitment. The total monthly rent and utilities came to approximately $40.00. Dr Woolson agreed to contribute about $24.00 per month; almost every other individual gave between $1 and $4.50, usually $2. When one considers that $1 in 1932 is equivalent to $18.77 in 2020, one sees a community offering considerable sacrifice as well as near universal participation.

The Assembly established committees to plan the gatherings held in their public room; to arrange flowers; to plan the Nineteen Day Feast; to organize and run the small library; and to ensure that cleaning services were sustained. At special times, they would show a film of 'Abdu'l-Bahá[9] and play a recording of His voice on their Victrola. They even had a movie camera and projector and would take and show films of their outings.

That same year, Clement and Leona Woolson received permission to make a pilgrimage to Haifa in the Holy Land, where they would visit the Shrines of the Báb and Bahá'u'lláh and meet the Head of the Bahá'í Faith, Shoghi Effendi. On 21 September 1932, the Assembly (and others) wrote and signed a letter to Shoghi Effendi, to be carried to him by Dr and Mrs Woolson. On 30 December, Clement Woolson 'gave a short address concerning their trip and then showed motion and still pictures of Acca, Haifa and other places visited'.[10]

Thus, the Abas family made connection, on a personal level, not only with the local community but with the international centre of the Faith. For many months, the women and children absorbed what was happening through 'continuous' conversations at home between Alice's father and grandfather, and also through 'general discussion'.[11]

It was in this context, in 1933, that the first mention

was made in the records[12] of Alice and Morris Abas attending Bahá'í meetings together with the older Kadrie children, Farhad Woolson,[13] and a few others. In April and May, Alice attended the Sunday school, which had a programme for both children and adults.

On Tuesday, 23 May 1933,[14] at 8:00 p.m., 'Alice Abas' is listed along with Morris, her father, and grandfather as attending a Holy Day observance: the Declaration of the Báb. The Woolsons were there with their son, Farhad. Mrs Kadrie had brought Kenneth, Melvin, and Bertha. Clement Woolson told the story of the Báb, as related in *The Dawn-Breakers* and, as part of the programme, Alice and Bertha Kadrie each read a prayer. This occasion commemorated the night on 22 May 1844 when the Báb, the Forerunner of Bahá'u'lláh, declared His mission to His very first disciple. Alice would gradually learn of the far-reaching implications of that historic night.

In November and December of that same year, Alice had occasion to spend time with a well-known Bahá'í teacher, Mrs Orcella Rexford, who came to offer lectures in St Paul. Several years before, Mrs Rexford had visited 'Abdu'l-Bahá in the Holy Land.[15] She had taught extensively both in North America and abroad, and was one of a few Bahá'ís who had designed a systematic way[16] to introduce the Bahá'í Faith into new areas and strengthen it in others. As a professional travelling lecturer, she offered a series of public talks on the science of colour, nutrition, holistic healing, numerology, and other topics. Typically, 300–400 people would attend the sequence. As the last class concluded, Mrs Rexford would invite anyone interested to attend a free meeting where additional spiritual information would be shared. At that time, she would introduce the Bahá'í Faith. Those wishing to learn more could join a free study class, usually run by someone in the local community. The St Paul *Record* notes plans for several follow-up meetings to engage interested members of Mrs Rexford's class. This was Alice's first exposure to such a systematic way of introducing the Bahá'í teachings to others.

Alice was struck by the current thinking Mrs Rexford's lectures conveyed about how to align one's life for success. She described how one's energies should be aligned and directed towards one's spiritual aim. How one presented oneself and organized one's life would affect the achievement of goals. This included many aspects, from the symbolic use of colour to the practice of good nutrition and holistic healing. Numbers were important, especially in one's name.[17] Although the latter was not a Bahá'í teaching, Orcella Rexford influenced a number of people to adopt numerically advantageous names.[18] Alice assumed the name 'Gayle' for this reason, symbolizing her evolving sense of identity and purpose. In the Bahá'í community, Gayle joined a youth group called The Northern Lights. On 14 February, this youth group held its first 'social' with 22 young people present. Gayle Abas gave a short talk, followed by games, music, dancing, and refreshments. On 1 August 1934, the Youth Group presented the programme for the Feast of Names. Dahela Abas, Gayle's younger sister, was present; Morris, Gayle, and Julian Abas all presented talks.

Gayle identifies 1933 as the year when she became confirmed in her recognition of the Faith and 1934 as when her 'service began'. Years later, she described the impact of learning of the life and teachings of Bahá'u'lláh. She wrote:

Personal Statement
The Significance of the Birth of Bahá'u'lláh for me
Personally

The significance of the birth and of the life of Bahá'u'lláh for me personally may be compared to the same differences between light and darkness. A curtain lifted in my mind, so to speak, and a new broad perspective of the purpose of life in its highest stages opened to my understanding. It was like stepping from one small world into the dimensions of the universe.

There was a new kind of inner energy derived from a stronger bond with God and with Bahá'u'lláh, a new sense of divine guidance in my daily life, and a general enrichment of my inner being. I felt a new kind of happiness that is not derived from material things, and a new and deeper meaning of life. There was an acute awareness that God endows each individual with the potential for achieving an admirable destiny which is related to the destiny of the human race. Bahá'u'lláh revealed the teachings and Divine Pattern for that monumental Kingdom imbued with a new universal power of harmony and fellowship, oneness and love. With such a luminous goal, the soul becomes rejoiced with inspiration and a sense of achievement. It is a source of unending happiness. To enrich the knowledge gained from the Bahá'í Teachings, we learn that the coming of Bahá'u'lláh is foretold in all the great religions.[19]

Gayle then cites statements from Hinduism, Judaism, Zoroastrianism, Buddhism, Christianity, and Islam that speak of an age when prophecies would be fulfilled, resulting eventually in what some call a Golden Age, an age of purity and peace, a universal civilization.[20] Gayle and the other youth came to realize that Bahá'u'lláh's teachings, while representing an independent Revelation, were closely interwoven with the progression of past great religions. The Báb and Bahá'u'lláh brought both a renewal and a fulfilment of prophecies engraved in past traditions. Their Writings asserted the oneness of human-kind, while bringing the social laws needed to realize that vision. Some of the Bahá'ís in St Paul could relate their own first-hand stories of meeting 'Abdu'l-Bahá, during his travels through the United States and Canada. The Bahá'í communities had direct communication with Shoghi Effendi, the grandson of 'Abdu'l-Bahá and the Head, or Guardian, of the Bahá'í Faith. This closeness to the early history and authenticated Writings of the Báb and Bahá'u'lláh, together with the continuing guidance of the Guardian, Shoghi Effendi, engendered a love and devotion that would cause many to leave their homes and travel throughout the world to make these teachings available to any who wished to learn together to pattern their lives according to what Bahá'u'lláh had taught.

3

The Woolson Family

As the Abas and Kadrie families learned about the
Bahá'í Faith, they also became more acquainted with Dr
Clement Woolson and his family. In later years, Gayle
asked three people who had been in St Paul at the time
to write their impressions of him. One of Sarah Kadrie's
daughters, Voroth Kadrie Degeberg, describes the first
meeting she attended:

> It was about 1934 when I first met Dr. Woolson, who
> was then Chairman of the St. Paul, Minnesota group. I
> think four of us children went to that first Bahá'í meet-
> ing with Mother and Dad. There were about 30 to 50
> people present. We sat down and waited, then from
> behind the curtain someone started a recording . . .
> it was a boy soprano singing one of the early Bahá'í
> songs. The lovely voice and verse set quite a mood and
> then Dr. Woolson stepped out. He had great physical
> attraction. We call it 'personal magnetism' or 'cha-
> risma' now-a-days. Tall, broad-statured, interesting
> face, high forehead, intense blue eyes . . . Laughter
> came easily with him. He had caught the magic of the
> Faith and made one long to attain it!
>
> And that's how I remember Dr. Woolson. A remark-
> able man, drawing people with his love and knowledge

of the Faith. His perception and ability to give people what they needed and more than that, to draw out the best in each one and inspire them to greater development. He was vitally interested in young people and they responded . . .[1]

Voroth's sister, Bertha, remembered him thus:

Dr. Clement Woolson was an individual who could change for the better the life or character of anyone who came in contact with him . . . I was only 17 at the time. My father and mother and some of us members of the family would go to the Friday night meetings, the Feast and special prayer meetings . . . He was always happy to see us – and ever with that beautiful, beautiful smile of his and happy, cheerful tone of his voice. I can still see that smile and hear him explaining many things he tried so hard to get us to understand . . .[2]

A former patient of Dr Woolson remembers how he treated her as a child:

I met Dr. Woolson when I was about 9 years old. I had fainting spells, possible convulsions, from the time I was three days old. I was on salt free diets, and treatments and drugs all my young life and it was when my Mother went in to get a repeat prescription filled for me that the druggist asked to whom it was to be given. He then told my mother that what I was taking was just drugging me and that he knew a doctor that might help.

I was nothing but skin and bones. I was taken to Dr. Woolson . . . X-rays and treatments were begun. I had a vertebra or two out of place in the neck area which would press on nerves going to the brain, cutting off blood supply, causing the fainting spells without warning. I went daily for treatments after school . . .

He seemed to be so knowledgeable. If I came in with some new subject I thought I could talk wisely about he would take up where I left off and astound me with his learning . . . He called me his adopted daughter. He did heal me. I think it was God's will . . . I could never have made it much further in life the way I was . . . He told me about the Bahá'í Faith, gave me a prayer book published in 1929 and which I still have and use regularly . . .

He paid for and supplied art materials for art lessons, but I really was not well enough to take genuine interest in them. Long after the hundreds of dollars my parents paid for my treatments were used up, he kept on treating me free and would not hear of any remuneration . . .

. . . I attended many Bahá'í meetings and dinners in his home, but the Faith was so new in this country and there was no real administration set up at that time so none of us could adequately appreciate what he was trying to share with us. He was the most powerful single influence in my young life. He saved my life physically and spiritually as I became a Bahá'í in 1942 . . .[3]

During this time, Gayle and others may have learned how Clement Woolson found the Bahá'í Faith in 1899 in New York as a young man of twenty. They may have heard about his service on the Council Board of the Spiritual Assembly of New York in 1900, and about the gatherings he attended at Saffa and Vafa Kinney's home on West End Avenue in New York City, with people from all over the world. Dr Woolson may have told of being among those who signed the petition to 'Abdu'l-Bahá asking that they be permitted to begin plans to build a House of Worship in Chicago.

In 1906, Clement Woolson had gone to Kirksville, Missouri to study at the American College of Osteopathy, now known as the Kirksville College of Osteopathic Medicine. It was here that he met Leona Harper, who attended the American College from June 1905 until June 1908, the date of her graduation. She then returned to Minneapolis, where her father, Dr Homer Harper, was also an osteopath and a devoted Bahá'í. Here she set up practice until January 1909, when Clement and Leona were married and established a joint practice in St Paul.

In 1912, Drs Clement (as delegate) and Leona Woolson (as alternate), both residents of St Paul, were privileged to attend the Fourth Convention of the Bahá'í Temple Unity, the committee established for coordinating the House of Worship building project. This took place during the extensive visit of 'Abdu'l-Bahá to North America. 'Abdu'l-Bahá spoke at the last session of the Convention on 30 April and the next day, 1 May, at the ceremony held on the land purchased for the future Bahá'í House of Worship, where He laid its cornerstone amidst a spellbound throng of believers. Later that year, on 5 September 1912, Leona

Orrol Woolson gave birth to a baby boy. In a letter to Martha Root in 1921, her father, Dr Harper, wrote that while 'Abdu'l-Bahá (known to Bahá'ís as 'the Master') was in Minneapolis, he, Dr Harper, had implored Him to go to the home of his daughter and Dr Clement Woolson in St Paul. When Dr Harper explained that the baby had been born just two weeks before and the mother was not yet up, the trip to St Paul was arranged. 'Abdu'l-Bahá arrived at the Woolson home on 20 September. Dr Harper states that He blessed the now two-week-old baby, rubbing His finger back and forth across his forehead. At the request of his mother, according to Dr Harper, 'Abdu'l-Bahá had already given the child the name 'Farhad', meaning 'fortunate'. At the Woolson home, Abdu'l-Bahá gave a talk on spiritual education, found now in the compilation *The Promulgation of Universal Peace*, pp. 323–327.[4]

A few years later, in about 1915, Dr Woolson continued his medical training at Loyola University. His name appears on the Chicago Bahá'í membership list for 1916, indicating residency there. After obtaining his diploma as physician and surgeon, he returned to the family home in St Paul.[5] During this general period, in 1918, Dr Woolson received the following Tablet from 'Abdu'l-Bahá:

> He is God!
> O thou who are enkindled by the fire of the Love of God. Verily, I read thy fluent letter which spoke of the praise of the Lord of Excellent Names and I begged of God to breathe the Holy Spirit into the soul of thy soul and to cause the lights of communion to shine

upon the heart of thy heart. Communicate with Me by whatsoever means (or way) thou wishest. Verily, I hear thy wonderful melodies in sanctifying and glorifying thy Glorious Lord.

If thou wishest to heal nervous pains turn with thy whole self unto the Supreme Horizon with thy heart free from all else save Him and with thy soul attracted by the Love of God. Then seek the confirmations of the Spirit from the Kingdom of Abhá, while touching (or laying your hands on) the place of pains, with all love, affection and attraction. And after all these matters have been confirmed with, be thou assured that, verily, healing will be attained.

Upon thee be greeting and praise!

(Signed) E. E. 'Abdu'l-Bahá Abbas[6]

By 1918, Dr Clement Woolson had returned to St Paul. He and his wife were known for their holistic approach to medicine; for their compassion; for taking time to listen to people's concerns; and for paying special attention to youth.

In her biography of Louis Gregory, *To Move the World*, Gayle Morrison relates the following about his visit to Minneapolis/St Paul:

In Minneapolis and St. Paul, Minnesota, a large number of meetings were arranged, especially in the black community. Mr. Gregory singled out the efforts of Dr. Orrol Woolson of St. Paul for particular praise, and she in turn wrote that 'the Spirit of 'Abdul Baha has

23

been in our midst.' A Minneapolis Bahá'í called attention to the twofold effect of Louis Gregory's presence: on the one hand, the Bahá'ís had become 'more united,' and on the other, they sensed an unprecedented public response, indicated by the fact that they had never had such meetings and so much interest shown.[7]

Years later, in the early 1930s, when the Kadrie and Abas families began attending meetings, the Woolson home was a centre of Bahá'í activity. For many years, Dr Woolson had been the Chairman and Mrs Woolson the Corresponding Secretary of the group and then Assembly. Their home is recalled as warm, welcoming, and joyous, embracing children and youth with a love they carried with them for many years.

However, as is often true of families, the dynamics within the Woolson marriage seem to have been more complex than was publicly realized. Details of the changes that took place are now obscure, for reasons unknown. Something happened to cause permanent separation. To date, information has not been found regarding Mrs Leona (Orrol/Nagene) Harper Woolson's subsequent life and service. There is one line in the *History of the Kadrie Family* in which oral history has it[8] that she was 'unfortunately committed to a mental institution'. At present, no written or publicly available records have been found to substantiate this account.[9] If true, it could explain the absence of information. What becomes pertinent to this story is how these changes then came into play in the life of Gayle Abas.

4

Marriage

The period from 1934 through 1935 brought significant change in Gayle's personal life and in that of the St Paul Bahá'í community.[1] Gayle had now moved beyond the family business and had begun working for Minnesota Employment Services. However, the sweetness of increased independence was mixed with the sorrow of another loss in the family in 1934: Gayle's maternal grandmother became the second person in the Abas household to pass away, following a considerable length of time in the hospital.

> My grandfather and mother would visit her frequently, particularly my grandfather who went daily. His conversations with her would include reference to the Bahá'í teachings. A few days before she passed away, she had an experience with Bahá'u'lláh, and suddenly felt well. She said to my grandfather and mother, as related to me by them together: 'Dr. Woolson's Bahá healed me.' I do not know whether she had a vision or a dream. In any case, she became free of her ailing condition. However, she did not live very long after that.[2]

In the 1930s, hospitalizations were longer than now, with less open discussion of medical conditions among family and friends. In later years, when Gayle wrote about her grandmother, she did not articulate personal impressions or feelings of loss, despite loving her grandmother deeply and having grown up by her side. Looking back, she emphasized two things: the qualities her grandmother brought to service within the family and the significance of the spiritual experience that seemed to bring healing during her last illness. She hoped her grandmother would be remembered as part of the family's legacy contributing to Bahá'í history. A single, wide gravestone in Oakland Cemetery in St Paul honors 'Kaloud Hider' and 'Kamel Hider', giving just the years of each one's birth and passing.

In the St Paul community, there were changes in the Spiritual Assembly membership. A few resignations resulted from turmoil not fully explained. As a result, Gayle, Kamel Hider (her grandfather) and Mrs Tetu were elected to the Assembly. Gayle became the recording secretary and treasurer.

Meanwhile, Gayle's relationship with Clement Woolson had become deeply personal. In a small, brown file envelope, carried with her throughout her life, she kept a few 'precious mementoes', some from this time. Among her snapshots of outings, family, and friends, she had one photograph enlarged and tinted with colour. She and Clement stand together, informally dressed, under a lattice arch of roses.

In the same brown envelope, she kept a few cards exchanged between them and her marriage license: Dr Clement Woolson and Gayle Abas were married in

Waukegan, Illinois on 23 April 1935 by M. J. Haney, Justice of the Peace. Rose Washick (Dr Woolson's assistant) and Sidney W. Wiegand (a relative of Dr Woolson) were the witnesses. The reader may notice with curiosity the absence of their immediate families and the location, far from St Paul. Gayle left us the brown envelope and no more.[3]

Directly after the wedding, as a newly-married couple, Gayle and Clement Woolson attended the 27th National Baháʾí Convention in Wilmette, Illinois, at which the members of the National Spiritual Assembly would be elected. Dr Woolson was a delegate, Gayle a visitor. What thoughts and dreams were in their hearts as they chose this occasion to inaugurate their life of service together? The Baháʾís were celebrating the completion of the dome of the Baháʾí House of Worship. Clement, now 55, had been there in 1912 when that spot was just a grassy knoll and the Master turned the earth with His own hands and dedicated the cornerstone, saying, 'The Temple is already built.' The maturing of Clement's spiritual and professional service had paralleled in time the erection of this magnificent structure from its beginning to the present, in 1935. Gayle had been born the year after ʿAbduʾl-Baháʾs visit to America. The building of the Temple took place as she grew up. Now twenty-one, her own adult life was just unfolding. She was newly married to one who was both mentor and cherished love. In their shared and private thoughts, the couple may have reflected on all they hoped to build together. They could not know then how brief their future together in this world would be, nor that Gayle would need to arise independently to respond to the call to action read out in the Convention.

They heard and studied the *Annual Report of the National Spiritual Assembly*. It focused their thoughts not on themselves but on the world. It included the following:

> ... Rather may we perceive ... the beginning of an era of greater maturity, larger responsibility ... Fourteen years ago the Bahá'í community was still as a child in the household of civilization, apparently bearing no responsibility for the fate of that household, and therefore concerned only with the joys and sorrows of the child's own growth, the dreams of its own future. Today, with the household in dire confusion and distress, the youth born of the new age is called upon to prove his birthright and demonstrate his capacity to achieve eternal peace, his elders having failed.

The report concludes with a statement about teaching and the importance of a unified community:

> Gratitude, however, must be expressed to all those teachers who during the year have answered the call to service and traveled to so many cities upholding the banner of the Faith. This circulation of thought and devotion ... is a great stimulus to the Bahá'í communities themselves as well as to the non-believers thereby attracted. But above all the firm unity of the local communities affords and will always afford the

only enduring foundation for the new era of vitality and spiritual zeal. The greatest teacher in the Cause of Baháʼuʼlláh is not a person but a community not only united together on the plane of personality but imbued with conviction that its essential purpose is to open the doors to the new souls.[4]

These words, penned by Horace Holley on behalf of the National Spiritual Assembly, would take on personal significance that Gayle could not then imagine, calling her to a maturity, responsibility, and dedication to the world well beyond her years.

Sitting there in the Convention, all reflected on what remained to be accomplished in building the House of Worship. Already, it had united the community in manifesting a vision voiced by Baháʼuʼlláh, guided by ʻAbduʼl-Bahá, and now being brought to completion through the Plans of the Guardian. Through this process, the Temple Unity, a committee formed to coordinate the House of Worship project, had evolved into the National Spiritual Assembly. The international flow of contributions had increased the sense of a world family collaborating as one. The House of Worship itself, when finished, would open its doors to all mankind.

Throughout her life, Gayle encouraged people to visit this special place. She always carried pictures of the House of Worship in her purse. She gave away postcards with a paragraph on the back as an invitation to visit the House of Worship and explained, in the most universal terms, its significance. She used them both for teaching in the United States and throughout Central and South America. She would show people how the building's design and purpose demonstrated spiritual principles. Always in the context of a conversation, she gave cards to taxi drivers, people waiting at the bus stop, post office clerks, and people in the shops where she made copies. She enclosed them in letters of thanks, sent both to express appreciation and to foster interest in making a visit.

After the National Convention, Gayle and Clement Woolson returned home to begin their married life in St Paul. Gayle has left no personal description of their first months of marriage beyond what is recorded in the *St. Paul Record of Various Activities,* which she got permission to copy and include in her papers as an historical record. During June, there were no Assembly meetings and only one in July and one in August, though typically the members had met weekly. Dr Woolson continued to serve as chairman of the Spiritual Assembly, Gayle as secretary.

After the 8 August meeting, there is no entry until 20 September, for which only the following is recorded:

> Gayle Woolson, secretary was appointed by the chairman, Dr. Woolson to conduct the meeting because he was unable to attend due to illness.
>
> > Gayle Woolson
> > Secretary

A week later, there is the following:

September 27, 1935 Friday.
Our beloved chairman, Dr. Woolson passed into the
Abha Kingdom[5] September 21, 1935. Meeting was
gathered in memoriam. All members took part in
prayer and reading.

Gayle Woolson, Sec'y.

As with her grandmother, Gayle does not write in detail
about the funeral service and burial. Dr Woolson's grave
may be found at the Acacia Park Cemetery, Mendota
Heights, St Paul. We do not know what intimations
either Gayle or her husband had of the imminence of
his death. He had been ill during the summer months.
Did they realize its seriousness and use this period as
a time of conscious preparation, or did the end seem
sudden and unexpected? Gayle later described his passing as from a sudden heart attack. Was she with him at
the time? Surely her loving family did much to assist her,
yet there was an aspect of the loss that had to be deeply
solitary and quite a shock for one just married, who
had just recently turned twenty-two years old. She had
already experienced what it is to live with the absence of
one she loved, first with the death of her little brother,
Haseeb, and recently, with that of her grandmother.
Losing Clement was profoundly different, representing
as it did not only the loss of her husband's presence, love,
and inspiration but that of her own imagined future.

Shortly thereafter, further changes took place in
the community. The Assembly decided to give up the
Midland Bank room. For a brief time, they held meetings

at the Woolson home. The newly-elected chairman of the Assembly, Edward Schmidt, often hosted meetings at his address, 741 Fuller Avenue, just blocks from where the Abas family lived. The community address list notes that shortly after Dr Woolson's death, Gayle and his son, Farhad Woolson, moved into the Abas family home. Gayle assumed responsibility for teaching the community children's class there.

The following April, as the first anniversary of Gayle's and Clement's wedding approached, Rose Washick, her friend and a witness at her wedding, sent her a card with a bride on the front and the printed words:

To the Bride
Wishing every happy thing / You'd like to have /the glad years bring,/ Hopes fulfilled and /dreams come true, / All that seems most dear to you, / And many joys / both new and old, / To bring you / happiness untold. (Signed) Rose

Inserted in the card, Rose wrote the following note, dated 22 April 1936:

My dear Gayle, Let each of these blossoms be a memory of the things you want to remember most, on this anniversary. Remember too, to be happy this day, and to be thankful for the great happiness that was yours, that little while. Keep in mind that someone is with you in spirit, at all times and desires your happiness to linger, for all the days to come. Love to

Grandparents Kamel and Khalud Hider (left), parents Hassen and Middíyyih Abas (right), and children Alice, Julian, Murrie, Edward, Dahela and Haseeb (left to right)

Alice and Murrie with unidentified person

Victoria, Loreli and Gerald

Clement Woolson, New York,
around 1900

Gayle Abas,
around 1935

In celebration of their wedding, Gayle and Clement

*Gayle at the time
of her wedding*

you my dear and bound in all the memories of that day. Rose [6]

In a letter written many years later on 6 September 1987 to her dear friend and fellow pioneer, Elena Marsella, Gayle describes two dreams she had of the Guardian, Shoghi Effendi. The first dream relates to her husband's passing, indicating her grief during that first year:

It was about a year after the death of my husband, Dr. Clement Woolson, who passed away through a heart attack 5 months after we were married. I was profoundly grieved and cried every day. One night I dreamt of the Guardian for the first time. I saw myself sitting at the edge of lake [sic] that was like a mirror in its serenity. I was crying with my head downwards and my tears were falling into his eyes. He said to me: 'Stop crying. Your tears fall into my eyes.' It was like a command, yet gentle and understanding. My crying spells were ended. I recall that the tears were pouring out like two narrow waterfalls directly into his eyes. I was sitting on a beautiful lawn of grass like a green carpet that was vast as in a park. The image of his face was about one foot under water and in the same position where the reflection of my own face would have been in such a mirror-like lake. When I woke up I thought to myself: there is nothing more graphic to demonstrate the closeness of the Guardian to us as believers than to say: 'Your tears fall into my eyes.'

She did dry her eyes; there was much to do. Among other things, she had to take care of Dr Woolson's affairs and figure out her own.[7] As Gayle gradually sorted through her husband's papers, she may have lingered over the Tablets from the Master and the letters from Shoghi Effendi. Among them are words penned to Dr Woolson by the Guardian at the end of a letter written in 1933, the year Gayle identifies as the time of her own awakening:

> Dear & valued co-worker: . . . I pray that the small nucleus now formed in St. Paul will under the guidance of Bahá'u'lláh and through your loving care develop into a flourishing community, ablaze with the fire of His love, and eager to establish far and wide the pillars of His all-embracing administration.
> Your true brother, Shoghi[8]

This passage seems prescient. Several from this very group in St Paul would travel 'to establish far and wide the pillars of His all-embracing administration'. Gayle did not know then how specifically she herself would be called to contribute to this work. For now, her Assembly service continued without missing a beat, most meeting notes written in her hand.

5

From Children's Classes to Teaching Teams

The sequence of Shoghi Effendi's communications and the response of the St Paul Assembly show careful study of and active response to each message. The Spiritual Assembly met on 9 February 1936, five months after Clement Woolson's passing. As Secretary, Gayle wrote the minutes in longhand, including an excerpt from a letter to the North American Bahá'í communities just received from Shoghi Effendi:

> This new stage in the gradual unfoldment of the Formative Period of our Faith into which we have just entered – the phase of concentrated teaching activity – synchronizes with a period of deepening gloom, of universal impotence, of ever-increasing destitution and widespread disillusionment in the fortunes of a declining age. This is truly providential and its significance and the opportunities it offers us should be fully apprehended and utilized. Now that the administrative organs of a firmly-established Faith are vigorously and harmoniously functioning, and now that the Symbol (The House of Worship) of its invincible might is lending unprecedented impetus to its spread, an

effort unexampled in its scope and sustained vitality is urgently required so that the moving spirit of its Founder may permeate and transform the lives of the countless multitudes that hunger for its teachings. That the beloved friends in America, who have carried triumphantly the banner of His Cause through the initial stages of its development, will in a still greater measure prove themselves capable of meeting the challenge of the present hour I for one can never doubt. Of the evidences of their inexhaustible vitality I am sufficiently and continually conscious. My fervent plea will not, I feel certain, remain unanswered. For them I shall continue to pray from all my heart.[1]

She began to find inspiration for action in such phrases as these: 'the phase of concentrated teaching activity . . . synchronizes with a period of deepening gloom . . . the significance and opportunities must be apprehended and utilized . . . an effort unexampled in its scope and sustained vitality . . . so that the moving Spirit of its Founder may permeate and transform the lives of the countless multitudes that hunger for its Teachings. My fervent plea . . . will not remain unanswered.'

How would the community individually and collectively respond?

The St Paul Assembly took steps to restore unity where there had been difficulties; to adjust to new financial constraints; to invite universal participation in activities; and to increase the teaching work. Letters were written to those who had pulled back, inviting them to attend meetings.

Miss MacKutcheon, Mrs Fink, and Miss Steinmetz visited the St Paul Assembly from Minneapolis. The *St. Paul Record of Various Activities* notes, 'It is hoped that this is the beginning of more harmony and union between the two assemblies.'[2] To economize, they continued to meet in people's homes; all were invited to host a Feast or Holy Day observance. At each meeting, there was a box for donations to the Fund for completing the House of Worship. The community sent in monthly contributions that ranged from $5.25 to $15.00 ($1 in 1936 = $18.50). Community members made efforts to attract new people and to visit isolated believers. They saw how efforts to establish unity became a magnet for further opportunities and how each small step taken led to a bigger one.

Despite personal constraints, Gayle's own service gained in scope and vitality. She continued to serve on the Local Spiritual Assembly. She was elected and served as delegate to the 1936 National Convention, to which the Guardian sent a cable that presaged the Seven Year Plan to come:

> Appeal to assembled delegates ponder historic appeal voiced by `Abdu'l-Bahá in *Tablets of the Divine Plan*. Urge earnest deliberation with incoming National Assembly to insure its complete fulfilment. First century of Bahá'í era drawing to a close. Humanity entering outer fringes most perilous stage its existence. Opportunities of present hour unimaginably precious. Would to God every State within American Republic and every Republic in American continent might ere

termination of this glorious century embrace the light of the Faith of Bahá'u'lláh and establish structural basis of His World Order.[3]

Shoghi Effendi sent a second cable to the National Spiritual Assembly on 30 May calling for permanent settlers to establish themselves in all the countries of Latin America.

Gayle absorbed and contemplated both. What part could she play in diffusing the light of the Faith in every state in America and province in Canada, and then in the countries of Latin America? Beyond the confines of St Paul, how could she help 'establish' the 'structural basis of His World Order'? Surely the way would be shown: her husband and father had so emphasized the role that young people have to play in establishing the new world-wide, spiritual civilization.

With her return to the family home, Gayle continued to teach the Sunday children's classes, comprised of her own siblings, the Kadrie children, and a few others. From this very class and these families, in later years, several would arise to offer lifelong service, both on the home front and in the international sphere. A letter written to her through the Guardian's secretary on 21 May 1936 elucidates the 'significance and opportunities' of this service to the children:

Dear Mrs. Woolson,

I am instructed by our beloved Guardian to thank you for your welcome letter of May 8th just received.

He is indeed quite pleased to hear from you and to learn of the good news of the progress of the Cause in St. Paul. He is specially gratified to hear that you are conducting a Bahá'í Sunday School Class, & wishes me to assure you of his best wishes and prayers for the success of your efforts in this connection. His hope is that this line of activity will provide you with the necessary equipment for teaching the Cause to the public. You should not feel discouraged or shy if you do not find yourself quite up to the task, but should rather strive to overcome your weaknesses in a spirit of courage & faith. Bahá'u'lláh will surely assist and guide you in your labours for the spread & establishment of His Cause. You should feel confident and persevere until your task is completed.

With warmest greetings from the Guardian to you & to all the friends in St. Paul,

Yours in His Service,

H Rabbani

wishing you success from all my heart & with the assurance of my prayers for your spiritual advancement,

your true brother,

Shoghi[4]

As in future letters Gayle Woolson would receive, Shoghi Effendi expressed gratitude and appreciation for her service, in this case, the teaching of the children's class. He did not stop there. Rather, he broadened her horizon, making of the task at hand a stepping stone that beckoned her to expanded vision and action. Gayle followed this guidance. Over the next three years, she moved beyond St Paul, accompanying experienced teachers, together introducing the Bahá'í Faith in other communities and states.

Over time, Shoghi Effendi continued to set the stage for the implementation of the *Tablets of the Divine Plan*. He needed the Bahá'ís of the West to grasp their place in the history of the Faith. To this end, he now introduced them to his translation of *The Dawn-Breakers*. In this context, in a letter to Martha Root dated 3 March 1931, he described the significance of the book and what its translation and production involved:

> I have just completed, after eight months of continuous and hard labour, the translation of the history of the early days of the Cause . . . The work comprises about 600 pages and 200 pages of additional notes that I have gleaned during the summer months from different books . . . I am now so tired and exhausted that I can hardly write . . .[5]

The book offers an eye-witness narrative of the tragic drama that ushered in the Dispensations of the Báb and Bahá'u'lláh. The accounts vividly depict the intense devotion and tragic martyrdom of more than twenty thousand people, many of them youth. As Rúḥíyyih Khánum explains in *The Priceless Pearl*, Shoghi Effendi's labour was more than simple translation: 'a literary masterpiece and one of his most priceless gifts for all time

. . . he may be said to have re-created it in English'.[6] He had Effie Baker[7] (of Australia) go through Persia, often heavily veiled, to take photographs that now form an invaluable historical record of each location as it was when early events took place. When the manuscript was finished, he asked Emogene Hoagg[8] to come from Vienna and type the final draft.

Published in 1932, *The Dawn-Breakers* was a work that the believers studied in depth individually, in communities, and at summer schools. It was within that context that the Guardian's cable of 30 July 1936 was received. In St Paul, the Assembly included its last paragraph in its minutes, written exactly as follows:

The dawn-breakers in previous age have, on Persian soil signalized by their acts the birth of the Faith of Bahá'u'lláh. Might not American believers, their spiritual descendants, prove themselves in turn capable of ushering in on a world scale the civilization of which that Faith is the direct source and sole begetter?[9]

Shoghi Effendi chose to use the words 'signalized' and 'usher in'. Webster's Dictionary defines 'signalize' as 'to make conspicuous: distinguish', 'to point out carefully or distinctly'. 'Usher in' is 'to serve to bring into being', 'to mark the beginnng'.[10] The martyrs signalized the birth of the Faith. Now a generation was being called to mark the beginning of a world civilization by taking the first steps to manifest both the spiritual qualities and instructions for action described in the *Tablets of the Divine Plan*.

As 'Abdu'l-Bahá before him, though in a different station, Shoghi Effendi laboured for the rest of his life to
awaken the consciousness and guide the movements of
those who arose to serve, shaping individual awareness,
uniting communities, and ultimately building the institutions that became the necessary pillars for the supreme
institution to carry forward the Covenant of Bahá'u'lláh,
the Universal House of Justice. The Guardian was able
to interpret the magnificent vision of Bahá'u'lláh's
Revelation, while encouraging the humblest souls to
take small steps that, insignificant in themselves, took on
meaning as part of the whole.

Thus, in St Paul, Gayle Woolson took her first small
step to teach in another state. The Assembly minutes
note the following on 15 September 1936:[11]

> 'Letter written to N.S.A. regarding giving lectures at
> Glenfield, N.D.
>
> G.W. Sec'y'

This concerned a trip she herself hoped to take. The
minutes continue in Gayle's handwriting, 'May we pray
individually and collectively for a thousand times greater
power to promote His Cause.'

It was not easy to see how her efforts could be
increased a thousand-fold. Within less than a year, Gayle
had become independent through marriage and then
had been suddenly widowed. She and her husband's son,
Farhad Woolson, were both living at the Abas family
home at 235 Fuller. The household's support system had

been weakened with her grandmother's passing and her father's move to North Dakota in 1934. The family business had suffered during the Depression, resulting in her father's move in pursuit of business interests that might support the family through these difficult times. Her grandfather, mother and younger siblings needed help. Dahela, her sister, had already assumed increased responsibility. Nevertheless, Gayle sought a way to increase her efforts.

If she could travel, the idea of the trip to Glenfield, North Dakota would be a natural extension of activity. With her father in Pillsbury, (possibly as the first Bahá'í to settle in that state), there was both a family connection and a network of her father's friends with whom to develop relationships. In her personal papers, Gayle states:

It was these initial efforts of Mr. Abas that led to a visit of two Bahá'í teachers to Glenfield in 1937.[12] These teachers were Mrs. Mabel Ives, the wife of the Bahá'í author Mr. Howard Colby Ives, and Mrs. Gayle Woolson . . . This trip was arranged by the National Teaching Committee through the National Spiritual Assembly of the Bahá'ís of the United States and Canada. After Glenfield, Mrs. Ives and Mrs. Woolson visited Carrington and Fargo, North Dakota. The following year, upon request of the National Teaching Committee . . . Mrs. Woolson and Mrs. [sic] Marguerite Reimer . . . visited Glenfield and Pillsbury as part of the itinerary of their teaching trip into North and South Dakota.[13]

Mabel Ives and Marguerite Reimer were among a few teachers who had developed systematic ways of introducing the Bahá'í Faith into new communities.[14] Both were outstanding teachers who understood how to enter new communities, make contact with organizations, gain newspaper publicity, and follow up with interested inquirers. Gayle's offer to travel drew to her the chance to accompany them, under the guidance of the National Teaching Committee. All that she learned, she would later put to good use in her decades of work in Central and South America.

The significance of these opportunities lay not only in the intensive teaching agendas undertaken but also in the individuals Gayle came to know. Mabel and Howard Colby Ives[15] had married in 1920. Inwardly transformed by encounters with 'Abdu'l-Bahá in New York, Mr Ives had left his Christian ministry, chosen a business path that involved travelling and meeting many people, and devoted himself to bringing the Bahá'í teachings to as many people and areas as he could. Doris McKay describes Mabel and Howard coming together in marriage as like 'two swift-running streams' together forming a river:

> They settled in New York City and tried first to earn as quickly as possible enough to free their activities completely for the life of teaching, which they felt must somehow be theirs. The fate of all of us spiritual children of theirs hung in the balance on the day that these two had a certain talk in which they faced the

facts: they might go on all the rest of their lives working as others did and dreaming of the future – or they could take hold of the apparently impossible by both horns and go *then*. In 1921 they sold or gave away all their immediate possessions, answered an advertisement for two salesmen and started on their long Odyssey.

. . . In 1934, after fifteen years on the road, Howard . . . wrote . . . as follows:

'You ask me how we can accustom ourselves to homelessness. Our own vine and fig tree is a natural desire to the children of men; there is nothing reprehensible in this desire. Bahá'u'lláh has provided for this in His Law, dignifying the home and hospitality as a means of serving God. Nevertheless, there are a few of us to whom He whispers in the ear "Make My Home thy Mansion, boundless and holy" . . . 'Abdu'l-Bahá's words "Homeless and without rest" ring in my ears . . . Rest assured that God does not take away an earthly home without providing a heavenly one *right here on earth* if we accept His Will with radiant acquiescence.'[16]

Travelling with Mrs Ives and experiencing first hand a portion of such a path was an early step in Gayle's own journey, many years of which would be lived in transit, discovering the whole world as her abode. On the occasion of their trip together, Mrs Ives gave Gayle a gift: her husband's new book, *Portals to Freedom*, recounting how his life was affected by meeting 'Abdu'l-Bahá during his travels in North America.[17] For Gayle, these descriptions would resonate with memories of her husband's stories. As Mrs Ives and Gayle prayed and studied together; prepared publicity; gave lectures; listened to the questions and concerns of those they met; and consulted about their learning, driving from place to place, they also shared personal reflections. A friendship developed which Mrs Ives articulated in the inscription she wrote in the front of *Portals to Freedom* on 2 July 1937:

> For Gayle
> In fond memories of our journeys together pioneering in the Path of God – and the eternal friendship which has resulted. May your services become greater and greater continuing until the last day of your life. And your faith become stronger and stronger in the unfailing assistance of the Supreme Concourse. May your life be crowned with spiritual victories in the Kingdom of Bahá'u'lláh.

Mr Ives would leave this world on 20 June 1941 in Arkansas, Mrs Ives on 18 June 1943, in Oklahoma City. From 1940 to 1944, Gayle would be at her first international post, in Costa Rica, with more than seventy years of service ahead of her. Through Mrs Ives, she learned that one could live for decades as an itinerant teacher, without one settled home. She learned from the love that motivated this way of life.

The second teacher with whom Gayle travelled was Marguerite Reimer.[18] At the time of their trip together, Gayle was twenty-four and Marguerite twenty-five. Gayle had formally identified herself as a Bahá'í in 1933/34; Marguerite in 1934. Both would serve the Faith consciously and consistently to their last breath, Marguerite passing away at ninety-four, Gayle at ninety-seven.

Marguerite was a Bahá'í of many talents whose family was distinguished in the Milwaukee community. Her father, Charles Reimer, was a prominent businessman, the owner of meat-packing plants, and one of five who founded the Green Bay Packers. He had been a Bahá'í for several years. Mr Reimer and Mr Hassen Abas were long-time friends, as a photograph Gayle kept of the two of them serving in Milwaukee suggests. At the 1934 Convention, Marguerite had been moved by a presentation by a young woman named Mary Maxwell.[19] At a later time, she heard Mary dramatize *The Dawn-Breakers*, bringing history alive in ways Marguerite had never experienced. Following the Convention, Mr Reimer arranged for Marguerite to spend the summer with Mary Maxwell and her parents, including time in Montreal. Their friendship was woven of many strands, including not only shared spiritual devotion but also their very human experience as only children who loved animals.

Marguerite had already spent a full summer at Green Acre Bahá'í School, where she went to weekly evening sessions in the cottages of Horace and Doris Holley and of Louis and Louise Gregory. She mentions that at Mr Gregory's gatherings, he invited each person to tell the story of how he or she had become a Bahá'í. The purpose of this was to show how one could teach the Faith through one's own story, demonstrating those teachings that had drawn him/her to study the Faith.

Marguerite became a valuable resource for learning the very skill the Guardian had encouraged Gayle to develop: public speaking. Inspired by Mary Maxwell's presentations, Marguerite had completed a four-semester programme at the Curry School of Effective Expression in Boston. This school, founded by Mrs Curry and led for many years by Dr Alexander Graham Bell as board chairman and Mr Curry as director, was distinctive. Rather than teaching mere technique, it taught students to utilize imagination, thought and emotion to create an inner awareness from which to project their outer delivery. The programme also benefited from Dr Bell's scientific research on hearing and speech. In 1932, the school had added radio broadcasting courses. The director at Green Acre had invited Marguerite to offer several public speaking classes during her studies.

Marguerite had been driving long distances since she was sixteen years old and had her own car. The Depression Era being still with them, her father had forbidden her to get a job, saying it was unnecessary and would take one away from someone needing to support a family.

By the time Marguerite and Gayle travelled together, Marguerite had already made two intensive trips to South Dakota, accompanying an experienced teacher, Mamie Seto. Mrs Seto would use the driving time to teach her and prepare for meetings and lectures at the next stop. One can imagine Marguerite and Gayle conversing, as they drove 4,500 miles in all! Marguerite describes it thus:

I made a third trip to the Dakotas with Gayle Woolson
. . . We were of a similar age and probably the first
youth travel teaching team in America, if not the only
one . . . She and I left from Milwaukee and stopped
first in North Dakota . . . I remember that her father
gave us a five-gallon can of black olives that we placed
in the car between us, and gradually consumed them
over the course of our journey.[20]

With what joy Horace Holley must have written the
following teaching report for *The Bahá'í World*, remembering Marguerite Reimer spending evenings with other
youth at his cottage at Green Acre, learning about the
Faith:

Miss Marguerite Reimer of Milwaukee . . . and Mrs.
Gayle Woolson of St. Paul, spent six weeks doing
follow-up work and teaching in new cities in the
Dakotas. Their trip covered 4,500 miles by automobile; more than thirty-three lectures were given; the
Faith was introduced into four new cities; the study
class in Lead, South Dakota, was strengthened with
five new members, and a class was left in Huron,
South Dakota. Of special interest in connection with
the teaching work of these two youthful teachers is the
many lectures given in schools and colleges. [21]

A report in *Bahá'í News* included the following regarding
their trip:

Of outstanding interest is the fact that many lectures were given in schools and colleges. At Spearfish, South Dakota, for instance, a lecture was given before the student body of the Black Hills Teachers College; attended by 175 students, 25 members of the faculty, and 2 clergymen.[22]

Gayle had followed the Guardian's advice to use the children's classes as a stepping stone to learn public speaking and introduce the Faith to new areas. Together, Marguerite and Gayle further developed a thirst to learn and a consecration to service that would become lifelong. Each one independently found her way to the international arena. A few years after Marguerite married, she and her husband, the future Hand of the Cause William Sears, would sail for Africa. Gayle's preparation commenced in 1939, leading to Latin America.

6

Preparing for International Service

During the first sixteen years of the Guardianship, Shoghi Effendi had been systematically developing elements of the Administrative Order, the whole machinery of which, he had explained, was intended for the pioneering efforts called for in the *Tablets of the Divine Plan*.[1] His 1936 messages to the North American Bahá'ís indicated that the time had now come for the first collective implementation of these Tablets, the full significance of which no one could yet fully grasp. The unfoldment of Bahá'u'lláh's Covenant was entirely new to human history, with its clearly designated succession and its organically developing Administrative Order, adequate to channel the forces of revelation into a new pattern of civilized life. Of the *Tablets of the Divine Plan*, the Universal House of Justice has written:

The Divine Plan, that sublime series of letters addressed by 'Abdu'l-Bahá to the Bahá'ís of North America between 26 March 1916 and 8 March 1917, constitutes one of the mighty Charters of His Father's Faith. Set forth in those fourteen Tablets, Shoghi Effendi explains, is 'the mightiest Plan ever generated through the creative power of the Most Great Name'. It is 'impelled by forces beyond our power to predict or appraise' and 'claims as the theatre for its operation territories spread over five continents and the islands of the seven seas'. Within it are held 'the seeds of the world's spiritual revival and ultimate redemption'.

In the *Tablets of the Divine Plan* 'Abdu'l-Bahá not only provided the broad vision necessary to carry out the responsibilities entrusted by Bahá'u'lláh to His loved ones, but He also outlined spiritual concepts and practical strategies necessary for success. In His exhortations to teach and to travel to teach; to arise personally or deputize others; to move to all parts of the world and open countries and territories, each meticulously named; to learn the relevant languages and translate and disseminate the Sacred Texts; to train the teachers of the Faith and especially youth; to teach the masses and, particularly, indigenous peoples; to be firm in the Covenant and protect the Faith; and to sow seeds and cultivate them in a process of organic growth, we find hallmarks of the entire series of Plans – each a specific stage of the Divine Plan shaped by the Head of the Faith – that will continue to unfold throughout the Formative Age.[2]

Mírzá Ahmad Sohrab formally presented these Tablets (originally revealed from March 1916 to March 1917) to the 11th Bahá'í Convention in 1919. It was a gala occasion, held at Hotel McAlpin in New York City, then the largest hotel in the world. May Maxwell of Montreal presented a talk, 'The Seed Sowing of the Ages', inspiring many to arise and travel to all countries to plant the new teachings in the hearts of men.[3]

In direct response to this gathering in 1919, Louis Gregory and Joseph and Pauline Hannen initiated a systematic teaching programme to reach all the US southern states. Notably, this trip, affirming the equality of all and the oneness of humankind, took place in the context of the worst series of racial riots to take place throughout the country in many American cities. A few individuals arose to travel internationally. Martha Root was first; she ultimately travelled three times around the world. Emogene Hoagg and Marion Jack journeyed thousands of miles through Alaska. Hyde and Clara Dunn moved from California to Australia. Leonora Holsapple, with May Maxwell's encouragement, left for South America and settled in Bahia, Brazil. E. R. and Loulie Mathews travelled to several continents. Such efforts created a remarkable number of connections in other countries; however, the task remained of nurturing these relationships and developing them into communities with the administrative structure necessary for the eventual establishment of the Universal House of Justice, the supreme achievement towards which the Guardian's efforts were aimed.

Now, in 1937, with the Guardian's First Seven Year Plan for North America, people were called not just to visit but to settle in new areas. Following directly and precisely the Master's instructions in the *Tablets of the Divine Plan*, and particularly those Tablets to each area of the United States and Canada, the Guardian summoned the community to establish centres in every state of the United States and every province in Canada. Implementing the Tablet originally revealed to the United States and Canada on 8 April 1916, he now called upon them to establish centres in every country in Central and South America and in the Antilles.

Gayle has stated that it was two years after this, when she heard the Guardian's cable to the 1939 Convention, that she felt impelled to arise to international service. This cable included the following:

GUATEMALA HONDURAS SALVADOR NICARAGUA COSTA RICA PANAMA CUBA DOMINICA HAITI IMMEDI-ATE OBJECTIVES. THOUGH POLITICALLY UNSETTLED RELIGIOUSLY INTOLERANT SOCIALLY BACKWARD CLIMATICALLY INHOSPITABLE THESE UNEXPLORED TERRITORIES HOLD FORTH INESTIMABLE PRIZES AUDACIOUS ADVENTURERS PATH BAHA'I SERVICE. DEARLY BELOVED MARTHA'S UNRIVALED EXPERIENCE INDOMITABLE FAITH INDEFATIGABLE LABORS WILL SOON REINFORCE POWERS RELEASED CONTEMPLATED CAMPAIGN. TASK ADMITTEDLY LABORIOUS HOUR LADEN WITH FATE PRIVILEGE INCOMPARABLE PRE-CIOUS DIVINELY PROMISED AID UNFAILING REWARD PREDESTINED IMMEASURABLE. APPEAL ALL BELIEV-ERS WHITE NEGRO ALIKE ARISE ASSUME RIGHTFUL RESPONSIBIILITIES.[4]

Gayle turned to the recently-formed Inter-America Committee for guidance. The correspondence exchanged offers insight into her preparation for pioneering. On 7 August 1939, a letter from Sara Kenny on behalf of the Committee suggested she go to Costa Rica:

> San Jose is the capital and largest city. In a report or sort of digest which one of the believers has made of the Central American Countries, he says that he feels Costa Rica to be the corner-stone for the Faith in Central America; he refers to it as the Greece of Central America, saying that its people are very evolved and intelligent.[5]

On 10 August, Gayle wrote back that going to Costa Rica would be feasible and that she would not need financial assistance. She intended to leave in mid-November, though she ended up sailing on a United Fruit Company boat out of New Orleans at the end of February 1940, due to difficulties and delays in obtaining the proper entry papers.

Meanwhile, she was studying Spanish with a Mexican teacher.[6] When asked about the alternative possibility of going to the Dominican Republic, she stated that her Spanish was as yet 'quite meager', and she would need a translator for some time.[7]

On 28 August 1939, Mrs Kenny wrote to Gayle,

> We have found that ones' (sic.) entry is much more assured if one enters as a tourist. This also holds true in conversations with such officials as consuls. It is advisable not to indicate that religious teaching is ones

(sic.) objective, but rather to say that one is there to study the language or simply to enjoy the hospitality of the country. [8]

On 11 September, the Committee advised that due to the social conditions in the Latin American countries, it would be very difficult for a young woman to gain the confidence of the people if she were travelling alone. Second, due to immigration restrictions, it would be best for her to study at a university, possibly St Thomas University in San Jose. Amalia Ford, 'a Mexican Bahá'í in the San Francisco Bay region' was suggested as a chaperone companion. Mrs Ford was fifty-five years old; she had one son about Gayle's age. The letter states that Mrs Ford 'feels that her main work is not pioneer teaching so much as assisting someone else and creating the necessary background and atmosphere for that other person'.[9]

In reviewing correspondence between Gayle and the Inter-America Committee, one already notes what became her consistent lifetime habit: to obey the guidance of institutions with alacrity and precision. Many years later, in notes made for discussion at a potluck supper at the home of Lee and Larry Olson, she noted, 'Writing to the committee was like writing to a mother'.[10]

While making these decisions and arrangements, Gayle continued her home-front teaching. At the request of the National Teaching Committee, she spent several months on her own in Cedar Rapids, Iowa, where no teaching work had yet been done. Initially, she was there during December 1938, and January and part of

February 1939. The *Bahá'í News* of January 1940 gives a summary:

> Mrs. Gayle Woolson has spent the months of December and January in Cedar Rapids, Iowa, where she has found many opportunities for teaching which have carried her also to the near communities of Marion, Mt. Vernon, and Iowa City. Her public engagements have included such groups as Rotary, Optimists, High Twelve (Masonic), Hi-Y Clubs of four high schools, Coe College, and Phonetian Club of Syrian Girls.[11]

Regarding her first visit, she wrote:

> in addition to contacting clubs where I could give a Bahá'í talk, I . . . [answered an advertisement to attend] . . . a meeting of the Unity congregation in order to try to find contacts. That is where I experienced my most treasured memoire of Cedar Rapids. That occurred about the early part of December, 1938. When the meeting was over and the audience was walking out, I happened to be walking next to a lady with whom I started a conversation about the Faith. She was very receptive. And when I told her that a new Messenger of God, Bahá'u'lláh, had come, the spark was immediately further enkindled in her soul and she asked eagerly, 'Where is He?' Her acceptance was instantaneous. She was Mrs. Marie Beals. We maintained contact, and her enthusiasm and devotion were an inspiration to witness. I gave her literature,

and as time went on I told her about the forthcoming
National Baháʼí Convention that I was going to attend
in April at the Baháʼí House of Worship in Wilmette.
She immediately decided that she would like to attend
it, which she did – the 1939 National Convention. She
had a beautiful, sweet soprano voice, and she sang at
the opening of one of the Convention sessions, thrilling the audience with the spiritual fragrance of her
song. Mrs. Beals was the first Baháʼí of Cedar Rapids,
as of December 1938.[12]

Gayle returned to spend part of September 1939 in Cedar
Rapids, Iowa, to ʻcontinue some pioneer work which I
started last winter'.[13] Excerpts from the National Teaching
Committee Minutes report that she was in Cedar Rapids
from 22 May to 22 June. Six new people were studying
individually and hoped to have a group study in the
fall. She was also there during parts of November and
December. In her final report on 20 November, before
leaving for Costa Rica, Gayle wrote that for 19 days she
accompanied Marvin Newport, who had come to reside
in Cedar Rapids to continue the work started. He spoke
at a number of organizations whose combined audiences
totalled about 500. Thus, he was able to benefit from
and follow up with people she had come to know, while
establishing his own connections.

Each of Gayle's travel teaching trips contributed sig-
nificantly to her preparation for international service.
Years later, at the 60th Anniversary of the opening of
Cedar Rapids to the Baháʼí Faith, Gayle reflected on

the teaching process. From each teacher – Mabel Ives, Marguerite Reimer, Gertrude Struven, Marvin Newport, Ruth Moffett, and Orcella Rexford – she had learned about a particular life story and witnessed each person's approach, interests and skills. The prominent teachers of that time were strong individuals with distinctive personalities. However, they were united by their love of the Báb, Bahá'u'lláh, 'Abdu'l-Bahá, and Shoghi Effendi, and by their dedication to the Covenant. In most cases, efforts were harmonized by placing the needs of the Faith above personal consideration. As the book *Century of Light* states, this was one of the distinctive aspects of these early times. By working with these individuals, Gayle gained confidence and became adept at entering new communities; identifying and befriending diverse groups; attracting publicity through newspaper and radio; and giving eloquent presentations of Bahá'í themes tailored to each audience. With these experiences complementing the consultation and guidance she received from the Inter-America Committee, she was now ready to spread her wings for flight abroad.

7

'Costa Rica, the Beautiful'

As Gayle continued working to obtain the documents required to enter Costa Rica, a message from the Guardian, now known as *The Advent of Divine Justice*, was published. In it, Shoghi Effendi depicted how the Bahá'í communities in Germany, Russia, Iran, and the Holy Land had been constrained by political forces, leaving the Bahá'í community in North America as the 'chief remaining citadel' with freedom to carry forward the work of the Faith. He identified elements of the *Tablets of the Divine Plan* to be applied in preparation for service in Central and South America. He clarified that pioneers would take the first steps but that responsibility for subsequent development in each country would be assumed by the inhabitants themselves. He delineated the accomplishments of the North American Bahá'í community during the previous 20 years. He outlined those spiritual qualities with which the Bahá'ís must equip themselves to rise up from the matrix of an ailing society to become 'heavenly, lordly, and radiant'.[1] He outlined the tasks ahead. Then, in an outpouring of love, encouragement, and faith, he included passage after passage from Bahá'u'lláh and 'Abdu'l-Bahá, giving all of the spiritual sustenance needed for open hearts to be transformed.

It was with this magnificent vision and precise

instruction that Gayle Woolson and a constellation of others left homes, extended families, familiar surroundings and friends to settle in areas hitherto remote and unknown, in North, Central and South America.

As they set off on these life-changing journeys, many they loved and who held the same beliefs had to apply Shoghi Effendi's guidance to treading a sometimes more perilous path. This was true for the Woolson, Abas, and Kadrie families.

In 1940, during World War II, the United States instituted a military draft for all young men from the age of 21 to 35. By the end of 1941, those aged 18 to 64 had to register; subsequently, those 18 and 19 years old were all called up. During the period 1940–1947, over ten million people were inducted into the military. Through Shoghi Effendi's guidance and foresight, Bahá'ís were instructed to apply for 1-A-O non-combatant status, obeying the government but seeking to serve in ways that would not require them to take another's life. The National Spiritual Assembly had a Selective Service Advisory Committee to assist Bahá'ís with taking proper steps. These young people arose to the very kind of maturity that had been mentioned at the 1935 Convention.[2] They entered the military when called, obeying their government and the Bahá'í intitutions, despite their conviction that the war itself would solve nothing. Such individual actions ensured the unity of the Bahá'í community. The non-combatant status legally formalized and collectively attained furthered the Guardian's goal of establishing the independent status of the Bahá'í Faith as an independent world religion that stood for peace.

The draft affected all the male youth in the St Paul Bahá'í community. Gayle's brothers, Julian and Edward Abas, both served, as did the husbands of her sisters. (Years later, Gerald Abas, her youngest brother, would be called to serve as a non-combatant in the Korean War.) Dr Woolson's son, Farhad, just a year older than Gayle, was drafted in 1940. Although this writer has found no further details, his military death is documented as taking place on 1 August 1942, his burial at Fort Snelling Military Cemetery in Minneapolis. He died one month shy of his thirtieth birthday, while Gayle was in Costa Rica. The eligible sons of the Kadrie family were also called to serve. Thus, the young men from the St Paul Bahá'í youth group all became part of the war effort.

As Gayle set forth on her own journey, it was therefore with a vivid and personal sense of 'the rumblings of that catastrophic upheaval, which is to proclaim, at one and the same time, the death-pangs of the old order and the birth-pangs of the new'.[3]

When she packed for her journey to Costa Rica, she included a small exercise book, every line and page of which were filled with her careful handwriting in pencil. The first few pages have Spanish phrases she might need to introduce Bahá'í principles. Following this are quotations from the world's major scriptures, reflecting the Guardian's instruction to study comparative religion.[4] These would be useful, as she later found that many in Latin America had scant information about faith traditions other than their own and were eager to learn more. This need ultimately inspired her to write her first book, *The Divine Symphony*.

Other notebook pages contained passages from a book popular at the time: *In Tune with the Infinite*, by Ralph Waldo Trine, one of the early authors to write about the power and significance of thought, habits, and character building in shaping one's life. Although not a Bahá'í, he wrote *In Tune with the Infinite* at Green Acre Bahá'í School in Eliot, Maine,[5] penning such words as these that Gayle then copied:

> The great central fact in human life, in your life and in mine, is the coming into a conscious, vital realization of our oneness with this Infinite Life, and the opening of ourselves fully to this Divine Inflow.[6]

This is followed by various quotations from this and another contemporary book with guidance about character building, morality, and the habits that allow one to reach one's fullest potential in spirit, mind, and physical well-being. She kept the notebook to the end of her life.

Gayle's account of her journey to Costa Rica and the four years she spent there, reprinted here, was first published in *The Bahá'í World*.[7]

COSTA RICA, THE BEAUTIFUL

When I first read the fortifying, faith-imbuing statement of Baha'u'llah: 'They that have forsaken their country for the purpose of teaching Our Cause – these shall the faithful Spirit strengthen through its power. A company of Our chosen angels shall go forth with them, as bidden by Him Who is the Almighty, the All-Wise. How great the blessedness that awaiteth him that hath attained the honor of serving the Almighty! By My Life! No act, however great, can compare with it, except such deeds as have been ordained by God, the All-Powerful, the Most Mighty. Such a service is indeed the prince of all goodly deeds, and the ornament of every goodly act.' I felt reinforced with an assurance that I would never hesitate or be afraid to go to any foreign country in the service of the Holy Cause of Bahá'u'lláh. It was, then, in response to the Guardian's appeal for pioneers for Latin America in his message to the 1939 Convention that I was privileged to go to the beautiful land of Costa Rica.

Costa Rica, the heart of the Americas, with its friendly, warm-hearted people of world renowned hospitality, its rich picturesque scenery and delightful climate, is a jewel among Latin American countries unsurpassed in its beauty and charm. The name of this tiny Central American republic lying between Nicaragua and Panama means 'Rich Shore' which bears eloquent testimony to the country's wealth of blessings.

It was on March 23, 1940, that Mrs. Amalia Ford, the other pioneer, and I boarded the United Fruit Company steamship, the S. S. Ulua, at New Orleans, and headed for Costa Rica where we were to carry God's new Message which Bahá'u'lláh proclaimed to the world to cure the ills that exist in society by establishing the Divine Teachings He revealed for the unification and spiritual regeneration of humanity.

On our way, the boat made a day's stop at Havana,[8] Cuba, where we were met at the dock by Philip and June Marangella, the first pioneers of that country.[9] We spent a wonderful and eventful day with these devoted pioneers who have lent such valuable services to the establishment of the Bahá'í Faith in Havana. We spent a memorable afternoon in their apartment that day where we were gathered with the first Bahá'í of Cuba, Sr. Perfecto Perez, and held a memorial meeting for Mrs. May Maxwell, the great international Bahá'í teacher, who had recently laid down her life in the path of God in Buenos Aires, Argentina. After thirty-eight years of consecrated, selfless service to the Cause of Bahá'u'lláh, 'her earthly life, so rich, eventful, incomparably blessed' was 'worthily ended'. She who had won the 'priceless honor (of a) martyr's crown' and who has been titled the 'Mother of the Latin races' is a shining example and great source of inspiration to all Bahá'í teachers.

We landed at Puerto Limon, the Atlantic port of Costa Rica, on March 29th, after an extremely pleasant week's journey. Landing on Costa Rican shores was like entering into a new world. A thrilling new world it was, indeed, for I found myself, all at once, amidst Spanish speaking people, with different customs, temperaments and way of being. Not knowing Spanish at the time made this world especially new to me; Mrs. Ford, though, was well-versed in the language. We were immediately impressed with the friendly, cordial attitude of the people making us feel welcome the instant we set foot on their soil.

A most picturesque and fascinating trip was the hundred mile journey inland from the port to our final destination – San José, the capital city. It is regarded as one of the most beautiful rail trips in the world. Along the coast are the usual palm fringed bays, inlets and rivers and the typical beautiful vistas of the tropics, while the interior is high up in the mountains. An ever changing panorama of large banana, cacao and coffee plantations, sugar cane, coconut palms, tropical fruit and flower trees, orchid plants, valleys, rivers and streams, native huts with their friendly peasant owners waving at the passengers is disclosed as the train winds its way up the mountains until the lofty peaks of the Cordilleras, backbone of Central America, appear majestically on the horizon.

No less exhilarating than the magnificent scenery is the invigorating change that takes place in the atmosphere, introducing a springlike tang in the air as one leaves the warmer coastal region and is carried to the bracing altitude of the interior. The view throughout this section of the journey may aptly be described as breath taking. The whole valley of the Reventazon River may be seen with one sweep of the eye with the rushing river itself appearing as a tiny, narrow ribbon of white foam a thousand or more feet below the train. The charm and delights of Costa Rica grew hour by hour, and a highlight was experienced as the train, approaching San José, made a steep, winding climb into the heart of the mountain. The heights were seen above where San José is embedded, and as we went higher and higher, it was as though we were ascending to some mysterious, unknown kingdom high up in the heavens. A heart-gripping emotion was sensed as we reached the capital, the new recipient of the light of Bahá'u'lláh's teachings for world unity, universal love and spiritual brotherhood, an emotion both of gratitude for the privilege of being a bearer of this glorious message to this virgin territory, and of awareness of the great responsibility which such a mission implied.

San José is a beautiful, modern city, bordered on all sides with inspiring mountains. In addition to the numerous attractive parks, one sees an abundance of trees and flowers, occasionally an entire tree covered with red, yellow or lavender flowers adorning its setting. It has approximately 80,000 inhabitants, the majority of whom are of almost pure Spanish descent. The altitude of the city is about 4,000 feet above sea level which gives it an ideal spring-like climate the year around with an average sea level temperature of 70 degrees, somewhat cooler at night. Every morning is a bright spring morning in San José. There is no autumn or cold winter. The trees, shrubs and grass are green, and the flowers bloom throughout the year. It has two seasons, the dry season from November to April and the rainy season during the remaining months when its [sic] rains in the afternoons sometimes until evening, but the mornings are generally lovely and sunny. San José has been becoming more and more a summer resort.

In Costa Rica, one finds a peaceful, peace-loving, hospitable people, rich and poor alike, and a tranquil atmosphere with none of the hustle and bustle of the large cities of North America. Life moves along in a leisurely sort of way, and the visitor eventually comes to realize that, after all, a little more of the 'mañana' spirit helps to make life more enjoyable. The beautiful innate qualities of the Latin Americans make them splendid Baháʼís. They are a people of exquisite human feelings. They are kind, courteous, loving, friendly, and tactful. They are extremely careful not to hurt anyone's feelings, a trait which is a natural inclination of their sensitive natures. They have great spiritual and intellectual capacity, possess a keen sense of humor and are poets by nature, as among them the ability to compose poetry seems almost universally prevalent. Because of these characteristics and the growing trend toward liberalism, the Baháʼí Teachings have found great receptivity in Latin America.

Our first opening in getting our Baháʼí work started in San José was made through the Chamber of Commerce where we inquired about groups interested in liberal thought. We were informed that Señorita Esther Mezerville, a former director of the Girls' College and a member of the Theosophical Society was the one to see. The kind gentleman giving us this information even telephoned her and made an appointment for us to see her. She was a charming, gracious lady of dignified bearing who listened to the Message with interest. She took us to visit Professor

Roberto Brenes Mesen, well-known Costa Rican edu-
cator, writer, and poet, and his wife. In the course of our
conversation, we were delighted to learn that he had
spoken in the Temple some years ago when he lived
in Evanston and taught at Northwestern University.
Miss Mezerville also contacted the president of the
Theosophical Society in our behalf, who invited us to
their hall where Mrs. Ford presented the Message. We
found the Theosophists receptive to the Teachings and
to be our true friends and collaborators.

Things moved fast for us and within a month after
our arrival, a weekly Bahá'í study class was established.
The few attendants we had were from the Theosophical
Society and other contacts that were made. At that
time, we were living in a pension (boarding house)
and the landlady gave us permission to use her dining
room for our class. A funny incident occurred after
our first meeting when the landlady had a sudden
change of heart, and as the friends began to arrive
for the second meeting, she firmly informed us that
under no condition could we have our meeting there.
We felt we had the right to use our own bedroom so
we invited the friends in there but the lady would not
allow us to use any of her chairs. With the use of the
edge of the bed, some of our suit cases and the one
lonely chair we had in the bedroom for seats, we hap-
pily carried on our meeting. Through the efforts of
one of the friends, a small apartment was soon found
for us where our meetings were conducted with freedom and regularity.

Rapid progress was made with the marvelous cooperation of the friends. One would bring a relative, another a friend to the meetings and they would take active part by speaking and presenting papers they had written on the Teachings. They showed wonderful ability to express themselves both in speech and in writing. After the reading of passages from the Bahá'í Writings, most interesting discussions would follow. Almost invariably, someone would bring, of his own volition, a commentary he was inspired to write on some principle or aspect of the Cause. We were fortunate in getting fine publicity early in the course of our work as one of the new believers [Esther Le Frank][10] was the owner and editor of the magazine, *Alma Tica* (meaning Costa Rican Soul), in which a section was devoted to the Bahá'í Teachings in each edition. Since the war, however, this publication has been temporarily discontinued.

The group grew to the extent that the following year, 1941, when the time arrived for the formation of the Spiritual Assembly, there were twelve Costa Rican Bahá'ís to take part in the election. In a letter from Shoghi Effendi to the Spiritual Assembly of San José, written December 17, 1941, by the Guardian's secretary, he said: 'Your Assembly will go down in history as the first Bahá'í Assembly in Central America, a great distinction and blessing, and the Guardian feels that if you continue to progress so rapidly you will soon be in a position to spread the Cause, through representatives of your Community, in other neighboring lands.

This would be of great value to the work of teaching these divine laws and truths, as then the Latin Americans would be hearing it from the lips of their own people, in their own language, which, of course, would be very effective.'

The progress continued and in the following year on April 21, 1942, a Spiritual Assembly was formed in Puntarenas, a seaport on the Pacific side, in the province of that same name, another one of the seven provinces of Costa Rica. It was very interesting how this came about. Our one prized Bahá'í family of San José [the Mirandas] was visited by a son [Genaro][11] living in Puntarenas who was, as yet, unaware of the Teachings.

Upon being told of the Cause and reading some of the literature, he became aflame with ardor and devotion, finding, at last, that for which his soul was thirsting. He took Bahá'í books and pamphlets back with him when he returned to Puntarenas and in his place of work, the custom house, during spare moments, he would gather a few of his intimate friends, also employed in the Custom House or at the pier, and read the Teachings to them. He became the first Bahá'í of Puntarenas, and seven of the men were interested. They expressed a desire to form a study class. It was just at this time that the chairman of the San José Assembly[12] was transferred to Puntarenas in his work, enabling him to help the new group with their meetings. As Puntarenas is only a four hour train ride from San José, I was able to visit them once a month. These men all became Baháʼís and with the transfer of the San José Baháʼí making nine, the Spiritual Assembly was formed.

In June of that same year, the legal registration of the San José Spiritual Assembly with the Costa Rican Government was completed. According to Costa Rican law, the San José Spiritual Assembly is considered the mother Assembly in the country and any other Baháʼí Assembly formed in Costa Rica becomes automatically incorporated under the registration.

In the second letter from the Guardian, through his secretary, to the Spiritual Assembly of San José, dated July 26, 1942, he said: 'The progress which the Baháʼís of Costa Rica have made during the past year is little short of astounding, and shows the deep receptivity the people of that country have to the New Message of God which Baháʼuʼlláh has proclaimed to the world. You must all indeed be both proud and grateful that you live in a land so tolerant of progress, and which enables you to establish the blessed institutions ordained by our Faith.

'The establishment of the new Spiritual Assembly of Puntarenas is a great step forward, and the legal registration of the Cause and approval of the government marks a milestone in the progress of the Cause not only in Costa Rica but in Latin America.

'The more the Guardian receives news from the Central and South American Republics, the more firmly he becomes convinced of the great capacity possessed by the peoples of Latin America. They are proving themselves to be both deeply spiritual and intellectual, and he cherishes great hopes for their future development and their contributions to this glorious Faith of ours.

'How wonderful that in less than a hundred years the message that originated in the heart of Persia should have spread to the heart of Central America, and kindled such love and devotion and hope as now burns in the hearts of the new believers in that distant continent!

'The Guardian hopes that you will not only succeed in establishing further centers in your own native land, but that the activities of the Costa Rican Baháʼís will spread to neighboring countries and aid in the establishment of the Faith there.'

The Message has also penetrated into other provinces of Costa Rica. The Theosophical group of the province of Alajuela invited the Baháʼís of San José to present the Teachings at one of their gatherings. A group of thirteen Baháʼís and friends made the trip and an interesting meeting was held. Much receptivity and enthusiasm was shown by the new listeners. We left books and pamphlets to be circulated among them. The ground of human hearts is so fertile now that wherever a teacher would go and remain a while, a group would easily be established. There does not seem to be enough teachers to supply the demand of the spiritually hungry souls that are craving Divine Light.

Our first Baháʼí of Puntarenas had an experience that resulted in the Message being taken into the Costa

Rican province of Cartago. One day when he was at
the pier in his city, he noticed that a man was watching
him very intently. For several days, whenever he saw
that man, the man's eyes seemed to be fixed upon him.
He inquired from among his friends who the man was
and one said he thought he was a detective. This made
our Bahá'í quite indignant; why should he be watched
by a detective, he was not guilty of any offense! One
day the man passed the Bahá'í's home and the two of
them exchanged glances and an 'adios', the customary
greeting. A few days later the man passed the house
again. Our Bahá'í was in the parlor of his home which
is built close to the sidewalk. The window and door
were opened so the man stopped and casually started
a conversation. Some Bahá'í books on a table caught
his attention. 'What kind of books are those?' he
asked. Our Bahá'í, thinking that the man was checking
up on him and perhaps suspected him of having some
kind of literature which he should not have, proudly
answered that it was religious literature. 'May I see one
of those books?' he requested. The Bahá'í handed him
one, and in his inner perturbation did not even notice
which book it was. The man calmly and observingly
turned the pages. He then asked if he could buy the
book. The Bahá'í answered that he could borrow it and
then if he felt he wanted it, he could have it. The man
thanked him and took the book. It was *Bahá'u'lláh
and the New Era*. The Bahá'í found out later that the
man was not a detective but a guard at the pier and
one whose soul thirsted for Divine Truth and he knew

that our Bahá'í had possession of some new religious teaching.

Every day for some days later, the Bahá'í noticed that the man spent all his spare moments at the pier in reading the book. After finishing it, the man asked for another, then another, having read in all, *Bahá'u'lláh and the New Era*, *Wisdom of 'Abdu'l-Bahá*, and *Some Answered Questions*. The man later told the Bahá'í that he was moving to the province of Cartago and that he wanted to take the books with him. Some time later he wrote asking for more literature and for pamphlets to give to his friends. He was referred to me as it was more convenient to send literature from San José. His letter to me was very beautiful and unique in his inspired expressions of devotion for the Cause. Here is a part of his letter translated into English: 'It was on the 20th of July of this year (1943) that, by coincidence, this Sacred, Unique and Unparalleled depository of Teachings, *Bahá'u'lláh and the New Era*, came into my hands. I consider this date memorable, glorious, as today I have nothing comparable; and for me it is an inexhaustible fountain of light, guidance, hope, certitude and assurance. My ultimate, one and only resolution is the upholding of this Holy Cause.' In a letter which he wrote to our Bahá'ís of Puntarenas,[13] he said: 'For twenty-six years I have dedicated my time to searching and meditating on religious matters and never in my life have teachings like the Bahá'í Teachings come into my possession. I am astonished, extremely satisfied and also always interested, but it is an interest which is well defined and without possibility of retrogression. In the reading, study and meditation of the Bahá'í Teachings, I feel great joy and ecstasy; it is something supernatural indeed. I feel the breath of the Holy Spirit in all my acts and occupations. It is in truth something supernatural that moves me. I am, I can say, a new creature, glory and thanks be to God.'

A very successful method used by the San José group to build up the meetings and make them better known was to occasionally invite some outstanding person of the city to be our speaker. We had such fine men as Professor Roberto Brenes Mesen, former professor of Northwestern University and distinguished writer and poet; Mr. Joaquin Garcia Monje, owner and editor of the widely circulated literary magazine, *Repertorio Americano*, who has been very cooperative and generous in giving space for Bahá'í articles and who is an Ex-Minister of Public Education in Costa Rica and a former director of the Public Library, and has had the distinction of being invited by the League of Nations to visit Geneva; Professor Jose B. Acuna, one of Costa Rica's outstanding educators and psychologists, who is now teaching at the Wonona Teachers' College in Minnesota; and Mr. Benjamin Odio, lawyer, who also gave us his invaluable and generous assistance in obtaining the legal registration of the Spiritual Assembly. We deeply cherish the friendship of these kind friends and shall forever be grateful; for their valuable help.

Visits from other pioneers are always very effective and helpful in the development of a group. It is hard to express how a pioneer thirsts for visits from fellow-pioneers while in those virgin and distant lands, especially when a Community is just a new one, and what a great joy, rare treat and fortification it is to see them, to talk with them, to derive the blessings of their association and assistance. If only more would come! Pioneers who visited us in Costa Rica, in the order in which they came, were: Gerard Sluter, Mathew Kaszab, Cora Oliver, Louise Caswell, Johnny Eichenauer and Virginia Orbison. Gerard Sluter visited San José while on his way to Colombia from Guatemala; Mathew Kaszab came from Nicaragua, Cora Oliver and Louise Caswell from Panama, Johnny Eichenauer from Salvador after also having visited Honduras and Nicaragua, and Virginia Orbison visited us on her way to Chile from the United States. Each has left his special contribution to the growth and strengthening of the Costa Rican Bahá'í community.

The San José Community is proud that two of its members have done pioneer work, Dr. David Escalante who cooperated with Mrs. Dorothy Baker in Venezuela and Sr. Gerardo Vega who has assisted with the work in Panama.

It is such a great thrill and source of immeasurable joy to witness, through the wondrous ways of God, the birth, establishment and growth of a Bahá'í Community in a virgin land. Throughout every moment of activity, as one door of opportunity opens after another in the promotion of the Holy Cause of Bahá'u'lláh, the pioneer is always vividly aware of the miraculous and mysterious workings of His Divine Spirit, aware of his own utter nothingness and of how he does nothing, that he is merely an instrument, a key in the Hands of the Great Door-Opener and that it is His Spirit and Power that do the work.

The interesting experiences, joys and blessings of pioneering are indeed abundant, and once a taste of pioneer service is had, it is like something that gets into one's blood and it does not seem possible to be content without it; and what is given and sacrificed, be it of oneself or any other contribution, is as nothing in comparison to what is received in return, in both the spiritual and material sense of the word. It makes us realize that a mystery of sacrifice is that there is no sacrifice, as 'Abdu'l-Bahá tells us.

Of my many experiences, the following is one I shall always cherish. One day in June, 1942, a Chinese family moved into an apartment adjoining mine. The next day, as I heard one of my new neighbors walking in the corridor towards my front door, I, too, went toward the door to meet him. My wide front door which gave entrance directly into the parlor was open, and there in the doorway stood a dignified Chinese gentleman; he was looking at the Greatest Name which was hanging on the wall facing the entrance. 'You are a Bahá'í!' were his first words as he shook my hand. 'I am Mr. Z. T. Ing, the Chinese Consul of Nicaragua.

This is the third time I have seen this Bahá'í symbol,' continued the gentle, soft-toned visitor. 'The first time was in China when I met a very friendly Bahá'í teacher (regrettably, he could not remember her name), then once in the United States, and now here.' He then went back to his apartment and brought his wife, a sweet, gracious lady who was dressed in a charming Chinese garb, and in introducing us, he said: 'Mama, she is a Bahá'í.' They expressed an excellent opinion of the Bahá'ís. A few days later, after Mr. Ing had finished reading the *Wisdom of 'Abdu'l-Bahá*, he said that the Bahá'í Teachings would find great receptivity in China as that is the way the Chinese think.

He had brought his family from Managua, Nicaragua, to San José to enjoy more comfortable climate but his work called him back there. He would make occasional visits to San José and on one of these visits, when he was attending a Bahá'í meeting, he made a beautiful statement about the Cause which thrilled and inspired us. He said, 'I have faith in the Bahá'í Religion because it is the essence of all religions and the basis of it is that it accepts all races on an equal basis. It is something which meets with the needs of these times and it satisfies within. I firmly believe it will replace all the existing religions of the world and it will be the one Universal Religion for all.'

During the stay of the family in San José, we became very good friends and they were so kind, so hospitable and loving that I felt a part of them. They even gave me lessons in eating with chopsticks though

I always ended up resorting to the fork if I wanted any nourishment.

The way some of the believers are attracted to the Cause is often reminiscent of *The Dawn-Breakers* and shows how many are long before prepared in the spirit to receive the Divine Message. One believer of San José [Isabel Porras] had a dream seven years before she learned of the Cause in which she was sitting at the foot of a tree when a venerable figure of Oriental appearance, with a white beard and wearing a beautiful white turban approached her and handed her a tray on which were some exquisite fruit and a crystal pitcher of water. He spoke to her in her ear and as he did so she beheld a magnificent temple. It was seven years later when her husband [Carlos Porras] who was attending the Bahá'í meetings brought home the Spanish version of the *Wisdom of 'Abdu'l-Bahá* and as she opened it and saw the picture of 'Abdu'l-Bahá on the frontispiece, she recognized Him as the venerable figure in her dream.

The pioneer, besides enjoying the many happy experiences which flower his path, is faced with difficulties as well. One of these that came my way was experienced when I received a cable from home notifying me of the grave illness of my mother and later of her passing. My family wanted me to come home but I did not feel I could leave my post. The situation was difficult because of very young brothers and sisters at home. It was my sister Dahela who took over our mother's place with the family responsibilities,

On the balcony of her apartment, San José

At work, Pan American Highway Department

With Pan American co-workers

Building friendships, Costa Rica, 1943

First Spiritual Assembly of San José, Costa Rica, 1941

Bahá'í community of San José, Costa Rica, 1944

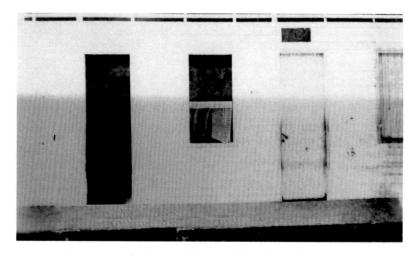

*Entrance to the home of Genaro Miranda in Puntarenas,
Costa Rica, where the initial Bahá'í meetings took place,
and continued there for a long time*

*First Spiritual Assembly of Puntarenas, Costa Rica, 1942
(Gayle with them, front row, centre)*

and though young herself, she valiantly shouldered her task. This enabled me to remain in Costa Rica and since then I have always rightfully referred to her as the 'pioneer at home' as had it not been for her, I would not have been enabled to remain in the pioneer field. It was soon after this that Mrs. Ford returned to the United States after a year and a half of devoted service.

My adventure in learning Spanish began upon my arrival in Costa Rica. In fact, there is no better school for acquiring a foreign language than to be in the country where it is spoken. At first I attended the girls' college known as the 'Colegio Superior de Senoritas' and although I did not receive instruction in Spanish there, I went to be among the students to hear the language spoken by them and the teachers and to practice by means of conversation with the girls. It was a most delightful experience. Outside of school, I had a private Spanish teacher from whom I received two lessons a week. The following year I attended the newly inaugurated University of Costa Rica. I made a special study of the verbs and concentrated much effort on learning the various conjugations. In my conception, once the verbs are grasped, the rest in Spanish comes easily. It is a beautiful, rich language and a key for unlocking the treasures of the Latin American soul.

The Costa Ricans love the English language and many of them speak it. They are especially eager to study it with some one from North America so as to hear the American accent. It was shortly after I arrived that I found myself with several students. The number of students grew as time went on and eventually I was also able to give Spanish lessons to a few English-speaking students. This work was continued until I was employed as secretary and translator at the Pan-American Highway Office which was set up in San José.

While in Costa Rica, I met people from various Latin American countries, and it was interesting to note how those from different countries spoke Spanish with different inflections, each having a typical melody peculiar to his country. One can recognize those from other countries by the 'song' in their speech. When I visited Guatemala after learning Spanish in Costa Rica, I was amused when Guatemalans would say to me, 'You come from Costa Rica, don't you?' They could tell, they said, because I spoke with the Costa Rican song. The people from Panama, Nicaragua, Guatemala and Mexico, for example, have a very marked inflection.

It was a jubilant occasion when the delegate of Costa Rica to the Centenary Convention [Rául Contreras] was informed by the National Spiritual Assembly that he would be enabled to go to the United States to attend that momentous event. He brought the letter to me to translate it for him and we could hardly believe it to be really true; we had not considered that such a great undertaking could be realized, making it possible for the Latin American delegates to attend that glorious celebration within the walls of our majestic Temple.

As we read this wonderful news, we were so over-taken by emotion and excitement, we did not know whether we were going to laugh or cry. Profound joy and gratitude filled our hearts. All the Latin American delegates must have felt that same emotion when they learned that an experience that occurs once in a life-time was to be theirs. Only the power of Bahá'u'lláh could accomplish such a great achievement, to bring together in love and unity representatives of these various Latin American countries with all those that would be gathered in North America, breaking down the barriers of distance, language and lack of means and demonstrating that spiritual brotherhood which is the salvation of all nations. This undertaking had a great effect not only on the Bahá'ís of Latin America but also on the other Latin Americans who learned of it, making them realize more deeply the scope and power of the Cause of Bahá'u'lláh.

After four years in the wonderful country of Costa Rica, the time had come for my departure. It had been like going through four years of school, a school of life, to better enable me to serve the Cause of God. The evening before I left, a happy close to my stay was occasioned by the one who was the first to open the doors to the Message in that country, Miss Esther Mezerville, a former director of the Girls' College and an outstanding member of the Theosophical Society not only in Costa Rica but in all of Latin America. She told me that she was going to speak of the Bahá'í Faith at their meeting that evening and so I attended.

After the kind words of the president who spoke of the important work of the Bahá'í Faith in Costa Rica, Miss Mezerville spoke of world unity as the sign and need of the times and said that in their endeavor to seek their ideal of world brotherhood, they must be alert to movements working toward unity in the world today. She then put emphasis on the great work of the Bahá'í Faith in fostering unity among all religions and races, and stated, 'I am now reading *Bahá'u'lláh and the New Era,*' as she drew the book out of her purse, 'and I am convinced that the Bahá'í Faith is the future religion of the world.' She recommended the investigation of the Teachings to her fellow members. Her beautiful words and the spirit and conviction with which she spoke them shall ever be engraved on my heart.

It was on April 18, 1944, that I left Costa Rica to spend three weeks in Guatemala City and then return to the United States. There were mixed emotions within me on that lovely bright morning as friends, both Bahá'ís and non-Bahá'ís, gathered to see me off at the airport and showered me with gifts, bouquets and corsages. The feeling of sadness on leaving these dearly-beloved friends was mingled with that of joy at visiting another Latin-American Bahá'í Community and then attending the Centenary Convention and seeing my family and friends at home again. As I boarded the Pan-American airship, I waved to the friends with a feeling of comfort in knowing that the Costa Rican Bahá'ís would staunchly carry on their vital task.

On the way to Guatemala, the plane made a short

stop at Nicaragua, Honduras and Salvador, and at each of these countries it was thrilling to have a brief visit with Bahá'í friends who were waiting for me at the airport.

Every moment of my visit to Guatemala City with our wonderful pioneer, Mrs. Florence Keemer, and the Guatemalan Bahá'ís was so filled with activity and glorious experiences that it, in itself, is a long story. Here is a beautiful, picturesque and colorful city; it is modern and sparkles with cleanliness. The streets of Guatemala are said to be the cleanest in the world. This beauty was glorified by its lovable people, equally as those of Costa Rica. Mrs. Keemer's radiant love and charm had won her many friends among whom there was an amazing receptivity to the Divine Teachings, and her excellent work was exemplified by the outstanding Bahá'í group I was privileged to know and work with for that short period.

There are indeed priceless treasures in store for anyone who arises to serve the Cause. 'The Almighty will no doubt grant you the help of His grace, will invest you with the tokens of His might, and will endue your souls with the sustaining power of His holy Spirit.

'All must participate, however humble their origin, however limited their experience, however restricted their means, however deficient their education, however pressing their cares, however unfavorable the environment in which they live.

'The field is indeed so immense, the period so critical, the Cause so great, the workers so few, the time

so short, the privilege so priceless, that no follower of
the Faith of Bahá'u'lláh, worthy to bear His name, can
afford a moment's hesitation.'[14]

* * * * *

During the first year that Gayle Woolson and Amalia
Ford were in Costa Rica, a letter dated 1 November 1940
arrived on behalf of the Guardian addressed to them:

Dear Bahá'í Sisters:

Your joint and welcome letters dated August 6th and
9th enclosing copies of reports you have submitted
to the Chairman of the Inter-American Committee
covering your teaching activities in Costa Rica, have
all safely reached our beloved Guardian, and he was
indeed immeasurably delighted by their perusal.

He feels truly proud and rejoiced at the notable
successes you have both so remarkably achieved, and
judging by the number of contacts you have already
established, the ground there seems to be quite fertile for the spread of the Cause. Though the number
of confirmed believers is only four, you should be
hopeful that through your painstaking and persistent
efforts, as well as through the guidance and confirmations of Bahá'u'lláh, you will be able to raise to nine,
and thus be in a position to proceed with the formation of your first local Assembly in that land. This is
the chief objective which the Guardian wishes you
to set as your goal for this year, and he himself will

earnestly pray that your joint endeavors to that end may be crowned with speedy and complete success.

With his loving good wishes and greetings to you, and to our four dear believers in San José, and assuring you again of his abiding appreciation of your devoted services.

Yours in His Service,
H. Rabbani

May he Who watches over and sustains His Faith, protect, guide and bless you always, and aid you to add fresh laurels to the crown you have won in the service of His glorious Faith.

Your true and grateful brother,
Shoghi [15]

As with the letter Gayle had received from the Guardian about children's classes, Shoghi Effendi acknowledged achievement in a context that then envisioned further expansion of effort. The death of Middíyyih Abas, her mother, in 1941, and Gayle's decision to remain at her post rather than returning home, lends poignancy to her perseverance and to her receipt of the Guardian's next message of 19 July, upon the formation of the Spiritual Assembly of San José. This letter was addressed to 'Mrs Gayle Woolson':

Dear Bahá'í pioneer:
Shoghi Effendi has instructed me to answer your most welcome letter of April 24th.

The Guardian was truly overjoyed by the news of

the formation of the Spiritual Assembly of Costa Rica. This constitutes a landmark in the southward march of the Faith of God, and you and Mrs Ford should feel the most justifiable pride and feelings of triumph at this truly great achievement.

The loving and ardent prayers of the Guardian will continue to be offered on your behalf and on behalf of the members of this precious new community and those who are not as yet declared believers.

Shoghi Effendi was very pleased to note that both you and Mrs Ford have been elected to the Spiritual Assembly. In this way you can assist the new Bahá'ís to understand and practice the administration through active participation with them in handling the affairs of the community.

The spiritual and intellectual nature of Latin peoples should tend to make them very profound and excellent Bahá'ís. The Guardian has the highest hopes for their future services to the Cause of God and the important contributions they will make to its unfoldment and establishment.

Assuring you of his profound appreciation for your services and his loving prayers for your future work,

Yours in His Service,
With Bahá'í love,
R. Rabbani[16]

It is interesting to note that Gayle's account of her journey published in *The Bahá'í World* does not include the personal communications written by the Guardian in his own hand. She seems to have quietly concentrated the vision and encouragement they contained into deeds. Shoghi Effendi's personal postscript to this letter, dated 19 July 1941, reads:

Dear and valued co-workers:
I wish to congratulate you most heartily on such a wonderful and glorious achievement.[17] Future generations will extol your labours, follow in your footsteps, and derive inspiration from your pioneer activities. I will specially and constantly pray that your numbers may increase, and your assembly flourish, and your hopes be fulfilled, and your influence extend far and wide. Persevere, and be happy.

Your true and grateful brother,
Shoghi

It was following the formation of the Spiritual Assembly of San José that Amalia Ford requested permission of the Inter-America Committee to return to California to be once again with her family. This request was granted.[18]

Meanwhile, the Spiritual Assembly pursued its next goal: incorporation. Gayle described her collaboration with Horace Holley in the process of preparing the necessary legal papers in an unpublished article entitled 'Remembrances of Horace Holley, Hand of the Cause of God'.[19]

While at that post I had contact with Mr Holley through correspondence when I was acting as representative of

the newly-elected Spiritual Assembly of the Bahá'ís of
San José, Costa Rica, the capital city (1941), and he
as secretary of the National Spiritual Assembly of the
United States and Canada relative to the preparation of
the documents for the incorporation of the Assembly
of San José. His assistance was invaluable in adjust-
ing the established Bahá'í By-Laws to Costa Rican law.
My task was to work as an intermediary with a Costa
Rican lawyer in the preparation of the documents.

In the obituary that Amatu'l-Bahá Rúḥíyyih Khánum
wrote for Horace Holley in *The Bahá'í World,* she noted
the following:

Horace Holley 'was largely responsible for drafting,
in conjunction with a Bahá'í lawyer, the American
Declaration of Trust of the National Assembly and the
By-Laws of a Local Assembly which have been made
by Shoghi Effendi the pattern for all such legal instru-
ments of the Faith in other countries.'[20]

Incorporation of Assemblies was a high priority of the
Guardian, as it established Bahá'í institutions as legal
entities, a status critical to the recognition of the Faith as
an independent world religion and to its ability to hold
title to property throughout the world.

It was when the Guardian was advised of the successful
completion of the incorporation of the San José Spiritual
Assembly that he wrote the following, dated 26 July 1942,
as quoted above in Gayle's account of her journey:

The progress which the Bahá'ís of Costa Rica have made during the past year is little short of astounding, and . . . the legal registration of the Cause and approval of the government marks a milestone in the progress of the Cause not only in Costa Rica but in Latin America.[21]

8

A World Celebration: Centenary of the Declaration of the Báb

Just as Shoghi Effendi's plans faithfully followed the instructions of the Báb, Bahá'u'lláh, and 'Abdu'l-Bahá, so also their timeframe coincided with significant anniversaries in the lives of the Central Figures of the Faith. Thus, the first Seven Year Plan culminated in worldwide commemorations of the 100th Anniversary of the Declaration of the Báb in 1844. Of this moment in history, Shoghi Effendi wrote:

> Thus drew to a close the first century of the Bahá'í era – an epoch which, in its sublimity and fecundity, is without parallel in the entire field of religious history, and indeed in the annals of mankind. A process, God-impelled, endowed with measureless potentialities, mysterious in its workings, awful in the retribution meted out to everyone seeking to resist its operation, infinitely rich in its promise for the regeneration and redemption of human kind, had been set in motion in <u>Sh</u>íráz, had gained momentum in Ṭihrán, Ba<u>gh</u>dád, Adrianople and 'Akká, had projected itself across the

92

seas, poured its generative influences into the West, and manifested the initial evidences of its marvelous, world-energizing force in the midst of the North American continent.

It had sprung from the heart of Asia, and pressing westward had gathered speed in its resistless course, until it had encircled the earth with a girdle of glory.[1]

Thus, for the 1944 Centenary, gatherings were planned in the Holy Land, Persia, the British Isles, India, Egypt, Iraq, Australia, Latin America, and North America. These were not isolated events but rather nodes in a single unfolding process that concentrated people, guidance, and the energy of universal love in gatherings generating new awareness and inspiration. The forces thus released would be translated into action and community growth as people returned to serve in their respective countries.

The 'All-America' Convention, held simultaneously with the 36th National Convention of the United States and Canada, formally opened at the Bahá'í House of Worship in Wilmette. On 19 May, as the time drew close to 8:00 p.m., participants approached the outer gardens in hushed awe. They often stopped to gaze up at the Temple as they walked along Linden Avenue, lined with spring-green trees and paved with red cobblestones, or came along Sheridan Avenue by the shore of Lake Michigan. Brilliant floodlights combined with lighting from within gave the building an ethereal presence, revealing what had truly become a majestic Temple of Light, with its white, deeply carved and lacy exterior ornamentation now complete – a goal of the Seven Year Plan.

Many who gathered that first night were themselves fruits of the Seven Year Plan, coming, as they did, from newly-opened states and provinces of North America and from twelve of the countries eventually represented from the south. The Centenary Program lists the following republics as having 'Participating Baháʼí Communities': Argentina, Bolivia, Brazil, Chile, Colombia, Costa Rica, Cuba, Ecuador, El Salvador, Guatemala, Haiti, Honduras, Jamaica, Mexico, Nicaragua, Panama, Paraguay, Peru, San Domingo, Uruguay, and Venezuela.[2] Of those, all but Bolivia, Haiti, Uruguay, and Peru had a representative present either in May, July, or at both times. The entire programme was unprecedented in its wide international representation, its unified consultative process, and the spirit of friendship and ongoing collaboration generated in a world still at war.

The Centenary offered Gayle an opportunity to welcome her co-workers from the south, serving both as a familiar friend and as official translator when needed. Interspersed in this process were poignant moments of homecoming. This was a place associated with her own spiritual awakening. It was here she had come with her husband just after their wedding and five months before his sudden death would precipitate a crisis that ultimately led to her service in distant lands. She greeted and embraced her father for the first time since her mother's passing. She saw her brothers and sisters, inspired by the same vision, though called to serve in contrasting ways during the upheaval of war. She saw friends from earlier times.

In her article for *The Bahá'í World*, Edna True reflects on the significance of this first gathering:

> To such vitally important and definite milestones in the growth of the Bahá'í Faith undoubtedly belongs the Centennial Celebration held in Wilmette, Illinois, May 19th to May 24th, 1944 . . . In spite of the manifold and seemingly insurmountable difficulties and regulations or [sic] travel in war-time, representatives from twelve of the Latin American Republics were miraculously enabled to participate in the epoch-making first 'All America' Convention, which was held during this Centenary, and in the July Conference which followed. In Foundation Hall of the Bahá'í Universal House of Worship, they had participated freely, in complete unity and harmony with the other delegates from the North American States and Provinces of Canada, in the important deliberations and discussions of the Convention, and had themselves taken a distinguished part in a practical and convincing demonstration of true equality without any distinction whatsoever of race, color, creed or class. With their horizons suddenly extended far beyond their own local and sectional interests, they found themselves concerned with the welfare and progress of the Bahá'í Community as a whole, and beyond the range of hemispheric solidarity, they caught a glimpse of the progressive unfoldment of the Divine Plan which

in its final stage will be world-embracing, bringing peace, security, and spiritual well-being to all mankind . . . The delegates assembled from all of the Americas, North, Central and South, turned homeward with fresh inspiration, renewed dedication, and firm resolve to carry ever forward the development and establishment of the Divine Plan, the pattern and certain unfoldment of which were now so clearly discernable. To the members of their respective communities, they carried with them a new conception and realization of the greatness and universality of the Bahá'í Faith, a clearer vision of the unfolding processes and of the hope and assurance it held for the whole world.[3]

During the days in Wilmette, the Latin American delegates were all invited to share input for the upcoming Plan. Together, they gained experience in consultation, the foundational process used in the administrative institutions to be raised up in their respective countries and around the world.

The resulting action plan included but was not confined to the following:

◆ Follow-up to countries where local Assemblies had yet to be established: sending pioneers to countries that did not yet have an assembly, including Bolivia, the Dominican Republic, Ecuador, Panama, Nicaragua, Uruguay, and Venezuela. By April 1945 all but Nicaragua had an Assembly.

Gayle on her way to the 1944 Centenary celebrations, Wilmette

Reunions at the Centenary: Gayle (right) with her father Hassen Abas and Cora Oliver, pioneer to Panama; and with her brother Edward and sisters Victoria and Loreli

NATIONAL BAHÁ'Í ASSEMBLY AND
LATIN - AMERICAN REPRESENTATIVES
JULY 9, 1944

*National Spiritual Assembly of the United States and Canada
with the representatives from South America*

*Centenary concert at Orchestra Hall, Chicago, 24 May 1944,
with the House of Worship as stage set*

*Bahá'ís serving in the military who attended the Centenary; pioneer John
Eichenauer, on his own in the second row; Gayle's brother Julian Abas is
in the back row, second from right*

Banquet for the Latin American representatives, July 1944

At Temerity Ranch, 1944, with the Inter-America Committee, Leroy Ioas, and prospective pioneers. Gayle and Louise Baker sitting on the floor

- ◆ Establishment of committees for the translation and publication of books, pamphlets, and newsletters. These were set up in Buenos Aires (Spanish), Rio de Janeiro (Portuguese), and Mexico (distribution of materials from Argentina and creation of circulars).
- ◆ Sending of itinerant teachers throughout Central and South America. At this point, Emeric and Rosemary Sala and Charles Mason Remey made extensive trips throughout South America. Mr Remey visited every centre where there were Bahá'ís. The Salas visited 19 countries.
- ◆ Planning and execution of the Central American Teaching Conference.

In addition to regular evening programmes, there were two major celebratory events whose significance was shared with the public at large. On 24 May Antoinette Rich conducted the Chicago Ladies Grand Piano Symphony Orchestra in 'An International Tribute to the Oneness of Mankind', held in Orchestra Hall, Chicago. The stage was set with a literal orchestra of pianos, arranged in a sequence of arcs that led back to a huge representation of the House of Worship itself. It was as though the pianos and therefore the music were ascending the steps of the edifice, as they played a new musical composition entitled 'The Making of the Temple'.

On 25 May, about 1,600 Centenary delegates, guests, and visitors assembled in a single location that could accommodate them all: the ballroom of the Stevens Hotel in Chicago. There they commemorated the fiftieth anniversary of the first mention of the Faith in the Western Hemisphere, which took place at what is now the Art Institute of Chicago. Following dinner, at 9:30 p.m., a culturally diverse array of speakers presented a radio broadcast from the hotel, framed at the beginning and end with inspirational music by opera singer Walter Olitski.[4]

Following these events, Gayle attended the session at Temerity Ranch.[5] Mrs Loulie Mathews, a member of the Committee, had with her husband established this school on their property in Colorado Springs, Colorado. In her Preface to the school programme, Mrs Mathews described how the school emerged through the intersection of their yearning to serve with the needs of the Plan:

> In 1929 I developed pneumonia of a type usually fatal. The family, frantic with anxiety, cabled Shoghi Effendi and he replied that my work was not yet finished and that he would pray that I might be spared to complete it. His prayers were answered. But the landmarks of a lifetime had to be abandoned. Under the shadow of Pike's Peak, in a wild valley, a new home was built and we named it 'Temerity' because of the courage required to begin life anew . . .
>
> In 1932 my health was sufficiently restored to cross the Pacific on a teaching journey. The success of this voyage encouraged us to ask advice of our Guardian. He replied that to go into Central and South America was the most important service, because the Faith must soon be established in these countries.

Before sailing I spent an hour with Martha Root. She described crossing the Andes on a donkey, with the peaks towering above her as she cried out the Greatest Name, that it might vibrate through the land. Shortly after her journey a landslide obliterated the pass and it has never been reopened. I remember the earnestness of our parting as she said, 'We must take no rest – all of our time belongs to God.'

The trek extended over many months. Each one of the picturesque countries of Central America were visited. The journey took us through the Panama Canal, down the west coast of South America, through the Chilean Lakes into Argentina and afterwards up the irregular and endless coast of Brazil. Following this journey the pioneers were called through Shoghi Effendi's 'Advent of Divine Justice' and before six years had passed, twenty-six believers were scattered among the Latin American people. They, like the disciples of old, pushed forward into untrodden paths.

Returning from Africa in 1939 to the Rocky Mountains which had become dear and familiar, I awoke one summer morn at dawn just as the valley was flooding with a carnival of light. One has no memories in the presence of the oncoming day. The sun is rising and you are standing witness to a new creation. In that instant of stillness that precedes the first sun rays, a message flashed across the vast spaces into my heart. 'This house, this land, does not belong to you; it has a high purpose of its own, above the needs of family or friends.' It was for a definite purpose life was broken; it

was that a work might be begun that is independent of
individual life. The Sun of Truth has conferred a blessing on these barren acres . . . The valley is a part of the
Divine Plan and will blossom as a rose in the spiritual
planting of the future.[6]

It was in this way that the Inter-America Committee
came to develop its training centre at Temerity Ranch.
Mr and Mrs Mathews and other committee members
had themselves travelled widely. Collectively, they had
first-hand knowledge of the languages, religions, and
cultures of the countries to which they would send pioneers. They developed a curriculum that included not
only Bahá'í subjects and practical travel information,
but an array of subjects important to understanding
the peoples the pioneers would befriend. These topics
included the following: Bahá'í history, Holy Days, calendar, and moral teachings; international studies such as
Bolshevism, Latin American relations and race relations;
religious/philosophical subjects such as prophecies of
the Old and New Testaments, Catholicism, the Papacy
and Guardianship, Rosicrucian teachings, Theosophy,
and the Socratic Method.

Additionally, on six evenings, the school hosted the
public for a series of programmes remarkable in their
integration of the arts, social concerns, spiritual teachings, and community participation. The first evening,
held in a Halfway House at 12 Boulder St., was a round
table discussion, 'What are the remedies for World
Chaos?' Presenters discussed problems of a modern

artist; problems for developing arts and crafts in a community; problems of a civic community and problems in international trade. On the first evening, Mark Tobey, a well-known artist who was also a Bahá'í, offered his perspectives. The second evening's speaker was from the local community: the President of the local Fine Arts Center gave an address and slide presentation with live piano accompaniment. Between these two was an afternoon programme on the theme 'The Rhythm of Creation'. It included three presentations: 'The Rhythm of the Seasons'; 'The Return of the Qualities'; and 'The Return of the Messengers of God', followed by several classical songs related to the theme. On the last day, the programme at the Arts Center focused on engaging community members in thinking of ways to increase 'Spanish American appreciation' and encouragement of Latin American people in the community.

Temerity Ranch was significant not only because it prepared pioneers conceptually but because it modelled ways to integrate the arts with presentation and discussion as a means to engage the wider community in spiritual and civic discourse. Gayle wrote that during the school the idea arose to use this programme as a framework for the first Central American Teaching Conference in Panama, later held in January of 1946. Using this template would create an economy of effort. As at Temerity Ranch, learning the framework would give participants confidence that they could then organize and execute future institutes and conferences in their own countries, feeling free to adapt its activities to the cultural and developmental needs of each community. This approach reflected the Guardian's guidance that pioneers must function as catalysts, empowering the Latin American believers and communities to become the protagonists of their own development and destiny. The combination of the May Convention and Celebration, the Temerity Ranch programme, and the July gathering described below lent a mounting impetus to the efforts of those returning or moving south to implement the upcoming Second Seven Year Plan. Gayle's article from *The Bahá'í World* describes the July programme and schedule of events in detail. Of the spirit of the gathering, she wrote:

> It was an echo of the convention which vibrated that same intense spirit of unity, love and brotherhood expressed amongst all the friends, and that same profound reverence and awe felt upon seeing the majesty and beauty of the Temple and the portrait of the Báb. Through the careful and excellent planning of the Centenary Committee and the kindness and hospitality of the friends in the Temple area, this special session was a great success . . .
>
> The Latin American delegates were deeply touched and expressed their profound gratitude and appreciation for the kindness, hospitality and generosity demonstrated by the North American friends. They felt that this experience has brought about a greater spirit of unity cementing the three Americas and that their carrying back this new fire and wider vision will exert great influence in their countries. [7]

9

International Travel

As September's trees became touched with gold and the first leaves fell in 1945, Gayle prepared to leave St Paul for what would be an extended period of international travel. The year and three months just spent with her family had been their first real visit since she had left to pioneer and since her mother had passed away. With the War now formally ended,[1] her brothers and brothers-in-law had been gradually returning home to their families to resume lives whose goals had been interrupted by military service. Cherishing memories of reunions, while also now anticipating new adventures, Gayle set off for Wilmette. Here, Edna True and other members of the Inter-America Committee offered instruction and guidance for her upcoming work. This journey south would initiate 'a period of two years of almost continuous traveling for the Faith, including visits to almost all of the countries of Latin America'.[2] The National Spiritual Assembly had asked that Gayle begin by accompanying Dorothy Baker during her upcoming visit to Mexico City, where the community needed assistance with some difficult matters.

Edna True accompanied Dorothy Baker and Gayle to the train station, as they left for Mexico. Once settled in their seats, Dorothy took out a copy of the newly published book by Shoghi Effendi, *God Passes By*.[3] Gayle had not seen it. The Guardian had timed its completion to synchronize with the 100th Anniversary of the Declaration of the Báb in 1944.[4] The narrative distils the first century of Bahá'í history; articulates the divine principles and historical forces at work; and creates a condensed template from which many histories will be written in the future. Gayle and Dorothy, both eloquent speakers, would have recognized with amazement how the Guardian distilled the whole Dispensation of the Báb on the first page, how factual precision was expressed in a prose that seemed to merge into poetry and song. The final sections of the book list achievements to which Dorothy, Gayle, and their contemporaries had themselves contributed, setting the stage for the Guardian's call to their generation to become 'spiritual descendants of the Dawn-breakers'.[5]

As they pored over its contents that day on the train, Dorothy showed Gayle the following passage:

> Finally, He [Bahá'u'lláh] said: 'Bid them recite: "Is there any Remover of difficulties save God? Say: Praised be God! He is God! All are His servants, and all abide by His bidding!" Tell them to repeat it five hundred times, nay, a thousand times, by day and by night, sleeping and waking, that haply the Countenance of Glory may be unveiled to their eyes, and tiers of light descend upon them.'[6]

At Dorothy's suggestion, they recited the prayer together 500 times, seeking assistance for the work ahead in

Mexico. Gayle has written that this experience would inform her approach to assignments in the future.[7]

Of their mission, Edna True wrote:

> In Mexico, which held the high distinction of being the first Baháʼí Community established in Latin America, the Spiritual Assembly was bravely facing internal and external problems, which seemed destined to be presented to young, new Assemblies, later proving to be but stepping stones to greater growth and fuller powers of resourcefulness. To give the assistance and wise consultation needed here, Dorothy Baker left for Mexico City in September 1945, remaining there for several weeks, counselling the friends, encouraging and helping them to meet, with faith and assurance, the difficulties and tests they were facing.[8]

For Gayle, as for so many others, Dorothy Baker was a spiritual example, a mentor, and a cherished friend. Many who knew her described her words and spirit being etched on their hearts and operative in their lives forever. While in Mexico, Gayle was moved by Dorothy's depth of prayer; by the gentleness and love with which clear vision was conveyed; and by the prayerful, creative steps that mysteriously led, without confrontation, to moments in which intractable problems yielded to unified solution. Leaving Mexico after two weeks, Gayle

continued her travels southward, making brief visits in Guatemala and Honduras before carrying on several weeks of intensive teaching in Managua, Nicaragua, with the group that had been formed there by Dr. Malcolm King. In late October, she was joined here by Elisabeth Cheney,[9] and as a result of the concentrated efforts of these two experienced Pioneers, this group of eight Believers was increased to sixteen, and the establishment of a Spiritual Assembly in the last remaining Latin American Republic was assured for the April election. From Nicaragua, Mrs. Woolson proceeded to San Jose, Costa Rica, where she had previously assisted in the formation of the historic first Spiritual Assembly in that country. During her two-years absence in the United States, this young community had sorely missed the wise and loving assistance of Mrs. Woolson, and its members were again in great need of guidance and teaching help.[10]

While Gayle was in San José in November of 1945, a meeting was arranged with the President of Costa Rica, His Excellency Teodoro Picado.[11] In an interview in 1998[12] Gayle attributed her courage in doing this to Dorothy Baker showing her the section in *God Passes By* that describes Martha Root presenting the Faith to government officials. Gayle said that her nature was 'timid and fearful' but that she wanted to serve and therefore arose to do so in any way possible. She relates the following:

An audience was requested with the President of Costa Rica, Dr. Teodoro Picado, in November 1945, and it was granted a week after the request was made. I went accompanied by Sra. Blanca Lacayo, one of the Baháʼís of San José. We had to go back and forth to the Presidential Palace for two days before we finally got our turn to see him. Before this exciting audience took place, one of the officials in the waiting room asked me what I wanted to see the President about, was it something connected with my passport? I assured him that I was not going to request anything of the President and that it was about a matter I wished to discuss directly with him. I was apprehensive lest he put obstacles in our path.

We were ushered into an elegant reception room, then the President entered. He was kind, gracious and cordial in his manner. After an exchange of greetings, I told him that I had not come to ask for anything, but rather I had come to bring him something. He laughed. The Message was explained to him and he listened very intently. He then said: 'I congratulate this Movement for its sublime ideals. These ideas are in accord with my thoughts and are completely pleasing to me. You have all my cooperation.'

I then gave him *Baháʼuʼlláh and the New Era* in Spanish, the pamphlet *El Alba de Una Nueva Era*, and a small glossy picture of the Temple in Wilmette. I explained about the architecture of the Temple and told him that the edifice stood as a symbol of the unity of all races and all religions. I explained about Baháʼuʼlláh and how the Prophets come from age to age in times of crisis to uplift humanity. Sra. Lacayo told him that there was a Bahá'í Community in San José and that it was incorporated.

He turned the pages of the New Era and these words caught his eye, which he read aloud: 'Bahá'u'lláh was born in 1817.' The way he pronounced Bahá'u'lláh's name impressed me very much as it was so beautiful and perfect. He then said, 'I am going to read this book with much interest. This is something that the world needs to lift the heart, especially in these very agitated times.'

As we said good-bye, he said, 'Whenever you pass through Costa Rica, come and visit us. This is your home.'[13]

Costa Rica received further support in December when Evelyn Larson of Chicago arrived, to remain indefinitely, Elisabeth Cheney visited, and Gayle later returned for a second stay.[14]

About a month earlier, the Inter-America Committee had initiated an intensive travel teaching project intended to strengthen all communities in Latin America. Charles Mason Remey, followed later by Emeric and Rosemary Sala, set off under the Committee's direction, to visit as many of the centres in Latin America as possible. This journey would involve much community preparation and intensive teaching. While these journeys had evident fruits, they also laid the foundation for future complications, due to Mr Remey's later defection from the Faith.[15]

To further stimulate regional development, the School at Temerity Ranch and the Inter-America Teaching committee sponsored the first Latin American Bahá'í Teaching Conference in Panama City from 20 to 25 January 1946. In her report for *The Bahá'í World*, Edna True noted that it would 'ever stand out as one of those portentious and definite milestones in the unfoldment of 'Abdu'l-Bahá's Divine Plan'. She continued,

> Although it was sponsored by the International School in Colorado Springs, Colorado and by the Inter-America Committee, the working out of all its details and the carrying out of its final plans were achieved with unusual efficiency by a special Committee, appointed by, and in consultation with, the local Spiritual Assembly of Panama City. To their devoted and whole-hearted consecration to their task and to the invaluable assistance so generously accorded them by visiting Bahá'ís, the ultimate gratifying success of this epoch-making occasion was in a very large measure due.
>
> The National Spiritual Assembly and Inter-America Committee were represented officially at the Panama Conference by Mrs. Amelia Collins, a member of both of these bodies. . . . Native Believers from ten of the Latin American Centers, and eight of the North American Pioneers gathered in Panama City, and in a marvelous spirit . . . each contributed his or her part to the well-rounded program of this Conference. Mornings were devoted to . . . an intensive study . . . of the Guardian's latest book, '*God Passes By*,' of administration and of teaching methods.

In the evenings, public lectures were arranged with talks on some of the basic Teachings of the Faith ... The largest and most impressive public session was held Friday evening, January 25th, in the main auditorium of the Inter-American University . . . Participating with two Bahá'í Speakers, Dr. Octavio Mendez Pereira, Rector of the University and Delegate from Panama to the San Francisco Conference for the establishment of the U.N.O., gave one of the principal addresses ... Dr Mendez Pereira spoke on 'The Problem of Peace in the Light of the San Francisco Conference' and brought out the need for a pact both more universal and more spiritual than that embodied in the U.N.O. Charter. Miss Elisabeth Cheney followed, delineating for her audience the 'Lesser Peace,' spoken of by Bahá'u'lláh ... As a glorious climax and fitting close to this important public meeting and to the Conference itself, Mrs. Gayle Woolson, in her address on 'The Most Great Peace,' unfolded the vision of that time when the 'Lesser Peace,' achieved mostly through the statesmen and rulers of the world, will be followed by the Golden Age of Bahá'u'lláh, when universal, supreme peace will be firmly established for all mankind and will be maintained through the functioning of a World State in which nations, races, creeds and classes will be closely and permanently united. Mrs. Woolson pointed out that this presupposes the spiritual regeneration of all humanity, because only the higher power of the Spirit can bring about such a state of unity and understanding. 'The express, the primal mission of Bahá'u'lláh,' she emphasized, 'is to unify all human beings in true oneness and to inaugurate a new and sublime era of spirituality, peace, brotherhood, and justice.'[16]

For several months following the conference, Gayle divided her time between Panama and Costa Rica. Subsequent to this, the Inter-America Committee asked her to concentrate her time in Colombia, which became her base as a pioneer for several years. She stayed partly in Bogota, taught in Cali, where the Masons opened their lodge to listen to the Message, and later made visits to Medellin, Cartagena and Baranquilla.[17] While in Colombia, she began what would become extensive travels throughout South America. One of her early trips, under the Committee's guidance, was to Guayaquil and Quito, Ecuador.

In Quito, the capital of Ecuador, pioneer Hascle Cornbleth had been teaching, assisted by friends from Guayaquil, with weekly meetings of about 15 each time. Helen Hornby described his collaboration with Gayle during her first visit to this country, which would later become her home for many years:

In September 1946, one of the most outstanding and dedicated pioneers to South America, Mrs Gayle Woolson, made her first visit to this country. She, as well as Haig[18] Kevorkian, was destined to return to Ecuador in later years and attain the spiritual bounty of being crowned valiant Knights of Bahá'u'lláh.

During her six day stay in Guayaquil she visited the office of the most important daily papers, spoke over radio and gave many talks to various lodges, societies and schools. She was well received everywhere she visited. At the Masonic Temple, the Governor of the Province, high officials of government, members of lodges as well as a number of high society women attended the conference. She left many new contacts for the Faith in that city.

She arrived in Quito 'Light as the spirit, pure as air, blazing as fire,' and 'unrestrained as the wind'. There believers and friends referred to her as the 'distinguished North American Lady' with great talents, an exceptional spiritual beauty with a great intellectual capacity. She remained in Ecuador for several weeks, initiating overwhelming activities for the Faith. One of her most outstanding feats was to give the Bahá'í Message to the President of the Republic of Ecuador in a very long interview. She gave innumerable talks. The most important was given in the Sucre Theatre to more than a thousand people. She proclaimed the Cause to business groups, military personnel, teachers and students alike in various schools and universities, as well as working closely with the Quito Bahá'í Group. The newspaper publicity was exceptional and sympathetic and commented on the many successful conferences she held. The fructiferous result of her visit was soon visible. Two of the old inactive believers of Quito returned and reaffirmed their belief in the Cause, requesting that their names be placed on the active list of believers . . . Five new contacts accepted the Faith, the first being the second Ecuadorian woman to enroll and the first for Quito, Señorita Rosario Vera Barahona, who would be privileged to be a member of the first local Spiritual Assembly of Quito.

Taking advantage of Mrs Woolson's visit, and with the cooperation of pioneer Hascle Cornbleth and the Bahá'í Group of Quito, an intense teaching campaign was systematically carried out. Five different groups invited her to give conferences on her return to Quito, and after her talk in the Sucre Theatre the directors of four different schools invited her to give talks in their schools. The highlight of her visit was when she and Hascle were granted an audience with the President of the Republic, Dr José Velasco Ibarra, on 3 October 1946. [19]

In his beautiful article in *The Bahá'í World*, 'Ilusiones', Hascle Cornbleth creates a vivid image of Quito and their time together:

In the city of Quito, capitol of Ecuador, there is a flower mart in the square of San Blas. It is nothing more than a row of rude tables upon which are displayed carnations. Long-stemmed, full-bloomed carnations with their salty fragrance. Scarcely ever anything else, except the wistful, tiny white blooms of gypsophila (baby's breath) often given you by the florist as a green or background for your bouquet. These the Indian Quichua women of the flower mart call

THE ART OF EMPOWERING OTHERS

'ilusiones'. Whether in Spanish the word means elu-
sive or illusion I do not know, but it is as descriptive of
the flower as is the Quichua word 'wah-wah' for baby.

In writing now of my experience as a Bahá'í pioneer
in Ecuador I am blocked for the moment; barred, as it
were, from collecting my thoughts beyond a recollec-
tion of startlingly large and fragrant carnations sensed
through a filmy veil of ilusiones.

There are other squares or plazas, of course, in
Quito of which the Plaza San Blas is one of the smallest. There is the Plaza de Independencia upon which
the Palacio de Gobierno faces. It was in this palace of
Government I was honored by witnessing the historic
interview by Mrs. Gayle Woolson, Bahá'í pioneer of
Bogota, Colombia with Dr. José Maria Velasco Ibarra,
President of the Republic of Ecuador. It was then he,
the President, said, 'I am happy to see there is a Centro
Bahá'í in Quito,' and likened the Bahá'í Message to
the opening of a window to allow fresh air to waft
through. It was over the Plaza de Independencia I
heard the President's voice rebound in strident tones,
'Bahá'u'lláh!', he voiced. What happened to my heart I
do not know, but, I felt I was carried out the window
over the plaza on the force of the intonation. 'Is this
how His Name is pronounced?' I regained my compo-
sure as Gayle assured him he had done well.

There is the park in Quito called the Alameda
upon which faces the presidential palace. It was in the
yellow room of the White House of Ecuador I escorted
Gayle Woolson on her interview, at the invitation of

the President, with his charming intellectual wife, Sra. Corina Porras de Velasco Ibarra. The first lady of Ecuador during our rather long visit excused herself to go into a bedroom to see the copy of *Bahá'u'lláh and The New Era* in Spanish, which her husband was reading. She then presented us each with a copy of one of her books of prose.

There is the Plaza Sucre in Quito upon which faces the national theater of Ecuador, El Teatro Sucre. The Teatro Sucre was put at the disposal of the Bahá'ís of Quito by the Minister of Education for a Bahá'í talk by Gayle Woolson. The theater was filled to the rafters. The loveliness of her person, the soft elegance in her manner of presenting the Cause of God enthralled the capacity audience into exhibiting a decorum of reverence.

There is the Recoleta in Quito with a guard at the gate for it is here that stands the Ministry of Defence. The Minister of Defence called a meeting in the officers' salon of this building where Gayle gave the Message, speaking on the attainment and maintenance of peace to about seventy-five of the high ranking officers of the Ecuadorian army. One of them, Major Carlos Suarez Palacios, was already a Bahá'í. The uniformed and caped assemblage hung on each word with the hunger and respect one gives true manna from heaven. Here was felt an air of awesome attentiveness.

Of all these things I hope Gayle will write in detail. There are many other facts of her visit in Quito of interest to the Bahá'í World; the intimate talks at table; the talks to groups and clubs such as the Rotarian and

Lions clubs; the cooperation of radio and press, for the Bahá'í Message was front page news in Quito for some weeks. The leading papers carried her picture and a full column or more on the front page several times during her visit to the 'city of eternal spring,' Quito . . .[20]

Gayle's account of this teaching trip adds further detail:

Mr Hascle Cornbleth, pioneer in Quito, and I were given an audience with the President of Ecuador, His Excellency José Valasco Ibarra. He is renowned in Latin America as an intellectual of high ideals. He received us with warmth and kindness. After the Message was explained to him, he said: 'I congratulate you for being in this great work. This is something truly magnificent. It is a great doctrine. Now in this time of crisis when there exist in the world such hate, prejudice, lack of understanding and limited nationalism, these universal teachings come to give a new horizon, a world concept. Everyone who comes here to see me comes to ask for something but you have come to give me spiritual renovation. These ideas should be spread with great intensity. It is not the quantity nor the multitudes that count, but the intensity with which these ideas are promulgated.'

He asked where I was giving conferences, and after I named various clubs and organizations he said that his wife was the president of the Women's Cultural Club, and that he wanted us to meet her and that a talk would be given at this club. He said he himself would arrange it with his wife. He rang for his secretary and told her to arrange an appointment for us with his wife, and instructed the secretary to send us an official car to take us there as their home was somewhat distant. He said: 'This will give the women something lofty to think about. They, too, should work for the betterment of the world as we men do. They should be doing what you are doing.' At this point, the Bahá'í concept of the bird of humanity having two wings, the masculine and the feminine, was explained to him and he enjoyed this very much.

We gave him *Bahá'u'lláh and the New Era* in Spanish, 'Appreciations of the Bahá'í Faith', and a card with the twelve principles and the address of the Quito Bahá'í Center. He asked for more information about Bahá'u'lláh pronouncing His name perfectly and asked if he was pronouncing it correctly. He asked about the origin of the Message and when did Bahá'u'lláh ascend. We explained to him the manner in which we work, that is, by establishing groups and assemblies that represent these ideals and about the Bahá'í Center in Quito and Guayaquil. He said he was happy to know that there was a Bahá'í Center in the city and he hoped that the persons in the group were sincere as their people have the tendency to become enthused about things for the moment and then lose interest. He added: 'The Center should plant its roots deeply so that it will be strong and permanent. This Center can influence the thought of the country.'

He asked how long I would be in Quito and said

that he would be very pleased to visit with us again before my departure for Colombia 'to talk more about these high ideals'. I asked him if he would give me a statement about the Bahá'í Faith for the World Order Magazine, and he said 'yes, with much pleasure'. We did not get to see him again before I left Quito as he went to Guayaquil for several days and returned a matter of hours before I left the country, so I was unable to get the statement at this time. As we were leaving his office, he stated that he was very glad we had visited him. A few days after this visit, we saw the President's secretary and she joyfully commented on how happy the President was after our visit with him.

As the President had promised, he personally arranged to have us meet the First Lady of the Republic, Senora Corina Parral de Velasco Ibarra, on October 16th. There was a delay in having this interview with her because she had been ill. The day set for the interview was the day before my return to Colombia which was my pioneering post at that time.

The secretary of the President had advised me of the hour of the appointment and told me that the president would have an official car sent to take us to the Presidential Residence.

We were grateful to God for such bountiful Divine Confirmation and still felt elated over the receptivity and enthusiasm of the President towards the Bahá'í ideals shown in our interview with him, at which time the light of the Spirit of Bahá'u'lláh seemed to inundate his office . . .

We were received by the gracious, charming and gentle First Lady of Ecuador in an elegant reception room. She was beautiful and walked, moved and sat with lovely dignity and grace. She told us of the work she is doing to advance the Ecuadorian woman and for the educational, cultural and moral elevation of the Indian children. She invited me to speak before the Women's Cultural Club upon my return to Quito and told Hascle that in the meantime he could present a written paper on any aspect of the Faith to read at one of their meetings. She said that she was interested in reading the Bahá'í literature and remarked that she would ask her husband for the books we had given him. She presented each of us with a book of poetry written by her and autographed and invited us to call on her again. One of the poems in her book, written in Spanish, which immediately caught my eye depicted how men have established frontiers that separate them from each other. It terminates with the question: 'Will they some day put up frontiers in the sky, too?'

At the conference given at Colegio Mejía for the Sociedad de los Graduados del Mejía (The Society of Graduates), there were present a Doctor Carlota Felix and Doctor Mercedes de Mora. They showed much interest in the Teachings and said they would like to cooperate with our new Cause . . .[21]

Helen Hornby relates:

A few years ago (mid 1970's), a lady telephoned the Bahá'í Center in Quito to seek information about the Bahá'í Faith. She was Ecuadorian but had been living out of the country for many years. She was a young lawyer in 1946 when Gayle spoke to a group of lawyers in Quito, she recalled, and was very impressed by the Bahá'í Teachings. All the years she was away, she never met a Bahá'í but did not forget her first contact with a Bahá'í, and as soon as she returned she began to make inquiries about the Bahá'í Faith (It is interesting that her sister had taught Spanish to a number of Bahá'ís at the Catholic University, including the writer). After receiving literature and visiting the Bahá'í Center, she accepted Bahá'u'lláh. After 30 or more years, the above-mentioned Doctor Carlota Felix refound the Faith! It appears that the seeds sown by Gayle were nourished by the spirit and became trees still bearing delicious fruits![22]

10

Colombia, a Call from Home, and a Return Trip through the Islands

'In June of 1946, at the beginning of the Guardian's Second Seven Year Plan, Gayle was sent as a pioneer to Colombia, where she stayed for seven years . . . until 1953.'[1] Among the goals of this Plan was the formation of two regional Assemblies, one each for Central and for South America. This accomplishment implied and depended upon a remarkable intensity of work outlined by the Guardian in a message of 18 August 1950:

The major task of insuring the breadth and solidity of the foundations laid for the establishment of the two National Bahá'í Assemblies,[2] through the preservation of the present Assemblies, groups, and isolated centers, must be scrupulously watched and constantly encouraged. The process of the dissemination of Bahá'í literature, of Bahá'í publication and translation, must continue unabated, however much the sacrifice involved. The newly-fledged institutions of Teaching and Regional Committees, of summer schools and Congresses, must be continually encouraged and increasingly supported by teachers as well as administrators, by pioneers from abroad, as well as by the native believers themselves. The highly salutary and spiritually beneficent experiment of encouraging a more active participation by these newly won supporters of the Faith in Latin America, and a greater assumption of administrative responsibility on their part, in the ever expanding activities to be entrusted wholly to their care in the years to come, should be, in particular, developed, systematized and placed on a sure and unassailable foundation. Above all, the paramount duty of deepening the spiritual life of these newly fledged, these precious and highly esteemed co-workers, and of enlightening their minds regarding the essential verities, enshrined in their Faith, its fundamental institutions, its history and genesis – the twin Covenants of Bahá'u'lláh and of 'Abdu'l-Bahá, the present Administrative Order, the future World Order, the Laws of the Most Holy Book, the inseparable institutions of the Guardianship and the Universal House of Justice, the salient events of the Heroic and Formative Ages of the Faith, and its relationship with the Dispensations that have preceded it, its attitude toward the social and political organizations by which it is surrounded – must continue to constitute the most vital aspect of the great spiritual Crusade launched by the Champions of the Faith from among the peoples of their sister Republics of the South. [3]

The National Spiritual Assembly of the United States and Canada sent Gayle to Colombia both to assist in this process and to serve temporarily as their legal representative in court proceedings that involved protecting the Faith against intense attacks. Ultimately, all accusations against the Faith were proved unfounded. Gayle also served as the coordinator of the Regional Teaching Committee for Colombia, Ecuador, and Venezuela, travelling through these countries and also visiting Peru, Bolivia, and the islands of the Antilles. [4]

Describing one trip, Horace Holley wrote the following for *The Bahá'í World*:

> Public meetings in nine of the cities of Venezuela, attended by governors of states, artists, writers, educators, prominent business men, Lions, Masons and Rotarians, as well as members of other organizations, accompanied by magnificent newspaper and radio publicity, marked the recent trip of Gayle Woolson through that country. [5]

Hascle Cornbleth gives a glimpse of the teaching work Gayle's trips often entailed. Having come to Colombia from Ecuador, he describes the following:

> Gayle Woolson and Leonor Porros [sic.] of the teaching committee for Colombia suggested I go to Mogotes, warning me it was a difficult trip over the mountains. I refused, with the excuse that I needed rest. Nevertheless, Gayle gave me the name of a young

man in Bucaramanga who was interested in knowing something of the Faith. So I boarded a plane for Bucaramanga where I went to the home of the young fellow, whose name was David Silva. He was so interested in our conversation about the Faith that he went with me about a mile out of town to a crossroads where I hoped to catch a bus to Mogotes. We talked there for some time before David said he would accompany me to Mogotes if I would wait while he went home and packed his bag. I sat on my suitcases in the scarce shade of an adobe wall for an hour or more before his return. Then we decided we had either missed the bus or it might not run that day. So we hitchhiked through several towns and stopped for lunch at a village in the foothills. We were fortunate in getting a ride on a truck all the way to Sanquil. We had to hire a cab to take us from there to Mogotes. It took hours through the rain over slippery roads to get to Mogotes, where we arrived long after nightfall. We put up at a dimly lit and dank inn, which I must say was not too clean – but we were tired and it was shelter. We opened the window and watched the rain pour down in a solid sheet as we lay on the thin pads over wooden slats that made our beds. We fell into a restful slumber, satisfied in having made the trip over the spine of the cordilleras of the Andes and caught a glimpse in Mogotes of one of the friends. Later I learned that Leonor Porros and Gayle Woolson, both of delicate frame and mild constitution, had made the arduous trip and washed the floor in that very room before they would sleep.[6]

In Cali, Colombia, Gayle had occasion to follow up on the 'first tests of combining correspondence teaching with visits of itinerant teachers'. In December 1945, Louise Caswell had spent time there and had sustained the relationships established through correspondence. In September 1946, Gayle responded to an invitation from the group, 'with the result that 13 adults and 2 youth were confirmed as Bahá'ís and a class of 20 is continuing to study.' Among the new members were 'a prominent physician and the grand master of the Masons of western Colombia'.[7] Such systematic collaboration and follow up was effective. In May 1947, we read in *Bahá'í News,* 'Cali, with an adult membership of 20 and 2 youth, will elect its first Assembly.'

In the midst of such intensive work that by then had spanned more than two years and several islands and countries, Gayle received an urgent message.[8] Her beloved father, Hassen Abas, was seriously ill and longed to see her once more. In 1941, when Gayle had learned of her mother's imminent passing, she had felt compelled to remain at her post in Costa Rica. Now, learning of her father's wish and realizing there was still time, she immediately made plans to fly home from Colombia to St Paul. The journey was long but now familiar.

Finally, Gayle arrived at the Abas home on Fuller Avenue. Greeted by family members, she came into her father's presence, walking on the same floorboards and looking through the same windows she had known as a child. The house held memories of a once bustling household, of wondrous spiritual discovery, as well as of the heartbreaking loss of her little brother Haseeb, then her grandmother, then her mother. Gayle and her family had one short week with her father. There would have been periods of prayer, of cooking and eating together and doing needed chores, of quiet sitting at the bedside, of deeper quiet, and, as Gayle had known with her husband, that moment when the person is irrevocably gone. In one of her notes, Gayle mentioned that the future Hand of the Cause Louis Gregory officiated at her father's funeral. Following this, the family needed to gather strength, administer the tasks that follow a death, and consider the needs of the youngest siblings, who had just entered adulthood. Hassen Abas was the last elder of their household. Now the reins of the family's destiny lay in the hands of the next generation.

Such profound transitions tend to require a time of contemplation and reflection before life energy is available for action. It seems therefore surprising, yet characteristic, that Gayle would accept an invitation to teach once again at Temerity Ranch, as reported in the *Bahá'í News* of 1948: 'The International School (Temerity Ranch) held two ten-day sessions, June 19 to July 1. The teachers were: Mrs. Loulie Mathews, Mrs. Gayle Woolson, Mrs. Marion Little, Miss Flora Hottes, and Mr. Leroy Ioas.'

The *Bahá'í News* also reported plans for her subsequent trip through the islands, which she offered in memory of her father, as she returned to Central and South America:

Gayle Woolson, after meeting for a day with the Inter-America Committee the end of September, left for Cuba. In accord with the desires of that country's Regional Committee, she is visiting the capitals of four provinces. From there, in late October, she will proceed to Haiti, the Dominican Republic, Puerto Rico and Jamaica, then back to Cuba briefly and on to Guatemala to attend the Central American Congress and School, which will be held simultaneously with those of South America.

The Regional Teaching Committees of South and Central America are enthusiastically and diligently undertaking and carrying out teaching projects. In Cuba a correspondence campaign was launched several months ago which succeeded in attracting inquirers from several provinces to investigate the Faith. The Cuban Regional Committee has been meeting twice a week to study and answer the correspondence which this kind of campaign involves.[9]

In the *Bahá'í News* of December 1948 we read:

Gayle Woolson has met with a warm response to the lectures on the Bahá'í Teachings which she has given before Masonic and Lions clubs in Havana and several other cities of Cuba. As a result, about 500 persons have signed cards requesting that correspondence lessons be sent them. (These were written and mailed out by Elisabeth Cheney.) Gayle explains the critical need for some kind of follow-up work after a teacher has given the Message and then moves on, if the seeds sown are to germinate and yield permanent fruit. The Regional Teaching Committee of Cuba is also following up, through personal correspondence, the contacts made by Gayle. Besides, Sra. Viva Lismore, of Havana, will go every two weeks to Matanzas to teach a class just formed there, and Julio Perez, also of Havana, will go every other Saturday to Pinar del Rio to teach another class.

On October 28 Gayle flew to Port-au-Prince, Haiti. She writes of the believers there: 'I have had to do much explaining to the friends on administrative points and it is encouraging to see their eagerness to learn and do things right.'

She also relates: "I went out to see the "Bahá'í Cultural Center" the other day. During the day there are classes for some thirty children who are learning to read and write, and they recite the twelve principles and the sayings above the nine doors of the Temple by heart. The school is just a little hut with a straw roof, just as all the little huts around it where these poor children live . . . At night, illiterate adults are taught and on Monday afternoons the sick are attended to by Dr. LaFleur and two nurses . . . The services of the school and clinic are wonderful and so helpful to these poverty-stricken people who turn to them for help.'

About mid-November Gayle will proceed to the Dominican Republic, and from there to Puerto Rico and Jamaica, returning to Cuba for a few weeks before going to the Congress in Guatemala.[10]

Teaching English at Academia Moderna, Honduras, 1945

First Spiritual Assembly of Cartagena, Colombia, 1947. Front row, left to right, with Gayle (centre): José B. Schuanes, Rafael B. Fortich, Patricio Villalba, José de J. Moyano. Back row, left to right: Ascanio Poñas R., Julio Pinado, Ernesto A. Florez, Indalecio Camacao, Alvin D. Gregory

Speaking on the Most Great Peace at the Second Bahá'í Latin American Conference, Panama, January 1947. Speakers also on the platform: Dr Tu Yuen-Ten, Minister of China in Panama; Dr Harold Sosted, Superintendent of Instruction for schools in the Canal Zone; and Mr Jorge Corgas, an Indian of the San Blas Islands

Visiting Havana, Cuba, 1948

*Out with friends, and
at the home of Viva
and Frank Lismore and
daughter Cynthia*

Visiting the Baháʼís in Port-au-Prince, Haiti, 1948

In rural Haiti, 1948

Visiting the Bahá'ís in Puerto Rico, 1948 . . .

. . . and in Kingston, Jamaica, December 1948

Children's class in Kingston, Jamaica (1947), given to Gayle by Mr William Mitchell, the adult in the back row, during her visit in December 1948. Wearing a tie, second row, is Mr Mitchell's nephew Glenford Mitchell, future member of the Universal House of Justice

Participants at the Bahá'í Teaching Congress of Central America and the Greater Antilles, Guatemala City, 1949, with representatives from Mexico, Guatemala, Honduras, El Salvador, Nicaragua, Costa Rica, Panama, Cuba, Haiti, Jamaica, Dominican Republic and Puerto Rico. Dorothy Baker, representing the National Spiritual Assembly of the Bahá'ís of the United States as well as the Inter-America Committee, is in the front row, 4th from left; Cora Oliver, pioneer in Panama, is in the back row, 3rd from left. Gayle Woolson, pioneer in Colombia at the time, took the picture so is not in the photograph

Dorothy Baker and Gayle at the Central American Congress, Guatemala City, January 1949

Back in Bogotá, Colombia, 1949. First Bahá'í Teaching Conference of Colombia, Ecuador and Venezuela, October 1949, attended by representatives from Bogotá, Barranquilla, Bucaramanga, Calí and Medellín, Colombia; Guayaquil, Ecaudor; and Caracas, Venezuela

With a close friend from a convent in Medellín, Colombia, 1950

In January 1949, the *Bahá'í News* described the following journey:

> Wonderful success seems to attend Gayle Woolson wherever she goes. While in Haiti she visited the goal city of Saint Marc, and the Masons there invited her to speak in the town's only theater. She offered to help pay for the rent of the theater, which represented a big expense to those people, but they would not accept it. Posters were put up all about the town and personal invitations were sent out, with the result that about 200 people came. They received the Message enthusiastically.
>
> The Regional Committee of the Dominican Republic sent in a thrilling report of the meetings held there during Gayle's visit to their island. Writes Elena Marsella, 'She swept through like a conquering queen but worked like an unpaid serf. All doors opened miraculously.' Copious and comprehensive articles giving resumés of her talks appeared in the largest newspapers of the country.
>
> Arrived in Puerto Rico, every door opened for her by a believer there of only one week, Mr. Irizarry. He is manager of a radio station and knows many important local people; consequently, radio time and newspaper publicity were made available, and Gayle and the pioneers of Puerto Rico, Edris Rice-Wray and Margaret Swengel, were presented to the high officials of Masonry, Lions, Rotary, and Elks, and given

speaking engagements before all of them to explain the Bahá'í Teachings.[11]

The same issue announced, 'The fourth annual Bahá'í congresses of South and Central America will be held simultaneously January 21 thru 24 in Guatemala City and Sao Paulo, and each will be succeeded by School sessions lasting from the 26th through the 30th.' The March 1949 issue included Dorothy Baker's assessment of the Central American Congress:

> The outstanding attainment of this Congress, Dorothy Baker thought, was the greater understanding which the delegates acquired of the Guardian and a tremendous deepening in their love for him. She was also much impressed by the maturity, diligence, hard work and steadfastness which they evinced.
>
> Dorothy Baker . . . gave as her judgment the principal factors for the smooth functioning and splendid success of the Congress: a.) the thorough planning of the National Teaching Committee for Central America, b.) the highly effective service of Natalia Chávez, the general Congress Secretary, c.) the fine and gentle leadership of the chairman, Dr. David Escalante, and d.) the arrangement whereby all the delegates lived at the same hotel and had their meals together at one table. She also made special mention of the splendid help contributed by Gayle Woolson, who took her part almost as one of the Latins themselves.[12]

In Gayle's own words, we have a summary:

> I had a very special experience of carrying out a teach-
> ing trip for three and a half months in 1948 and early
> 1949 in the Greater Antilles, or West Indies, covering
> Cuba, Haiti, Dominican Republic, Puerto Rico and
> Jamaica, and back to Cuba. That trip was made under
> the auspices of the Bahá'í Inter-America Committee.
>
> The trip was one of the most fascinating and excit-
> ing episodes of my teaching work as a pioneer. It
> started with the sadness of the recent passing of my
> dear father, Hassen Abas, at our family home in Saint
> Paul, Minnesota, and culminated with the happi-
> ness of seeing many new doors open for our beloved
> Faith among those islands and the holding of a <u>major
> teaching conference in January 1949 in Guatemala
> City, Guatemala for the whole Central American area
> including the islands of the Greater Antilles.</u>[13]

Gayle's first visit to San Salvador was in 1949. In late
January that year she participated in the Congress for
Central America, Mexico, Panama, and the Antilles,
which took place in Guatemala. After the congress various
attendees, including Gayle, visited San Salvador on their
route to the south, and celebrated a reunion.

The *Bahá'í News* of July 1949 reports the following
regarding the work of the Teaching Committees and the
role of North American pioneers:

With the arrival of Eve Nicklin in Lima, Peru, and Natalia Chavez in Panama City, about the first of June, the two new National Teaching Committees are launching upon their year's work. In accordance with the policy of placing responsibility more and more into the hands of the Latin American believers themselves, only Eve in South America and Gayle Woolson in Central America are North American pioneers who are members of these committees.[14]

Gayle kept correspondence with her siblings from this period, showing how she felt it important to stay closely in touch, despite the demands on her time. These include several letters exchanged with her youngest brother, Gerald, who tenderly addresses her as 'Gaylita'. They become particularly significant as 1949 turns into 1950 and conscription begins for the Korean War. He turns to her for loving support and spiritual guidance as he obeys the Bahá'í guidance to apply for non-combatant status. One of the older Bahá'í women in St Paul helped him with the forms, now that his father was gone. After the war Gerald would use the G.I. bill to follow the family interest in holistic healing and become a reflexologist. He and his future wife, Gladys, would later become steadfast pioneers to Arkansas, where he would dedicate much service to the indigenous communities nearby.

Throughout her travels, Gayle relied on prayer and on institutional guidance. At times, a sense of assistance also came through dreams. One of these occurred in 1948, shortly after Gayle and Elena Marsella had been together

in the Dominican Republic. Of that time, Gayle later wrote
to Elena Marsella:

> My visit through the islands in 1948 was one of the
> happiest experiences, and my visit to the Dominican
> Republic and working with you were especially sig-
> nificant.
>
> For some time, I have wanted to relate to you an
> experience that initiated in your apartment and cul-
> minated in Bogotá, Colombia, my pioneering post at
> that time . . .
>
> The day that I was to leave I tried to move a heavy
> suitcase from the bedroom to the living room so as
> to make things easier for the taxi driver who was to
> pick me up to take me to the airport. That effort of
> moving the suitcase was because the afternoon before
> that day you had a difficult time finding a taxi driver
> who would be willing to go up to your apartment to
> get my luggage . . .
>
> In lifting the largest and heaviest one I heard a crack
> in my back so I left the bag in the bedroom and won-
> dered what in the world had happened to my back.
>
> My trip was to Puerto Rico and localities in
> Colombia until I got to my residence in Bogotá. There
> was some discomfort in my back all the while but not
> so much because those places where I went before
> Bogotá were warm areas. In Bogotá, 8,000 feet above
> sea level and where it is cold and rains 8 months of
> the year, my back pain got worse. There were no such
> things as chiropractors or osteopaths there so I just

withstood the pain thinking I would have to wait until I returned to the United States (in 2 or 3 years) before seeing a doctor. The pain increased to such a degree that in order to lay down I would help myself by holding the edge of the mattress and slowly go down on my side. In order to get up I would also hang on to the side of the mattress and rise up slowly.

One night I had a dream of the Guardian. I was to have an interview with him and I saw myself walking towards a beautiful marble building where he was living. It was black bespeckled marble. On my way I saw people of this world, and people of the other world in vapory bodies, moving about just as one does on ordinary down-town streets. Finally I reached the building where I was to see the Guardian. It was like a beautiful bank building. I entered and went to the room where he was. As soon as I went in he stood up from behind a beautiful desk where he was sitting. The room was huge and rectangular and all the four walls had book shelves with books from the floor to the high ceiling. He was beautiful and young reflecting loftiness, purity, spirituality, humility, and loving-kindness. The desk was ultra-modern. The top border of it was shaped something like this: [in the letter, she drew a wavy line] and was light brown.

To the left of the desk was a comfortable living-room chair. That is the only furniture that was in the room. He invited me to sit down and then he started to talk. As he was speaking, he was seen standing in a low pulpit continuing to talk. He emanated such an exhilarating spirit that I felt as though I was basking in rays of light. (I sometimes compare the feeling I had to a bird basking in sunshine.) It was such a heavenly, ecstatic feeling that I thought to myself: 'I wish I would never have to move from this spot.' (I did not recall anything he said.) But the time came when the interview was over. He walked with me out of the door which led to a rather narrow vestibule. He was at my left. He lifted his right hand, protruded the middle finger and made a vertical downward gentle sweeping motion over the part of my back where I had been suffering pain. It was like a feather touch. Through this miracle I was healed.

... Perhaps the problem of my back was a slipped disk. This is the first time I have written out my experience in such detail and that is because I am telling it to you. [15]

Elena Marsella and Gayle shared a friendship in service and had similar spiritual attributes. Following this island teaching experience, both would become Knights of Bahá'u'lláh, reaching remote islands through difficult journeys and witnessing the seemingly miraculous opening of doors where others might have seen none.

11

The Regional Spiritual Assembly of South America

Several years of development led up to the Convention to elect the first Regional Spiritual Assembly of South America on 21 April 1951, followed by a three-day study session. At the 1944 Centennial Convention, Latin American delegates had experienced international fellowship, consultation and planning under the dome of the Bahá'í House of Worship in Wilmette. Subsequently, regional teaching committees had been established in each country to foster local initiative. In June 1947, the first National Teaching Committee of South America (CEBSA) had been formed, 'transferring even more of the responsibility of the Inter-America Committee to South America as a further step in affording them the necessary training in the conduct of teaching projects and of stimulating a spirit of mutual fellowship and interaction among the believers.'[1] For several years, Teaching Congresses, with delegates attending and consulting, had set the pattern for future Conventions. In *The Bahá'í World* we read:

The first of the twin historic Conventions called to elect these new National Spiritual Assemblies was held in Lima, Peru . . . with eighteen of the twenty-seven official delegates present in person and seven voting by mail. Representing the Bahá'ís of the United States were Paul E. Haney, chairman of the National Spiritual Assembly, and Miss Edna True, former secretary of the Inter-America Committee.[2]

Lima was where pioneer Eve Nicklin, later named the 'mother of the Bahá'ís of Peru' and a gentle, sensitive friend to all, had first settled ten years before. It was where she had nursed John Pope Stearns, the first pioneer to Ecuador, through his last painful months with cancer of the tongue. Eve and Gayle would serve together on Regional Assemblies for ten years, until each country had its own National Spiritual Assembly. Of this first Convention, Eve wrote:

The hotel where the event took place was right on the same street where I had lived in the beginning. Naturally, my thoughts went back to those days of struggle against the language, climate, loneliness, trying to gain contacts for the Faith and all the things a pioneer has to face in the pioneering field. But how different was that day! All those experiences could be counted as pure joy. I shared some of these experiences with Edna True and Paul Haney, those two beloved representatives who were sent by the Assembly of the United States of North America.[3]

The Guardian gave the new Regional Assemblies three over-arching goals: to consolidate the Regional Assembly, to promulgate the teachings of the Faith, and to enrich the spiritual life and deepen the understanding of its avowed supporters. Sent with his message to them was a gift:

> As a token of his love and as the first precious relic for its national archives, the Guardian also presented to each Assembly through Mrs. Amelia Collins, Hand of the Cause of God, a lock of the blessed hair of Bahá'u'lláh.
>
> Messages were read from each of the other nine National Spiritual Assemblies and each delegate was presented with a picture of 'Abdu'l-Bahá in a special souvenir folder bearing a greeting from their 'brothers and sisters in Europe, under the Divine Plan'.[4]

The members elected to the first National Spiritual Assembly of South America were the following: Edmund Miessler of Brazil, Margot Worley of Brazil, Eve Nicklin of Peru, Gayle Woolson of Colombia, Estéban Canales of Paraguay, Mercedes Sanchez of Peru, Alexander Reid of Chile, Rangvald Taetz of Uruguay, and Manuel Vera of Peru. The article in *The Bahá'í World* concludes:

> Thus began a new stage in the evolution of the Administrative Order in Latin America . . . to the end that they would be prepared and ready by Riḍván 1953 to assume their full and independent roles as 'pillars

of the Universal House of Justice' and participants in the global crusade.

While Gayle's international service continued after the Convention, her home base remained for a time in Colombia. The early South American Bahá'ís faced difficulties inherent in the inner and outer transformation required to establish communities expressive of the teachings and values of the Faith. The details lie beyond the scope of this narrative. Some are ably documented, year by year, in Helen Bassett Hornby's *Heroes of God: History of the Bahá'í Faith in Ecuador*. These challenges had a direct and continual impact on Gayle's life of service. In various roles, she, with a few others, was often called to encourage believers to overcome misunderstandings, to clarify misconceptions, and to unite around the teachings of Bahá'u'lláh. A core of steadfast believers, guided by the institutions, remained united. However, the community's growing pains at times involved personal invective and later manifested themselves in several instances of Covenant-breaking. Gayle demonstrated clarity of vision born of continual prayer, study and memorization of the Writings. She showed unwavering loyalty and openness to learning from her mentors and collaborators. Most important of all was her wholehearted obedience to the Writings, the Guardian and later, to the Hands of the Cause. Despite situations that might have disillusioned many, she continued to hold in her mind the 'vision of celestial perfection',[5] fulfilling her responsibilities with trust in the ultimate destiny of the

Faith and in the divine assistance available with each step of service.[6]

In her history of the Bahá'í Faith in Ecuador, Helen Hornby describes the conditions under which the Bahá'ís laboured in 1951:

> In spite of the fact that it was often very difficult to get the believers to meet as a group and to perform the assigned tasks given by the Guardian, he never mentioned their frailties and shortcomings to anyone. He wrote letters of encouragement and often of camaraderie to them and continued assigning new responsibilities added on to the unfinished and often untouched ones. He never spoke of their incapacities or lack of ability; rather, he addressed the potentialities in the individual in such a unique way that one aspired to be what 'the Guardian said I am' [sic]; and to attain the goals which 'he just said I achieved'.[7]

In the same section, she includes a few examples of letters he wrote to these embryonic communities after the election of the first Regional Spiritual Assembly of South America. On 11 July 1951 his secretary wrote to this new Assembly on his behalf:

> He feels sure these two new National Bahá'í Bodies[8] will greatly enrich the Bahá'í World Community, and accomplish noble feats in the service of Bahá'u'lláh.
> It is truly significant and inspiring to think that there are now four National Assemblies[9] in the New

World. It shows what vitality and promise these young nations have, and these characteristics will aid them in their Bahá'í service.

Your Assembly is called upon to direct and safeguard the activities of our Faith in a truly vast and impressive area. But the very newness of the work . . . the great need of the people, both aboriginal and European in origin, to hear of Bahá'u'lláh, is stimulating and challenging, and must call forth the best in every believer.

Now that you have the privilege of building from the very beginning a new National Institution he feels special attention should be devoted to laying a deep and permanent foundation. The basis of all successful work in this Faith is that true brotherhood and unity should prevail amongst the believers. To promote unity and love amongst the friends is your first duty.

Your second is undoubtedly the teaching work . . . Next to this comes support of the National Fund . . .

The Guardian feels that special efforts must be made to enroll the primitive peoples[10] of South America in the Cause. These souls, often so exploited and despised, deserve to hear of the Faith, and will become a great asset to it once their hearts are enlightened.[11]

Gayle would continue to heed this call when she settled in Ecuador by going often with others to visit and work with the Quechua people in Otavalo and its environs. Over time, this small beginning yielded remarkable long-term fruits.

Shoghi Effendi also described the maturing of the relationship of the two Latin American 'daughter' Assemblies to its 'parent' Assembly in North America:

> It is truly inspiring to think that in relatively so short a time the Bahá'í Community of the United States should have given birth to these two beautiful daughter-Assemblies in the southern part of the New World. He therefore, considers it wise and proper that for a few years your Assembly should keep in close touch with its 'parent', who, like all parents, has had the benefit of long years of experience, and passed through many trials, and is therefore in a position to help you with advice and other support.
>
> For the first time in Bahá'í history we see constellations of National Bodies, so to speak, cooperating for the good of the Faith: In Africa, England is working closely with the N.S.A.'s of Persia, Egypt, India and the United States. Upon the success of the close cooperation between your Assembly, that of Meso-America, and the United States during the coming years will depend, to a great extent, not only the speed of achievement in the future, but also plans to be undertaken by the National Bodies of the New World.
>
> All your work will be watched by the Guardian with the keenest interest, and his loving prayers be offered for your success and guidance.[12]

A year later, the Convention for the second election of the Regional Assembly of South America was held from

29 April to 5 May 1952, at the Hotel Allá en el Sur in Ezeiza, about an hour from Buenos Aires, Argentina. Among Gayle's papers are a copy of Minutes[13] she took of this four-day Convention and the subsequent three-day Convention school, affording a window into both the functioning of the Assembly during its first year and the proceedings of the Convention.

This second Convention was honoured by the presence of Hand of the Cause Dorothy Baker. The friends were deeply moved by the recent passing of Hand of the Cause Sutherland Maxwell, the architect of the Shrine of the Báb. They felt blessed to attend a memorial service for him at the nearby resting place of his wife, the famed teacher May Maxwell. Nineteen of the 25 delegates elected were in attendance; additionally, there were 20 visitors from the Bahá'í community of Buenos Aires. This Convention coincided with significant developments at the World Centre: four years before, Israel had attained statehood. The Guardian had seen fit then to take a significant step towards the establishment of the Universal House of Justice by appointing the first International Bahá'í Council. He guided them in developing a formal relationship with the government, in caring for the World Centre properties, and in carrying out the work of the Guardian. In 1951, he had named the first contingent of Hands of the Cause appointed during his ministry. The gathering reflected the rapid evolution of the Faith and its institutions, together with the Guardian's keen appreciation of the critical nature of time and the opportunities of a given moment.

The activities began with an elegant reception, in the form of a dinner provided by the Bahá'í community of Buenos Aires. Seventy people attended. Following dinner, the Chairman of the Spiritual Assembly welcomed the participants. Then Salvador Tormo[14] welcomed all to the Convention. He and his wife had given a beautiful property to the Faith to be used as a Bahá'í School. It was just next door to the hotel and would be used for the deepening sessions following the Convention.

The officers elected for the Convention were Margot Worley, Chairperson, and Bolivar Plaza, Secretary, both Latin believers. As the first order of business, the Convention sent a message to the beloved Guardian. They proceeded according to the agenda planned by the National Assembly. In the evenings, they had programmes of music and drama, including skits of how assemblies should and should not function, and individual teaching conversations.

Edmund Miessler reported to the Convention on behalf of the National Spiritual Assembly of South America. Excerpts from his tribute to the National Spiritual Assembly of the United States include the following:

It seems appropriate here to express the profound appreciation of this Assembly for the constant guidance and material assistance which our parent National Assembly has showered upon us. At the first Convention, we had the benefit of the presence of its members, Paul Haney and Edna True, chairman and recording secretary of that Assembly. At our January

Delegates at the election of the first National (Regional) Spiritual Assembly of South America, Lima, Peru, 1951, with representatives of the Bahá'ís of the United States: Paul Haney, chairman of the National Spiritual Assembly of the United States (back row, centre) and Edna True, former secretary of the Inter-America Committee (2nd row, 2nd from left). Gayle is in the front row, far right

First National (Regional) Spiritual Assembly of the Bahá'ís of South America, 1951. Front row, left to right: Edmund J. Miessler (São Paolo, Brazil), Margot Worley (Bahía, Brazil), Eve Nicklin (Lima, Peru), Manuel Vera (Lima, Peru); back row, left to right: Alejandro Reid (Punta Arenas, Chile), Gayle Woolson (Bogotá, Colombia), Estéban Canales (Asunción, Paraguay), Mercedes Sanchez (Lima, Peru), Rangvald Taetz (Montevideo, Uruguay)

First National Spiritual Assembly of Central America, Mexico and the Antilles, 1951. Front row, left to right: David Escalante, James V. Facey, Elena Marsella, Artemus Lamb; back row, left to right: Louise Caswell, Zenayda Jurado, Cora Oliver, Raquel J. François de Constante, Natalia A. Chávez. Elena Marsella was a good friend to Gayle and later became a Knight of Bahá'u'lláh to the Gilbert and Ellis Islands.

Hand of the Cause of God Dorothy Baker with the newly elected National Spiritual Assembly of the Bahá'is of South America, Ezeiza, Argentina, 1952. Front row, left to right: Gayle Woolson, Eve Nicklin, Dorothy Baker, Margot Worley, Mercedes Sanchez; Back row, left to right: Bolivar Plaza, Rangvald Taetz, Edmund Miessler, Guillermo Agilar, Manuel Vera

Delegates to the 1952 Convention attending a memorial service for Hand of the Cause of God Sutherland Maxwell at the grave of May Maxwell, Quilmes, Argentina, 1952

The grave of May Maxwell as it is today

First Indian group in Ecuador, in Vagabundo, Imbabura Province, 1953

meeting, Horace Holley met with us to give us counsel. He is the corresponding secretary. Now, at this
Convention, we have the presence of an officer of
that Assembly, Mrs. Dorothy Baker,[15] member during
many years. We have been helped more than words
can express by their wise and loving counsel.[16]

He continued, speaking of the Guardian's messages re-
garding the upcoming Holy Year and the dedication of the
House of Worship in Wilmette; the four Intercontinental
Conferences to be held; the building of the Shrine of the
Báb; the appointments of the International Council and
of Hands of the Cause of God.

The report reviewed the activities of the National
Assembly during its first year. The Assembly had met
four times: the first meeting lasted ten days; the second,
ten days; the third, eleven days and the fourth four days.
They noted two new local Assemblies and two lost. In
South America, there were 53 new Bahá'ís registered. Two
schools had held important sessions: Loncoche, in Chile,
and Ezeiza, in Argentina. The Bahá'ís had participated in
two South American Congresses of non-governmental
organizations, one in La Paz, Bolivia, and one in Quito,
Ecuador. The other important development was the preparation and adoption of the Constitution of the National
Spiritual Assembly.[17] The same Constitution was adopted
by the National Spiritual Assembly of Central America.
The delegates had gathered ideas reported from various places, particularly including those from Cali, to be
shared continentally.

Committee reports covered the following areas: Teaching, Youth, Children, Radio, Publications, Teaching among the Indigenous, International Schools, the Bulletin, Archives, Legal Matters, the National Treasury, and the Bahá'í History of South America.

The Convention had an important discussion on the messages of the Guardian that gave instructions regarding the plan for the four Intercontinental Conferences to be held in Africa, America, Europe, and Asia. The Faith had now extended to 124 countries of the world, and Bahá'í literature had been translated into 90 languages.

The new National Spiritual Assembly reflected the growing strength of the continental Bahá'í community, with only three pioneers and six members native to South America.[18]

Gayle typed her personal transcription of Dorothy Baker's presentations. They convey the spirit and content through which she moved her audience. She encouraged all to meet tests by invoking the wellsprings of spiritual assistance available, rather than by engaging the difficulty on its own level. Throughout the programme, she related the history of the Faith to the call of the present hour. For example, Gayle noted her as saying the following:

A little before the Convention, the Guardian advised the Bahá'í world of the death of Mr. Sutherland Maxwell, one of the Hands of the Cause of God, and architect of the Shrine of the Báb, and requested that the National Assemblies hold memorial services appropriate for this valuable Bahá'í brother. The wife of

Mr. Maxwell, Mrs. May Maxwell, is buried in Buenos Aires, and it is in the Quilmes Cemetery,[19] where her sepulcher is, that they paid homage to Mr. Maxwell with a beautiful service and floral offering. All the delegates contributed for the exquisite flowers, and there was money left over from the generous contributions they gave, and for that reason, they decided to send the remaining sum for the Shrine of the Báb, others adding more for this purpose. [20]

In a message on behalf of the Guardian, the memorial is mentioned:

> The loving sympathy conveyed by your Assembly on the occasion of Mr. Maxwell's passing was much appreciated, and he was glad to see the friends held a meeting at the grave of dear Mrs. Maxwell.[21]

The message also commented,

> He was particularly pleased to see the Plan you have formulated for the coming year; it seems a well-balanced one and possible of achievement – a most important point, as otherwise the friends become discouraged if they fail.[22]

Following the close of this Convention and school, Gayle returned to Ecuador, to which she had transferred her residence from Colombia. The National Spiritual Assembly of South America and the followers of

Bahá'u'lláh everywhere were now preparing for the Ten Year Crusade. Its inauguration in 1953 would coincide with the 100th anniversary of Bahá'u'lláh's intimation of His mission while imprisoned in the Síyáh-Chál; its scope of action would embrace the entire world.

12

'Paradise ... because reached In time'

In 1953, following elaborate preparation, the Guardian's Ten Year World Crusade was inaugurated with four international conferences that spanned the globe. The gathering for Europe was held in Stockholm, Sweden; for Africa in Kampala, Uganda; for North and Latin America, in Wilmette, Illinois; and for Asia, in Delhi, India.

In Wilmette, people gathered from throughout the western hemisphere and beyond, including those from newly-opened Latin American countries, Caribbean islands, and North American states and provinces. As participants and guests approached the House of Worship, they were greeted by even more than the majestic vision of its domed structure, clothed in intricate, ethereal ornamentation. Walking along the garden pathways, climbing the wide skirt of steps and walking inside, they entered a light-filled space, newly transformed by similarly complex, interwoven designs. Both sunlight and evening illumination created a sense of grandeur that evoked hushed meditation and prayer. At last ready for 'dedication to public worship', the House of Worship could now welcome all, symbolizing in its design and variegated gardens the oneness and potential harmony of a diverse humanity.

Central to the 1953 programme was the Guardian's message sent to the Conference in Wilmette. In it, Shoghi Effendi set the new Plan in historical context; depicted milestones achieved along a path six decades long; and focused the four National Spiritual Assemblies of the western hemisphere[1] on specific goals. He also wrote about his gift to each of the Conventions worldwide – a copy of a photograph of Bahá'u'lláh, offered for viewing at those sacred events.[2] Twelve Hands of the Cause were present in Wilmette. As the Guardian's representative, Rúḥíyyih Khánum presented the message, which included these words:

> The hour has now struck for the national Bahá'í communities dwelling within the confines of the Western Hemisphere – the first region in the western world to be warmed and illuminated by the rays of God's infant Faith shining from its World Centre in the Holy Land – to arise and, in thanksgiving for the manifold blessings continually showered upon them from on high during the past six decades and for the inestimable bounties of God's unfailing protection and sustaining grace vouchsafed His Cause ever since its inception more than a century ago, and in anticipation of the Most Great Jubilee which will commemorate the hundredth

anniversary of Bahá'u'lláh's formal assumption of His prophetic office, launch, determinedly and unitedly, the third and last stage of an enterprise inaugurated sixteen years ago, the termination of which will mark the closing of the initial epoch in the evolution of 'Abdu'l-Bahá's Divine Plan. Standing on the threshold of a ten-year-long, world-embracing Spiritual Crusade these communities are now called upon, by virtue of the weighty pronouncement recorded in the Most Holy Book, and in direct consequence of the revelation of the Tablets of the Divine Plan, to play a preponderating role in the systematic propagation of the Faith, in the course of the coming decade, which will, God willing, culminate in the spiritual conquest of the entire planet.

It is incumbent upon the members of the American Bahá'í Community, the chief executors of 'Abdu'l-Bahá's Divine Plan, the members of the Canadian Bahá'í Community acting as their allies, and the members of the Latin American Bahá'í Communities in their capacity as associates in the execution of this Plan, to brace themselves and initiate, in addition to the responsibilities they have assumed, and will assume, in other continents of the globe, an intercontinental campaign designed to carry a stage further the glorious work already inaugurated throughout the Western Hemisphere.

The task, at once arduous, thrilling and challenging, which now confronts these four Bahá'í communities involves: First, the formation, under the aegis of the National Spiritual Assembly of the Bahá'ís of the United States, and in collaboration with the two existing national assemblies in Latin America, of one national spiritual assembly in each of the twenty Latin American republics as well as the establishment of a national spiritual assembly in Alaska under the aegis of the National Spiritual Assembly of the Bahá'ís of the United States of America. Second, the establishment of the first dependency of the Mashriqu'l-Adhkár in Wilmette. Third, the purchase of land for the future construction of two Mashriqu'l-Adhkárs, one in Toronto, Ontario; one in Panama City, Panama, situated respectively in North and in Central America. Fourth, the opening of the following twenty-seven virgin territories and islands: Anticosti Island, Baranof Island, Cape Breton Island, Franklin, Grand Manan Island, Keewatin, Labrador, Magdalen Islands, Miquelon Island and St. Pierre Island, Queen Charlotte Islands and Yukon, assigned to the National Spiritual Assembly of the Bahá'ís of Canada; Aleutian Islands, Falkland Islands, Key West and Kodiak Island assigned to the National Spiritual Assembly of the Bahá'ís of the United States of America; Bahama Islands, British Honduras, Dutch West Indies and Margarita Island, assigned to the National Spiritual Assembly of the Bahá'ís of Central America; British Guiana, Chilöe Island, Dutch Guiana, French Guiana, Galapagos Islands, Juan Fernandez Islands, Leeward Islands, and Windward Islands, assigned to the National Spiritual Assembly of the Bahá'ís of South

America. Fifth, the translation and publication of
Bahá'í literature in the following ten languages, to be
undertaken by the National Spiritual Assembly of the
Bahá'ís of the United States of America: Aguaruna,
Arawak, Blackfoot, Cherokee, Iroquois, Lengua,
Mataco, Maya, Mexican and Yahgan. Sixth, the consol-
idation of Greenland, Mackenzie and Newfoundland,
allocated to the National Spiritual Assembly of the
Bahá'ís of Canada; of Alaska, the Hawaiian Islands
and Puerto Rico allocated to the National Spiritual
Assembly of the Bahá'ís of the United States of
America; of Bermuda, Costa Rica, Cuba, Dominican
Republic, El Salvador, Guatemala, Haiti, Honduras,
Jamaica, Martinique, Mexico, Nicaragua and Panama
allocated to the National Spiritual Assembly of the
Bahá'ís of Central America; and of Argentina, Bolivia,
Brazil, Chile, Colombia, Ecuador, Paraguay, Peru,
Uruguay and Venezuela, allocated to the National
Spiritual Assembly of the Bahá'ís of South America.
Seventh, the incorporation of the twenty-one above-
mentioned national spiritual assemblies. Eighth,
the establishment by these same national spiritual
assemblies of national Bahá'í endowments. Ninth,
the establishment of a national Ḥaẓíratu'l-Quds in the
capital city of each of the aforementioned republics,
as well as one in Anchorage, Alaska. Tenth, the formation of two national Bahá'í publishing trusts, one
in Wilmette, Illinois, and the other in Rio de Janeiro,
Brazil . . . [3]

The Guardian's call galvanized believers throughout the western hemisphere. In an unprecedented response, the following five members of the National Spiritual Assembly of the United States, once elected, would resign their positions in order to go to unopened countries and territories: Elsie Austin, Dorothy Baker, Kenneth Christian, Matthew Bullock, and Mamie Seto. Many others responded in kind.

Years later, speaking in Cedar Rapids in 1998, Gayle recalled,

His message was so beautiful and so exciting. This was my feeling. You wanted to get up and go somewhere. The National Spiritual Assembly of South America had asked me to go to Ecuador to help with two non-functioning Assemblies. What a dilemma! I wanted to go to one of those territories! I wanted to be on the honor roll.[4] I had experienced enough not to be afraid to go anywhere, even by myself. But then, the National Spiritual Assembly had asked me to go to Ecuador. I knew there was nothing I could do. One afternoon, shortly after lunch, I took a nap. Later, when still half asleep and half awake, I was getting ready and I heard a voice: 'Why don't you go to the Galápagos?' I thought, 'Galápagos?' I realized the Galápagos belonged to Ecuador, so I was mystified. I wrote to Dorothy Baker about my dilemma.

Dorothy Baker entranced all at the Convention when she spoke of the Guardian's call to serve and prefer the

historically downtrodden, now destined to arise to hitherto unimagined heights. Referring to her pilgrimage,
she said the following:

> He told of 'Alí Na<u>kh</u>javání. He spoke of the fact that
> this intrepid youth had gone into the jungles of Africa,
> as you have no doubt been hearing, and, assisted by
> Philip Hainsworth of Britain, they lived with the Teso
> people; they ate the food of the Teso people; they slept
> on straw mats or leaves, or whatever it is that you sleep
> on among the Teso people. The rain falls on your head
> and salamanders drop in your tea, if there is tea. And
> they stayed! And they did not say, 'Conditions do not
> warrant it because these people eat herbs and things
> that would just kill us.' They stayed! Is there an 'Alí
> Na<u>kh</u>javání, then, in America? At the present, no. I
> mean, up to the present. Is there a Philip Hainsworth?
> Up to the present, no.
>
> Now, the dark-skinned people, he [Shoghi Effendi]
> said, would have an upsurge that is both spiritual and
> social. The spiritual upsurge will rapidly bring them
> great gifts because this is an act of God and it was so
> intended. And all the world's prejudiced forces will
> not hold it back, one hair's breadth. The Bahá'ís will
> glorify and understand it. The social repercussions of
> race suppression around the world will increase at the
> same time, and frightened, the world's forces will see
> that the dark skinned peoples are really rising to the
> top – a cream that has latent gifts only to be brought
> out by Divine bounties. Where do the Bahá'ís stand in

this? Again and again he pointed out that the Bahá'ís must be in the vanguard of finding them and giving them the base. For the social repercussions will at times become dreadful, if we do not, and we shall be judged by God.

I thought that I was rather a fanatic on the race question, at least a strong liberal, but I sat judged by my Guardian, and I knew it. My sights were lifted immeasurably and I saw the vistas of these social repercussions, coming because of our spiritual negligence through the years, and I saw the Indian tribes dotted about this continent unredeemed, waiting – waiting for an 'Alí Na<u>kh</u>javání . . . God forbid, that in even this coming year we fail in this . . .

God grant that we may raise up our heroes who will dedicate their lives to the Indians, to the great dark skinned races, to the Eskimos, to the Negro peoples so brilliant, so promising in our national life. Which one will be our 'Alí Na<u>kh</u>javání?[5]

Gayle took Mrs Baker's words to heart as she once again set off for South America, now to establish her residence in Ecuador, home not only to the Galápagos Islands but to a large indigenous community. The Guardian had given the South American communities their goals:

As associates of the chief executors of 'Abdu'l-Bahá's Divine Plan, the members of the South American Bahá'í community . . . have a great and splendid task to perform . . . They stand on the threshold of a new Era

marking the inauguration of their Mission beyond
the borders of their homelands. Their responsibilities, which are continually growing as they themselves
mature, are twofold. They must devote their attention
henceforth to both the multiplication and consolidation of the institutions they have already established
throughout the South American Republics, and assiduously endeavor to implant the banner of the Faith
in the nine territories and islands assigned to them
as their share in the prosecution of the decade-long
world spiritual Crusade recently launched by their
fellow-believers throughout the world.[6]

Helen Hornby describes in detail the difficulties encountered just to have someone settle in the Galápagos
Islands, let alone achieving the rest:

Three believers offered to pioneer in the islands: Haig[7]
Kevorkian, Francis Steward and Gayle Woolson. Haig
was offered the post the year before by the National
Spiritual Assembly and he accepted. He ran into
obstacle after obstacle trying to settle in the Galapagos
by the prescribed date and the National Assembly did
all they possibly could to facilitate his arrival on time
but to no avail. The Guardian initially asked that the
pioneers be in their posts by October 16, 1953 . . . but
that was not possible in some cases.

The National Assembly of the United States had
decided, based on information received from their
investigation of the Islands, it was too primitive and

not a place for a woman to pioneer, especially a single woman. Therefore, they did not accept the offer of Francis Steward . . . Later it was learned that Gayle Woolson had written to the Hand of the Cause of God, Mrs Dorothy Baker, confiding in Mrs Baker about her desire to settle in the Galapagos and asked for advice. On 11 September 1953, the Western Hemisphere Teaching Committee was informed of her request and responded with the following letter:

This committee feels that you could both settle this post and continue the consolidation work in Quito, by establishing your residence in the Galapagos and by spending some time in Quito on your way to and/or from N.S.A. meetings. We are sure you could do this and, if you agree, will recommend this arrangement to both N.S.A.'s.

You probably realize that this is a difficult post. We have been doing some research on the Islands which indicate that not only are the living conditions rugged, but also that they may be dangerous. On the other hand, it would appear extremely difficult for most people to obtain permission to go there and we believe that you could.

We know that you want to enter the vanguard of soldiers called for by our beloved Guardian.

However, we want to warn you of our findings and are enclosing a brief digest of them.

We suggest that you go there with the intention of settling, subject to the approval of the N.S.A.;

and that, if you find it impossible to stay there, you make a survey of the Galapagos sending us your suggestions as to how this goal can be won.

Evidently the Committee had not consulted with the National Assembly regarding Gayle's offer and received their opinion, for on 26 September 1953, the National Assembly of South America received the following cable from the National Spiritual Assembly of the United States: WOOLSON IMPOSSIBLE GALAPAGOS REASONS ALREADY DISCUSSED.

. . . Then on October 21, Haig wrote to the National Spiritual Assembly of South America asking if they were still saving the post of the Galapagos for him. They assured him that it was waiting for him and they felt sure he was the ideal person for this post. In the meantime the Guardian extended the time for the pioneers to get to their post to Riḍván 1954. Time passed and it appeared Haig would not make it before Riḍván because even after arriving in Ecuador he would have a lot of red tape to go through in order to travel to the Archipelago de Colon, the Galapagos. Being aware of this and the lateness of the hour, the National Assembly cabled the National Assembly of the United States on February 22, 1954: SETTLEMENT GALAPAGOS NOT CERTAIN BY RIDVAN WELCOME ASSISTANCE . . .

The National Assembly of South America also investigated the conditions of the Archipelago and learned among other things that it was not a suitable place for a woman without a family to attempt to live;

there were no hotels or boarding houses – women and girls alone were often raped; that one island was a penal colony and not a fit place for ladies. Having received such information, it was determined that it was not suitable for Francis or Gayle to go there alone, besides, permission would not be granted by the Ecuadorian Government for a woman to go alone. But when it appeared that Haig would not be able to make it before Riḍván the National Spiritual Assembly of the United States gave Gayle permission to go with the understanding that she must have a woman companion. She could only find a non-Bahá'í friend to accompany her for a short period of time, Mrs Rebecca Kaufman, who promised and then changed her mind about going due to some obstacles.

Gayle's problems continued – in Quito she made arrangements to take a boat from Guayaquil to the Islands. So she arrived in Guayaquil early to finalize the arrangements for the trip and had quite a shock when she was told that she could not sail on the boat contracted for her by a Sr. Munoz because it was a military boat and she had been given a permit to sail on a commercial boat. Sr. Munoz kindly wired the Commander in Quito for special permission for Mrs Kaufman and Gayle to sail on the military boat with this permit but it was not granted. (Gayle obviously felt that Mrs Kaufman's problems would soon be resolved in time for her to accompany her). Then Gayle was informed that a commercial boat was scheduled to leave the end of the month. She reported to the Assembly:

I explained to him that I would gladly go on his commercial boat but that I could not wait until the end of the month . . . I went to see the head commander in Guayaquil, who is under the commander in Quito, and he kindly sent a wire . . . recommending a special permit for my sailing on the military boat. He suggested that I go back to Quito and make personal efforts too, and as I didn't want to take any chance of being denied again, I took the plane . . . and went to Quito to the Ministry. I saw the Commander and the permit was given for both Rebecca and myself. It has all worked out wonderfully and this is the only boat on which I could have gone in order to get to the Galapagos in time . . . Another miracle was that the boat was supposed to leave last Friday, then it had to be delayed until Monday and due to this I had the opportunity to continue my efforts . . . The Hand of God was seen in the whole arrangement but for a time I had lost all hope of going on that boat and even talked to an aviator to get prices for a special trip in his little plane (but it turned out to be a little too dangerous and expensive). [8]

In her personal papers, on an unfolded envelope, written in pencil, Gayle left the following additional reflections on her preparations for the journey:

As the day of our departure from Quito to go to Guayaquil was approaching, Rebecca advised me that she would not be able to go with me. What a big disappointment that was, and there was no one else available to replace her. I would go alone, knowing that Bahá'u'lláh would take care of me. There were other occasions when I had gone alone to virgin cities to teach the Faith. But, of course, they were not like the Galapagos. But I was not afraid. The important thing and above all else, I was to get to the Galapagos and on that last boat before Riḍván 1954 in order to fulfill this goal of the World Crusade.

So off I went to Guayaquil, taking an early flight in order to do all I had to do such as buying some items there instead of in Quito to avoid extra luggage from there, and to go to the boat company. Also, I had to go to the All-American Cable Company in Guayaquil to find out about cable facilities in Galapagos from where I had to cable the date of my arrival so that the Guardian could be informed about this additional goal. The information was that the only way to cable out from the Galapagos would be to leave a deposit of the amount of the message at the All-American Cable Company and have the text cabled from there in the morning.

When I went to the boat company to buy my ticket the day before the scheduled sailing, I was told that the permit from the Ministry of Defense had not yet been received. What a shock! Had the earth opened up and swallowed me, I could not have been more stupefied. They said they would send a radiogram requesting the permit by radio.

So I went back to my hotel room to pray. I prayed the Tablet of Aḥmad nine times. When I was toward the end of my prayers, I lay down on the bed to complete the ninth prayer. As I was praying, I felt as though I were lying on a berth on a ship and could feel the gentle rocking with the waves of the sea. I knew that was a sign for me and that everything was going to work out so that I could be on that boat. I couldn't see how but my whole trust was in the help of Bahá'u'lláh.[9]

As it happened, Rebecca Kaufman did join her. She and Gayle left the port city of Guayaquil on 5 April 1954, travelling on a military ship to arrive at San Cristobal Island, the major island, on 9 April. 'After a short stay at San Cristobal, they continued their journey to Santa Cruz Island, arriving on 11 April. That is where they resided.'[10] They notified the National Spiritual Assembly of South America. On 10 April 1954 the following cable was sent to Shoghi Effendi:

SHOGHI EFFENDI
HAIFA ISRAEL
GAYLE WOOLSON ARRIVED GALÁPAGOS APRIL NINTH
BAHAI LIMA

The Guardian replied on 12 April 1954:

ASSURE WOOLSON LOVING PRAYERS
SHOGHI

Thus was her name recorded as one of Knights of Bahá'u'lláh – souls who, under the Guardian's guidance and in their love for Bahá'u'lláh, underwent improbable journeys to some of the remotest and most inhospitable places on earth assigned in 'Abdu'l-Bahá's *Tablets of the Divine Plan*. Thus, in this global Plan, the light of the new Revelation was diffused to illumine almost all the countries and territories of the earth.

Decades later, on a paper with details of conversations at a fireside, Gayle noted, 'Galapagos . . . paradise because reached in time'.

One day, when she was in her nineties and details of short-term memory seemed of diminished importance but her soul could still express its concise wisdom, she was asked what was important in making decisions for one's path of service. She replied, 'To know the value of time'.

In some ways, the boat journey had been like travelling back in time as well as forward in the present. It was 605 miles across open sea to an archipelago of islands that were tops of gigantic volcanoes strung over thousands of miles of ocean, some on either side of the equator. They had an ancient feel: some were more than eight million years old. Stars were plentiful in the night sky. The famed turtles and tortoises, or 'galápagos', could grow up to 500 pounds in weight and live for 150 years. Charles Darwin had arrived there 120 years before. Landing first on San Cristobal and then doing much of his research on Santa Cruz, it was here that the rich but isolated flora and fauna inspired him with insights leading to his theory of evolution. Now, two unlikely women came ashore to make friends and introduce teachings by which humanity could unite and achieve a new worldwide spiritual civilization.

When Gayle and Rebecca landed at San Cristobal and then pulled into shore on Santa Cruz, there were about two hundred people on the island, including Ecuadoreans, Australians, British, Germans, North Americans, Norwegians, and Swiss. Most lived on haciendas in the mountains. Gayle and Rebecca found a place on the coast where there were about 25 or 30 houses. There were no hotels or houses to rent, nor did the island have stores, general electricity or running water. There was one nurse, a first aid station, a doctor and a dentist who visited the island on occasions.[11]

The Swiss carpinter [sic.] of the island, Adolf Heni, kindly emptied his shed where he stored tools and wood planks so that the two ladies could lodge there. It had the rare convenience of a pump of slightly salty water, which all homes did not have, and the luxury of 19 papaya trees. They were able to arrange in the shed their two army cots, a gasoline stove, kerosene lamp and a few other household items, and some canned goods. Two wood stools and the edges of their cots were used for seating and a built-in counter served as a table.[12]

In later years, Gayle still enjoyed the taste of coffee with a little salt, as it evoked that place and time.

A few families sold basic items in their homes such as

bread, sugar, flour, and periodically a few farmers from the 'hills', the agricultural section of the island, would bring some vegetables and meat to sell. Occasionally a fisherman would show up with a fish for sale. Bathing took place in swimming suits at a bay. The salt from the Pacific Ocean would be rinsed off afterward at the pump in their yard with less salty water. Mail came in or went out only about once a month when the military boat came in.

Living on Santa Cruz Island was like rustic camp life. The proprietor of the shed did not want to charge any rent for its use. He said it was not worth anything. However, upon Gayle's insistence that he accept some payment, he agreed to receive the equivalent of $3 US dollars per month . . . [13]

Gayle spent most of her time looking for a place in which Haik Kevorkian could live upon his arrival and making acquaintance with people, starting with those close by. Gayle identifies some of their friends in the caption for a photo taken at their home:

Gayle and Rebecca and friends in the yard of their lodging quarters. The gentleman at the left, Adolf Heni, is the carpinter [sic.] and proprietor who rented the shed to the ladies. The other at the right was an islander from Canada, Frank Balbar. The two children at the right are of the Horneman family. The two at the left, it is believed, are of the Castdalen family. These two families of European background lived in the 'hills'. Mrs Alfreda Horneman, the mother of the two children, was the first person of Santa Cruz Island to whom Gayle conveyed the teachings of Bahá'u'lláh. The two gentlemen were among the contacts to whom the Bahá'í Message was given by her.[14]

Gayle often used pictures and poetry to introduce the Teachings. She explained,

> The approach used in sharing the Bahá'í Faith was generally by showing photographs of the Bahá'í House of Worship in Wilmette, which always impressed the viewer . . .The beautiful architecture of the Temple, lace-like and ethereal, and the significant idea of the nine sides, nine doors and nine gardens were a source of fascination.
>
> To convey the meaning of the temple, Gayle would use a poem by the American poet, John Greenleaf Whittier, who was a contemporary of Bahá'u'lláh . . .

One Brotherhood for Evermore

Great God, unite our severing ways;
No separate altars may we raise,
But with one tongue now speak Thy praise

With peace that comes of purity
Building the temple yet to be,
To fold our broad humanity.
While flowers of love its walls shall climb,

Soft bells of peace shall ring its chime,
Its days shall all be holy time.

A sweeter song shall then be heard –
The music of the world's accord,
Rejoicing o'er the broken sword.

That song shall swell from shore to shore
One hope, one faith, one love restore,
One brotherhood for evermore.[15]

Additionally, she had a chart she would use to explore the way the teachings of the founders of all religions unfold through history in a progressive way. At that time, she found that people in South America were eager for knowledge of Faiths beyond their own Christian tradition.

Haik arrived on 29 May 1954. He, too, was named a Knight of Bahá'u'lláh for the Galápagos Islands, as his preparations to come had begun before the deadline. By coincidence, Haik's and Gayle's families both hailed from Syria. Haik was born in October 1916 in Aleppo; his father had embraced the Cause in 1911 in his birthplace, Gaziantrep Aintab, Turkey, and then he and his family had visited the Guardian in Haifa on their way to Argentina. Later, in 1940, when May Maxwell and her cousin Jeanne Bolles arrived in Buenos Aires, Haik was the only local believer to speak with her before her sudden passing the following day. He offered to come by the hotel. She declined, as she needed to rest. Following her passing,

Haik devoted himself to caring for the grave of Mrs. Maxwell and it was his charming custom always to visit her resting place on the anniversary of her death. The cemetery caretakers befriended Haik and permitted him to visit even after closing hours. Struck by his devotion, the present caretaker once asked Haik's fiancée, Miss Aurora de Eyto, 'Was she his mother, or a relative?' It was Haik's pleasure to accompany any Bahá'í visitor to Buenos Aires who wanted to visit the grave. On the eve of his departure for Galápagos Islands – although Miss de Eyto was not yet a Bahá'í – he asked her to visit Mrs Maxwell's resting place during his absence and ensure that it was properly cared for.[16]

In the 'In Memoriam' for Haik Kevorkian in *The Bahá'í World*, we find Gayle's tribute to him:

Haik was very devoted and possessed a friendly and outgoing personality. His warmth and sincerity won him many friends. Although he generally displayed a jolly attitude his nature was deeply serious. He had great spiritual depth and was well grounded in the Bahá'í Teachings He was at ease in conversation and had a ready supply of charming anecdotes and analogies with which to illustrate his points. He was casual in his manner and had a delightful sense of humour. He worked diligently on the island of Santa Cruz and won friends and sympathizers for the Cause there and established some contacts on the island of San

Cristobal and the penal colony island of Santa Isabela which he also visited.

Upon arrival, Haik brought with him two communications – one, that Gayle had again been elected to the National Spiritual Assembly of South America, and another appointing her to the first contingent of Auxiliary Board Members for the Americas. It was clear that she needed to return to the mainland.

Gayle, Rebecca, and Haik were together on the island for nine days, making contact with friends and acquainting him with the environs of his new home. One of the closing events before Gayle and Rebecca left the Galápagos Islands was a shishkabab dinner prepared by Haik, who was an expert cook. She has a photograph that shows how he created the barbecue out of rocks, which were plentiful in the area, and used metal skewers he had brought with him.

Soon after this, the same military boat on which they had come arrived unexpectedly. They asked and got permission to leave on this boat on 13 June, going to the mainland earlier than expected, instead of waiting until July for the commercial. Gayle felt it was important to get back, catch up on the news, and learn the plans for her work. Rebecca felt ready to return to Quito and resume her own life. They were cut off from communications by more than their remote location. The Galápagos were in a strategic military position. Authorities and inhabitants were conscious that the world did not yet have a durable peace. The international relations between Peru and

Ecuador were delicate. Helen Hornby explains:

> Fearing that they would be thought of as spies, the
> National Spiritual Assembly (of South America) in
> Lima would not send cables nor letters to Gayle directly
> nor could she correspond with them directly. However,
> on 21 June 1954 Gayle notified the National Assembly
> of her present whereabouts and the status of the islands:

> > My stay in the Galapagos was exactly two months
> > and I am very grateful for having had the experi-
> > ence of going there. Life is so different there that it
> > seems like being in another world. Haik arrived on
> > May 29th and Rebecca Kaufman and I were there
> > nine days with him before we came back to the
> > mainland. The three of us held the Nineteen Day
> > Feast of 'Light' together, on June 5th, although
> > Rebecca is not yet a Baháʼí. I was happy to have
> > been able to give seven people of the island the
> > Message, most of whom are now studying our lit-
> > erature. The seventh of these was a resident of the
> > island who traveled on the same boat with us on
> > the way back. He has 'Baháʼuʼlláh and the New Era'
> > which I loaned him and when he returns to the
> > island in about three months, Haik can carry on
> > from there. I will let him know about it. We con-
> > nected Haik with all of our contacts and friends,
> > and he moved into our little one-room house after
> > we left. I feel that he will be very successful there.
> > When he went to the Galapagos, he had as a cabin

mate a young man who lives in Santa Cruz. They became very good friends, and he is also studying the teachings now. [17]

Haik's experience in the Galápagos after they left is described in his 'In Memoriam' article:

Haik left a diary of his experiences at his post. The entries speak eloquently of his efforts to be patient in awaiting opportunities to speak of the Faith, of his loneliness, of his prayers for his fiancé and 'all my dear ones who have passed away, including Dorothy Baker, Philip Sprague, May Maxwell...' He lived in a small hut without sweet water or lights, unaccustomed to the limited diet of the island which offered no vegetables and only rarely meat. The solitude on the island, the environment, and the peace he found there helped him to meditate. Throughout the years he corresponded with the Guardian and drew much strength from Shoghi Effendi's replies which were full of encouragement. The quality of Haik's faith was profound and exceptional and it withstood even the painful test created by the estrangement from the Cause of some of the members of his family.

A friend who knew him well and served with him has provided this tribute: 'I was always deeply impressed by Haik's uprightness; he did and said what he felt to be right, an admirable quality in a world so lacking in rectitude. He was most generous, especially with the poor and disadvantaged. I heard of his giving away his clothes on more than one occasion when he came in contact with the underprivileged.'[18]

Helen Hornby's account of Haik Kevorkian's two years in the Galápagos Islands is based largely on correspondence, as Dorothy Campbell, as the secretary of both the National Spiritual Assembly of South America and the New Territories Teaching Committee, kept in close touch. In a letter dated 7 June 1954, shortly after his arrival, he wrote to her:

> Life down here is very primitive . . . When somebody is here (they) can really appreciate what it means to have an electric light, or to have a bathroom, even a small shop on the corner street of your house where you can buy small things that you need – you miss them all, but with all this you can understand better the life of 'Abdu'l-Bahá, who had to suffer for a life time and understand better His Sacrifices . . .
>
> Unemployment and lack of food were among the tests Haig had to face. The very little food he was able to obtain was often shared with guests who he invited, or who called unexpectedly. Additionally, there were endemic problems of alcoholism and rape and generally low moral standards. These had been among the reasons for initially advising against a woman going to the islands alone.[19]

According to Hornby, there were no churches on Santa Cruz but just a 'wooden hut with a few fabricated saints'.

However, there was a priest who came from another island who was alarmed to discover that there was a new person teaching a new religion on the island. 'He warned the people to "beware (of) these people because they have some truth with some poison in it which is enough to kill your souls forever."' This opposition was to continue, together with increased interest aroused among some of the inhabitants: 'it was the island school teacher, a native Ecuadorian, Senor Moyses Mosquera Zevallos . . . who, on January 8, 1955 was the first to accept the Bahá'í Faith in the Galápagos.' Haik remained on the island for two years that were very difficult, both because of the social conditions and because of specific opposition from both the priest and the Mayor.

Dorothy Campbell's letters continued to be a source of sustaining encouragement. Below is an example:

> I am sending you some 'Time' Magazines which I have on hand and will send you others from time to time as I can. Your life and work there will not be easy, Haik, but it will have its great compensations, not the least of which is to know that you have filled the heart of the Guardian with great joy and that the Hosts of the Supreme Concourse will surround you constantly and give you a power that you've never had before. Our sacrifices always bring us great rewards and one of them . . . is to come to a deeper realization of the sufferings Bahá'u'lláh and 'Abdu'l-Bahá underwent. You will have great confirmations there, Haik, and we shall be praying constantly for you and for your teaching work.[20]

Through service on the National Assembly and the Auxiliary Board, Gayle continued to be in touch with Haik and the difficulties he faced, as well as with the Bahá'í community on the Galápagos Islands, as the Bahá'í presence there gradually increased. Haik returned to Buenos Aires in January 1956. He married his fiancée, Aurora de Eyto, on 19 October 1957. They had two sons; one died as a young child. Haik served throughout his life until his passing, at age 54, on 3 August 1970.

It was not until 1977 that the first Spiritual Assembly was established in Santa Cruz. For many years, Gayle kept in touch with individual believers in the Galápagos Islands and later entertained thoughts of pioneering there once again. In later years in Evanston, she continued a habit of sending a Riḍván letter of greeting to each of the countries where she had pioneered, including one individually addressed to the Galápagos Islands.

13

New Dimensions of Service

With her return to Quito, Gayle contemplated the contents of the envelopes Haik had brought for her. As previously mentioned, the first concerned her election to the National Spiritual Assembly of South America, the second her appointment to the first Auxiliary Board for the Americas.[1]

She resumed her work with the National Spiritual Assembly, a service that was demanding but somewhat familiar. The Auxiliary Board was a new institution, called into being by the Guardian as announced in a cablegram in 1952:

> Call upon fifteen Hands from five continents . . . to inaugurate historic mission through the appointment, during Riḍván 1954, of five auxiliary boards one each continent, of nine members each, who will, as their adjuncts, or deputies, and working in conjunction with the various National Assemblies functioning on each continent, assist, through periodic systematic visits to Baháʼí centers, in the efficient, prompt execution of the twelve projected National Plans.[2]

With Rebecca Kaufman, near their new home, 1954

Adolf Heni, standing left, who rented the shed to Gayle and Rebecca. At right, Frank Balbar, islander from Canada. The children are from the Horneman and Castdalen families from the hills. Mrs Horneman was the first person from Santa Cruz Island to whom Gayle spoke of the Bahá'í Teachings. The men both learned of the Faith

Scenes from the Galápagos Islands, with Rebecca Kaufman, and the barbeque with Haik Kevorkian

Knights of Bahá'u'lláh Gayle Woolson and Haik Kevorkian

*In Ecuador, with Haik Kevorkian and
Auxiliary Board Member Katherine McLaughlin, 1954*

In 1954, Shoghi Effendi indicated that the moment for action had arrived:

> The hour is ripe for the fifteen Hands residing outside the Holy Land to proceed during Riḍván with the appointment, in each Continent separately, from among the resident Bahá'ís of that Continent, of Auxiliary Boards, whose members, acting as deputies, assistants and advisors of the Hands, must increasingly lend their assistance for the promotion of the interests of the Ten Year Crusade.[3]

Nine were appointed to the Auxiliary Board for the Americas. Gayle (Ecuador) and Mrs Margot Worley (Brazil),[4] who were both already serving as full-time itinerant teachers for South America, were assigned to this continent. Both were also serving on the National Spiritual Assembly of South America.[5] Gayle promptly replied to the Hands for the Americas:

> A copy of your cable of April 30th to the National Spiritual Assembly of South America concerning the appointment of the Auxiliary Board for the Americas was given to me by Haik Kevorkian upon his arrival to the Galápagos May 29th. The honor conferred upon me by being included among the members of the Board has filled me with a feeling of great joy and a grave sense of responsibility, and I assure you that I shall do everything within my power, reinforced by Divine Assistance, to fulfil the tasks assigned to me.[6]

On 22 June 1954, they replied:

> We are delighted to know you are back in the arena of
> service – not that pioneering in the Galapagos Islands
> wasn't magnificent, because it certainly was! However,
> Haig Kevorkian can fill that post, while you help us
> mightily in our great task of forming the new National
> Spiritual Assembly.

On 12 July 1954, they wrote regarding the goal of the
Ten Year Crusade that was to be the focus of her assignment:

> We are delighted that you are now available for this
> intensive work in preparation of formation of new
> National Spiritual Assemblies.

A letter dated 27 May 1954 from the Hands stated:

> We are embarking upon a new work of tremendous
> and far-reaching importance in the evolution of the
> Faith of Bahá'u'lláh. Our constant hope and prayer
> must be that, as representatives of the Guardian,
> we shall receive divine assistance to render services
> which will bring joy to Shoghi Effendi and lighten his
> overwhelming burdens.

The American Hands suggested that Gayle and Margot
Worley each assume responsibility for five of the
ten countries designated to form National Spiritual

Assemblies.[7] They also identified three main objectives for the consolidation work:

> We feel very strongly that our most urgent continuing responsibility will be the consolidation work in the ten countries of South America where National Assemblies are to be formed by 1963, and that priority must be given to these goals. This consolidation work includes the strengthening of existing communities, the multiplication of groups, and the bringing of groups to Assembly status in these countries.
>
> We are aware of the problem presented by the vast distances separating the countries and Baháʼí communities of South America. The funds at our disposal for travel expenses will not be adequate to cover all of the teaching circuits which would be desirable. However, we must arrange for at least one visit by a Board member to each country during the current year.
>
> In your own case, we are assured by the National Assembly of the United States that your regular living budget will be continued as heretofore.[8] Your transportation expenses will be met from the new Continental Baháʼí Fund which has been established in accordance with the instructions of our beloved Guardian . . .[9]

While this is a narrative of Gayle's story, her service is representative of work being done by a small band of people throughout the Americas. For a full decade (and longer than that for many), they sacrificed personal needs and concerns to this most important work, convinced that the achievement of the goals held significance, not only in the moment but for the future development of a world spiritual civilization.

Multiple responsibilities often fell to a few individuals. Gayle and Margot Worley thus added yet another layer to a pattern of service that would continue to the end of the Ten Year Crusade. Already, the National Spiritual Assembly of South America was responsible for making systematic visits to Bahá'í centres and for the efficient execution of the Regional Plan. Now, as Auxiliary Board members, Gayle and Margot shared increased international responsibilities. Both Margot's and Gayle's experience and particular talents made them well suited to the work ahead.

The American Hands of the Cause structured the visits of their Board members to ensure efficient, unified coordination:

> The Hands will prepare the way for each visit by notifying the National Spiritual Assembly, local Assemblies or other Bahá'í bodies concerned, obtaining their cooperation and advice, extending all possible information to the member of the Board carrying out the project, and making the necessary financial arrangements. All expenses of Board members engaged in projects initiated by the American Hands, which cannot be personally sustained by members, will be defrayed from the Continental Fund.[10]

Thus, for a given visit, the Hands would request specific collaboration between Assemblies and the Board member, depending on the need. During the first year, the Board members tried to cover all areas with intensive work. A single trip might combine inspiring expansion activities with careful attention to consolidation. In the second year, as the timeframe became more constrained, they were guided to narrow their focus to assisting weak groups to become strong, and larger groups to achieve Assembly status.

Initially, Gayle had been asked to come to Ecuador from Colombia to assist with some challenging situations in two communities with Assemblies, Quito and Guayaquil. Now, upon her return from the Galápagos, the National Spiritual Assembly requested that she immediately visit the port city of Guayaquil. Its Assembly had been the first formed in Ecuador (in 1945) with the assistance of Virginia Orbison, including in its membership a dynamic group of young Ecuadorians. This work developed on the foundation of teaching work laid by Ecuador's first and devoted pioneer, John Stearns. Over time, several pioneers, travel teachers, and Hands of the Cause patiently encouraged its development.

The community had struggled to establish unity, a clear understanding of the Faith, and a self-sustaining dynamic. The Assembly had been lost and now needed to be restored. Gayle knew the Bahá'ís in the community from previous meetings together. Her visit at this time would be followed by many others. She met with each of the believers, gathered them together, and encouraged activities. The community was then assisted in April by the coming of new resident pioneers, Ervin and

Wilma Thomas. Restoring Guayaquil to Assembly status involved developing trust among the believers, patiently clarifying understanding, strengthening individual relationships, encouraging unified collective action, and reaching out, by example, to acquaint new people with the universal teachings of Bahá'u'lláh. By 21 April 1955 the Assembly was re-established.

A letter from Gayle describes how, while following a systematic plan, they remained alert to new possibilities that would unfold as they moved forward. On 6 August 1954, she wrote to 'The American Hands of the Cause of God: Mrs Corinne True, Mr Horace Holley, Mr Paul Haney':

Beloved Friends:

Thank you very much for your letter of July 25th...

I am happy to inform you that very good contacts have been made in the cities of Ibarra and Otavalo, Ecuador and that a meeting is being arranged for next Monday, August 9th, at the city of Riobamba, Ecuador, on my way to Guayaquil. All three are virgin cities.

My plan had been to leave for Guayaquil this week, but due to the fact that I could not arrange an extension to my visa which expires this week, I had to make a trip to the frontier of Colombia in order to re-enter with a new visa for Ecuador. On the way I had to stay over night at the city of Ibarra. I was accompanied by a friend . . . At the local Turismo where we stayed, I met a lady who was my seat companion on the plane a year ago from Cali to Quito. She is now employed at the office of that hotel. We had talked about the Faith practically all the way during the plane trip and she showed much interest. I had lost track of her until now. Her name is María Giai. While we were conversing at the hotel, María excused herself to go to talk to the wife of the manager and came back to tell us that the manager's wife and also the manager knew of the Bahá'í Faith and were interested in it. Then the manager's wife came to meet us and she told us that she and her husband, who previously lived in Quito, had learned of the Faith through one of the Bahá'ís here, Hans Levy, and that they had 'Bahá'u'lláh and the New Era'. This couple's name is Colonel and Mrs Pablo Borja. Mrs Borja suggested that if we could stay an extra day in Ibarra, she would be able to arrange a meeting with some of their friends. This was done and on Tuesday, August 3rd, a fine group of 15 people, not counting us, gathered together for the meeting. Sincere interest was shown and they expressed the desire to have me come back to speak to them when I return to Ecuador after my tour. I am sending more books to the Borjas and also pamphlets to the interested friends. Among that audience which attended was the president of a bank, a director of a school and the brother of a bishop.

I was interested in contacting someone in the city of Otavalo as it is a city consisting principally of Indians. Another lady at the hotel, the cashier, who was friendly, gave me the name of . . . the president of the Central Bank of Otavalo. As this place is only 45 minutes away by bus from Ibarra, the following morning . . . María and I went there. I talked to (the bank president) and he showed sincere appreciation of the Bahá'í ideals. He said that when I come back I should notify him in advance and he will invite a group of friends to a meeting. I consented to do this and left a pamphlet with him. I will plan to contact both Ibarra and Otavalo after my teaching tour in Bolivia.

One of the Quito Bahá'ís, Sr. Luis Arguello, has relatives in the city of Riobamba which is about six hours from Quito by bus. He has consented to accompany me there next Monday and has written his relatives to arrange a meeting. From there I will go on to Guayaquil arriving the 10th or the 11th.

I beg your prayers for continued confirmations for these new cities.

With heartfelt love and warmest Baha'i greetings,

Faithfully,

Gayle Woolson

About her trip to Riobamba, Gayle writes:

Mr Luis Arguello, a Baha'i of Quito, and I went to Riobamba, where a group of 10 of his relatives gathered to hear the Message. A second meeting was held the next day. Interest was shown by some of them and we left literature for them to study and I told them I would visit them again on my way back to Quito.

One wonders at the mysterious forces at work. A simple trip to obtain a new visa on the way to Guayaquil included seemingly chance encounters that opened doors to meeting people in new areas. An entire fabric of connections would emerge in the area around Otavalo, bringing forth over time the sustained development of communities in that mountainous, indigenous area, fulfilling a primary goal of the Guardian in all of the Americas. A journey intended to strengthen a community and restore an Assembly resulted also in first steps towards the multiplication of groups in new areas.

Meanwhile, following these encounters, Gayle reached Guayaquil. On 7 September, she wrote to the Hands for the Americas:

In Guayaquil, where I was for three and a half weeks, I had intense activity giving public talks, and re-organizing the group there. About fifteen newspaper articles came out in their papers . . . The majority of the Bahá'ís of Guayaquil were cooperative and I feel sure that their Assembly will be reinstated next April. I spoke at the University, three high schools, the Masonic Temple, over two radio stations, the Rosacrucian Center and the Lions Club. The director of one of the schools enthusiastically expressed that the Bahá'í ideals were in accordance with his way of thinking and said that the doors of his school would always be open to us. This public activity did much to stimulate the Bahá'ís and get them back into activity after a year and a half of recess. They will meet every Friday at the home of Juan Luis Aguirre, and every other Saturday will have a deepening class. On my way back to Ecuador from

Bolivia, I feel that I should spend about a week with them.

From here, she proceeded to an NSA meeting in Santiago, Chile, with a stopover in Peru.

Gayle's reports provide a detailed picture of how she carried out tasks assigned.[11] Over many years, she had become skilled in using a single visit to assess the needs of an area and tailor her work to accomplish multiple objectives.

Amidst the intensely scheduled work of this time, the Hands of the Cause guided the Auxiliary Board members to consider the true well-spring of their work, the inner focus that yields success. On 12 October 1954, the Hands for the Americas wrote to 'Mrs. Margot Worley, Mrs. Gayle Woolson, and Mr. Esteban Canales' (for Central America) the following:

We feel profoundly that the pivot round which all success revolves is the station we attribute to the Faith in our own hearts.

Surveying the many teachers who have represented the Faith in North America over a period of years, we realize that their essential differences were not eloquence or its lack, experience or lack of experience on the public platform, nor thoroughness of knowledge of the teachings.

Their real difference was determined by the inner attitude they held toward the Faith – whether it is a social movement with liberal principles, or a pure mysticism, or an organization of doctrines and laws – or the channel through which Revelation flows into the world at this time. That is, the spiritual nature and divine essence of the Cause of Bahá'u'lláh.

Perhaps we fail to explain our thought clearly. Our purpose is to appeal to all members of the Auxiliary Board to give force and freedom to his [sic] concept of the station of the Faith as pure religion. Herein lies our capacity to teach in the real sense – guiding the souls whom Bahá'u'lláh has prepared for His message. We hope that by reflection you can complete our thought.[12]

Following the NSA meeting in Santiago, Gayle made the planned visit to Bolivia. Extracts from her report to the American Hands from Bolivia on 23 November 1954 offer an example of her continued intensive work, careful analysis, and precise narration. The report covers her visit to Sucre from 4 to 20 October, to Oruro from 21 October to 1 November, to Cochabamba for three days, and finally to La Paz from 4 to 24 November. In her own words:

These four cities (excluding Cochabamba) can be considered as the field to be developed as a basis for the future National Spiritual Assembly of Bolivia. Both Sr. Angel García and Sr. Estanislao Alvarez of La Paz have offered to make occasional visits to these cities ... However, the presence of resident pioneers would, of course, be the quickest way to develop assemblies in the three cities outside of La Paz. In accordance with your letter of October 19th, I will also keep in touch through correspondence with the contacts and friends in these cities.

Gayle thus identified those communities that could become the strongest Assemblies and therefore the foundation upon which the National Spiritual Assembly could be established. She identified and engaged local people to make additional visits, while also noting that pioneers would be valuable. She herself followed up with individuals and communities through correspondence. In a letter dated 12 January 1955, the Hands for the Americas asked their Board members to 'undertake a friendly and informal correspondence with pioneers in virgin areas of the Western Hemisphere'. The same day, they wrote a letter to Gayle asking her specifically to correspond with pioneers in the Galápagos, a practice she continued to her last years. (Throughout her life, Gayle kept up a worldwide correspondence. An individual recalled that during her years in Haifa, Gayle could often be seen sitting on the steps near the Shrines writing letters to the friends in Central and South America.)

In her report in November 1954 she goes on to state, 'The case of Sucre is . . . a matter of starting all over again. We made a new beginning there, and before Mr and Mrs Angel García and I left Sucre, we gathered a group of 10 who are interested in studying together.' She then lists specific names with identifying details regarding each one's situation, and continues:

In regard to our public diffusion work in Sucre, Mr
García and I collaborated in giving talks at the high
schools. With a letter of authorization from the
superintendent of high schools, Mr García spoke at
the three girls' high schools and I at the three boys'
high schools as well as at the Normal College. We also
participated jointly at a public meeting held at the
auditorium of the university under the auspices of the
Department of Culture of the University. Mr García
gave a 15 minute radio talk almost every evening we
were there, making 13 in all . . .

Our last night in Sucre, we had a fine meeting with
the friends who are desirous to study together and
prepare themselves to form part of the Bahá'í nucleus
of that city. We organized them and left Sucre feeling
satisfied with the results and hopeful of a better future.

Rather than concentrating directly on the discourage-
ment of the believers, Gayle worked with others to infuse
the community with a new spirit by engaging them in a
fresh wave of publicity and teaching. Thus, people were
drawn together with renewed understanding and made a
plan to deepen understanding with regular group meetings.

The section of the report about her time in Oruro
(21 October to 1 November) describes both systematic
efforts of the Bahá'ís to reach a wider audience and the
receptivity of institutions and individuals encountered.
Gayle wrote:

I met . . . a Baháʾí of Oruro, and a university student. He could not collaborate with me as he had just recently been released from a six months imprisonment caused by false accusations against him[13] maintaining that he had participated in propaganda against the government in a clandestine radio station. He explained that his complete freedom would not be obtained until December so he preferred to remain home most of the time until then. He visited me two or three times, and met with the group of six people whom I had invited the last day I was there. I was interested in having him meet them so that he would establish relationship with them for the benefit of future activities which he can start in January. He seems like a fine person and is eager to help develop the Faith in Oruro. The other Baháʾí who lives in Oruro is Edmundo Mérida, also a university student. He was out of town so I could not meet him . . .

In Oruro I had the excellent collaboration of Dr Oscar Uzín, a mason [sic] whose name and address was given to me by the head of the masons in La Paz. He is a lawyer and professor of commercial law at the Oruro University. He invited me to the Rotary luncheon where I was asked to say a few words about the Faith. Three members of the Lions Club were also there and they invited me to the Lions dinner that evening where I was presented as a Baháʾí and the chairman spoke briefly of the Baháʾí ideals when he presented me.

The Department of the Extension of Culture of the

University sponsored a talk at which 150 were present and the talk was broadcast over the University radio station. Another talk was given at the same auditorium of the university and also broadcast under the auspices of a women's club called Sociedad Femenina de 10 de Febrero. Other talks were given at three high schools, to the English class at the University, at the Politechnical School of the University, at the Club of the Yugoslavian colony and at the Theosophical Society. Six 15 minute radio talks were also given over Radio El Condor. I had the kind collaboration of the newspaper of the town and seven Bahá'í articles appeared, one of them being in the form of verse written by a columnist whom I met at the Rotary Club making reference to the talk to be given at the university which was to be the following day . . .

Several persons showed interest in deepening their knowledge of the Faith. Six of these attended a meeting at my hotel the last day I was there. One of them is the director of the Poly-technical School of the university. He and another friend requested to buy the whole Bahá'í library that is available in Spanish. In January . . . will contact these friends and others whose names I have given him to invite them to regular meetings which he has offered to start. Mr Alvarez of La Paz will go there at that time to help them get started.

Of her time in La Paz, she wrote, 'My public activities in La Paz consisted in giving talks in seven different departments of the university.' The report continues with a list of several professors she met, their level of interest and comments regarding their perspectives and possible follow up.

In La Paz, she found that only eight of the 22 Bahá'ís listed were active. She made contact with each, assessed his/her interest in the Faith and situation, and proceeded with natural next steps. She documented each encounter, to facilitate others in following up. Some were having difficulty with the Bahá'í teaching to avoid partisan politics. The Catholic Church also held great sway over the minds of the community. From time to time, she came in touch with those who had been given misinformation or who had confused ideas about the teachings of the Faith. The report reflects skill in gaining people's trust, inviting them to share their thoughts and concerns, clarifying issues, and observing what the process revealed of the true nature of a person's intent and interest.

Gayle concluded her report, 'Stay in Bolivia – 2 months – has cost me about $110.00.' When the Hands sent her a reimbursement check, she declined it, saying that she had just been giving information; she did not need the funds. This report offers an example of how one Bahá'í served the goal of strengthening local communities as the necessary foundation for each country to achieve an independent National Spiritual Assembly by 1963. Throughout Latin America, the Hands of the Cause, their newly-appointed auxiliaries, travelling teachers and local Bahá'ís dedicated their energies to this goal set by the Guardian.

After her return from Bolivia, Gayle made the

follow-up trip to Otavalo and Ibarra mentioned in her letter to the Hands of the previous August. Otavalo was a four-hour bus journey from Quito and on this journey she was accompanied by Luis Arguello. As was their practice, they contacted civic organizations. The Rotary Club invited them to make a presentation, resulting in newspaper coverage as well. The director of the local library attended, was attracted, embraced the new teachings, and offered his apartment for meetings. Gayle gave several other talks which she followed up by corresponding with about 25–30 individuals, including both professionals and students.[14]

The 'fabric of connections' mentioned earlier in this chapter would bear fruit. Around 1956, Gayle wrote the following regarding an individual from Otavalo who, with his family, were drawn to the Faith:

> Raúl (Pavón)[15] found the Faith in the following manner. One day while in his twenties, he went to the municipal library in Otavalo. The Director who was a Baháʼí, Mr César Vásquez, spoke to him briefly about the Faith and told him he would put him in contact with some Baháʼís where he could get further information. This was around 1956 . . .

As Raúl Pavón found himself increasingly drawn to the Teachings, he would leave books around the family home, which his parents, Clementina Mejía De Pavón and Segundo Pavón Barrera, could pick up and read in their own time.

The result of the investigation was that Dona
Clementina embraced the Cause in July of 1960. In
December of the same year, her husband Segundo
wrote a perceptive letter to the National Teaching
Committee explaining that he had made a thor-
ough investigation of the Faith, having studied *The
Covenant of Bahá'u'lláh* and *The Dispensation of
Bahá'u'lláh* as well as the communications his wife
had been receiving from the Assemblies and committees. He related that through his study he had come
to recognize Bahá'u'lláh. 'I have found the light with
which the Lord our God has deemed to inspire his
Divine Messengers to spread true faith in God, and
being convinced of this reality, I desire to be accepted
as a new believer in the Faith of Bahá'u'lláh.' The light
he found at that time was to guide his life until the end
of his time on earth.

The Pavóns were both born in Otavalo, a small
Ecuadorian city in the Province of Imbabura, the
province that holds the largest concentration of indigenous Bahá'ís in that country. As this century [20th]
opened, they were children growing up among the
native people, learning Quechua, the lingua franca of
the Andes, and learning also to appreciate the qualities and the culture of a greatly underestimated and
disparaged people. They acquired those humane qualities and that spiritual nature that distinguished their
years as Bahá'ís and gave them the unique ability to
identify with the Quechua-speakers they served.

They married in 1920 and had nine children, two

of whom died young. They lived to see all their sur-
viving children and a number of grandchildren accept
the Faith. Their lives were, even before their exposure
to the Faith, devoted to humanitarian objectives. Mr
Pavón was a civil servant, who well understood the
needs of the Indians, and his wife, a loving mother to
her own children, was also widely known as Mother
Pavón, a beloved 'mater familias' for all who needed
her.

Early in their marriage they purchased a farm in
Cachaco, miles from any city, so that their children
could be raised in a healthy and spiritual environment.
It was in a jungle-like area with no transportation,
not even roads. An undependable train which ran at
irregular intervals at some distance from their home
was the only means of travel in or out. They could not
have foreseen at this time that the farm would become
a school under Bahá'í auspices and a training institute
for the native believers of Ecuador. Seeing the needs
of the children of Cachaco, who were without educational facilities, they opened a school in their home,
supporting it from the proceeds of their farm insofar
as possible.[16]

Of Raúl's mother, widely known as Mother Pavón for her
consecrated work with the indigenous people, the campesinos, and children, Helen Hornby writes:

In spite of the hardship she suffered from time to time,
she never complained and always saw someone else in

greater need. On one occasion she and her husband heard that there was a mother in the market-place trying to sell her partially paralytic four year old child, who was also mute. Disregarding the fact that they had a house full of children of their own, they went and bought the child, fearing that someone would take him who would not give him love. He grew up with their children as one of their own brothers. There is no doubt that it was through their love and their unwavering faith that they were able to teach the child, including how to utter a few words. José Manuel Perugachi is a man now and a very devoted Bahá'í – ever ready to be of service, even beyond his physical capacity.[17]

Many in the Pavón family dedicated their lives to the Faith, using their property as a site for intensive institute programmes and literacy and children's programmes. Raúl Pavón and his sister, Isabel Pavón de Calderón, both later served on the Continental Board of Counsellors for the Americas. In later years, Hand of the Cause Dr Muhájir found in Raúl a dear friend and one who shared his vision of ways of teaching whole populations. Raúl was instrumental in establishing a community-based Bahá'í radio station to enhance communication with the widely-scattered Quechua people through their own language, music, and cultural expression. To this day, the radio station continues and new generations of Raúl's family continue to serve with the same spirit, in Ecuador and beyond.[18]

It was also through Raúl Pavón that Rufino Gualavisi learned of the Faith and became an outstanding teacher among his own Quechua people, as well as others. It is said that he would go first to villages, announce the Message, gather the names of those who responded, and invite the people to prepare for an upcoming visit from Raúl Pavón, who would then visit and share the teachings in greater detail and depth. Through their mutual accompaniment and collaboration, thousands responded. Decades later, in March 1990, the *Bahá'í News* offered the following tribute at the time of his passing:

Rufino Gualavisi Farinango, a renowned indigenous Bahá'í teacher, died March 23, 1990 in Otavalo, Ecuador. Mr Gualavisi taught the Faith to thousands of indigenous people and campesinos and helped open many difficult areas of the country (Ecuador) to the Faith, often accompanied by his spiritual father and teaching companion, Counsellor Raul Pavon. Although beaten and imprisoned at various times, he remained steadfast and never once wavered in his teaching efforts. He is buried in the cemetery 'Parques del Recuerdo' in Quito, on the left side and adjoining the resting place of his good friend and staunch admirer, the Hand of the Cause of God Raḥmatu'lláh Muhajir. On learning of Mr Gualavisi's passing the Universal House of Justice cabled the National Spiritual Assembly of Ecuador: 'Deeply saddened new passing outstanding sacrificial teacher Cause God Rufino Gualavisi. His noble qualities, his loving nature, his immense services indigenous masses native land never to be forgotten and worthy source pride your community. Urge holding befitting memorial meetings his blessed memory throughout country. Assure fervent prayers Holy Threshold for progress his radiant soul Kingdom on high. Kindly extend heartfelt condolences family and friends.[19]

Once again, we see the mysterious process by which one connection led to another, a single person, such as the librarian, becoming an instrument through whom Raúl Pavón and then many others responded. It was thus that the work continued, through crisis and victory, expansion and consolidation, to establish a firm basis for the National Spiritual Assemblies to be formed as a foundation for the Universal House of Justice.

14

A Pilgrimage Framed by Teaching Trips

In February 1956, Gayle made her first pilgrimage to the Holy Land, where in addition to visiting the Shrines of the Báb and Bahá'u'lláh, she met the Guardian, Shoghi Effendi, less than two years before his passing. On her way there, she spent time in two of the countries she was assigned as a Board Member: Colombia and Venezuela. The May 1956 issue of *Bahá'í News* reported:

> Mrs Gayle Woolson: Bahá'í Centers visited have been Cali, Medellín, Bucaramanga and Barranquilla, Colombia, spending a week in each city. In Venezuela she visited Caracas and Valencia, and spent a day in Curacao. Mrs Woolson devoted a month to Valencia, holding two meetings a week and giving public talks at high schools and local clubs affiliated with international organizations.[1]

Once in Haifa, the pilgrims would usually have their evening meal in the Pilgrim House with Shoghi Effendi, Rúḥíyyih Khánum, and others living in Haifa. The Guardian used these times to learn from the pilgrims about conditions in their countries, to give guidance as needed, to share news of recent developments in the Holy Land and abroad, and to broaden the vision of all.

Years later, in 1986, Gayle described in an interview her first dinner, as a pilgrim, with the Guardian:

> When I went to see him, you can imagine how I felt ... At that time, I was the only Westerner. The others were Persian ... He would put the last pilgrim (which, in this case, was Gayle) at the head of the table and he would sit to the right. I didn't know how I could eat. Everyone ate so I had to eat. When he was with us, it seemed that everything else disappeared. He would talk. He was so holy. He was like a pure angel. When he was finished eating, he would stand and we would stand too. We would leave. I would come back to the world with a thud. The Guardian's presence was so great that everything else would disappear.
>
> He had a marvelous picture of the whole world and the future of the whole world.[2]

As always, Gayle kept careful notes, often taken in shorthand or written close to the time of each conversation, then typed in final form. She recorded both questions the Guardian asked and comments he made regarding particular issues being encountered in South America. Beginning with his profound awareness of the present, the Guardian's comments penetrated to the heart of processes and took on added significance over time. Among her 'pilgrim notes'[3] is this account written on 16 February 1956:

When I conveyed to him the loving greetings of the Baha'is of South America, he said: 'I am pleased with Latin America.' Then he asked: 'How are the friends in South America?' 'Are they working? Are they progressing? Are they firm in the Cause of God?' I answered: 'Yes, but we still have a long way to go before we can say it is satisfactory.'

Then he asked: 'Are they now familiar with the Institution of the Hands?' I said yes and that we had received the visit of some of the Hands. He said: 'I am looking forward to the time when there will be a Hand in South America and one in Central America.'

I asked: 'How can we create a greater sense of individual responsibility in South America?' He said: 'They must be encouraged to have it. They need much encouragement. The Assemblies there are nascent, not even infant yet, just nascent, that is why we must be patient.'

He said one Hazira was destroyed (referring to one in Teheran) but 40 were gained. He asked me about the countries that had their Haziras and endowments in South America. He then said: 'It is very important that they all get these before April. The present Haziras are only temporary. This is just a start. They will be improved upon in the future.'

It is essential that the Bahá'ís do not become involved in politics especially in Latin America where the governments are very unstable. The Bahá'í Faith is supra-national, supra-natural. It is divine. We are above politics. Becoming involved in politics is particularly dangerous in Latin America. We are patriotic but not nationalistic. We are more than patriotic. We uphold patriotism but maintain that it is not enough. We are above nations and above parties ... We love the world and by loving the world, we love our own nation. Bahá'u'lláh said: 'Let not a man glory in that he loves his country but rather in that he loves his kind ...'

It is not enough to convert to the Faith. The new believer must develop spiritually and arise to teach others. Conversion should not be the goal of the teacher. The goal is that the new believer should arise to teach others. This is why progress in Africa is so extraordinary. The new believers go out and teach others.

The friends must teach with determination and patience. If the process is slow, they must not become discouraged, but to have determination is important.

As to how to attract the Indians, he said: Attract them through friendliness and kindness. Give them preference in everything; not only equality but preference, preferential treatment. Teaching the Indians is very important ... Then they must take part in the administrative activities of the Faith. Do you remember what the Master said about the American Indians? He compared them with the Arabs at the time of Muhammad. The Indians must be given preferential treatment. The Bahá'ís must treat them just the opposite of the way the others treat them. Amongst the Bahá'ís, the minorities in any country must be given preferential treatment. If there is a tie between two believers for anything, and one is of a minority group, there must not be a second vote. Preference must be given to the believer of the minority group . . .

The National Assembly of South America must encourage the believers, it must stimulate them. They must become re-created, become aflame. It is easy for the Latin Americans to be set aflame, they must not lean on the North American. We must have unity in essentials, but in non-essentials we must stimulate diversity so that each country will have its own spirit in the work and not the North American spirit . . .

Work with the weak places, not the strong ones. Give special attention to the weak ones until their roots are firmly planted.

More sacrifice is needed. The more sacrifice is involved, the more effective the Bahá'í work will be. Of course, all work is effective, but the degree of effectiveness is greater when sacrifice is involved . . .

In three years, the 2500 centers we had in the world were raised to 3700. One-hundred of these were in Latin America. The Faith is now established in 243 territories. There are four islands left that do not have pioneers and it is because they are privately owned. We are now entering into the third phase of the world Crusade which will be the most brilliant phase as its objective will be to create 50 NSAs to amplify the basis for the Universal House of Justice. We have 12 NSAs now, we will have three more in Africa this year, and 13 next year, four of which will be in Latin America and one in Alaska.

The first phase of the world crusade lasted one year and consisted of the opening of the virgin territories. One-hundred were opened. The second phase lasted two years, during which time forty Haziras were purchased. the third phase will have as its main objective the widening of the basis for the Universal House of Justice. by establishing more NSAs. [4]

These notes demonstrate that however overwhelming the presence of the Guardian may have been, Gayle nevertheless paid attention to the details of his discourse. The awareness he instilled would inform her work as she returned home to assist with the completion of the Ten Year Plan. The Guardian's comments not only offered an assessment of the present but also articulated principles of the Faith central to its unfoldment in the future. Patience and persistence were needed to nurture 'nascent' communities. While the Guardian stressed the gradual nature of individual and community growth, he never diluted the vision. He was clear that the Faith is 'supranational' and 'supranatural', transcending allegiance to anything less than the oneness of humankind.

In two handwritten notes among her papers,[5] Gayle records the Guardian's farewell and explains the gifts she was to carry on his behalf:

The first gift:

1956 Scarf given to Mrs Woolson by the Beloved Guardian.

The sacred hands of the beloved Guardian handed

this scarf to me with a gift for Colombia, Ecuador, and Brazil at the time of my pilgrimage in February of 1956. The last blessed evening when he bid me fare-well and said:

'Your reward in the Abhá Kingdom shall be great.'

The next year I was employed in October of 1957 at the lowest possible level for a bilingual secretary and through the bounty of God, I worked myself up to the highest level within that category – with high marks in Spanish according to the official evaluation – 5 in speaking, 4+ in reading.

This 'reward', as she sees it here, represented a major transition. Upon her return to Ecuador, Gayle was instructed that the time had come for her to become financially independent from the stipend given by the National Spiritual Assembly of the United States, due to the exigencies of the Plan and development of the Faith. Now 44 years old, Gayle had to find employment for the first time during her residence in South America. As she states, she saw 'the bounty of God' in the way she not only obtained work but was shown a path that led to a stable government position with USAID, advancement, and ultimately a small pension essential to her liveli-hood. Once again, obedience to the admonition in the *Tablets of the Divine Plan* to learn the language of one's country would be confirmed.

The second gift:

Pilgrimage February 16 to 25, 1956
  Given to me by Shoghi Effendi with his own hands
on last day of my pilgrimage, February 1956. In this
cloth was wrapped a gift of piece of curtain from
Shrine of Báb for NSAs of Colombia, Ecuador &
Brazil.

On her way home, Gayle resumed her teaching trip,
returning first to Colombia and Venezuela, then pro-
ceeding to Ecuador, Peru, and Colombia, stimulating
community growth by sharing news of the pilgrimage
and the meeting with the Guardian. The *Bahá'í News*
offers the following summary:

In March 1956, she returned from pilgrimage in Haifa
and planned to convey the inspiration received from
the Guardian with Bahá'ís in Caracas, Venezuela;
Barranquilla, Bucaramanga, Bogota, Medellín and
Cali, Colombia; Quito, Ecuador; Guyaquil, Lima,
Callao, Huancayo, Arequipa, La Paz, Cochabamba
and Sucre, before the Convention of the Bahá'ís of
South America.[6]

The following year (1957) saw two interim regional
National Spiritual Assemblies established in South
America, one for the northern countries and one for
those in the south. Gayle was elected to that which
served the northern countries of Brazil, Peru, Colombia,
Ecuador, and Venezuela. Additionally, through long and
unwavering local effort, together with the beneficent

contributions of the Guardian, Mrs Amelia Collins, and the National Spiritual Assembly of the United States, Ecuador was able to complete the purchase of a building for a Centre, or Ḥaẓíratu'l-Quds (Ḥaẓíra) as they were called. This completed a goal of the Ten Year Plan, together with the 3,154 square meter endowment property for a future temple, purchased in 1956 north of Lake San Pablo, near Otavalo.[7]

Filled with gratitude for the international support in their hard-won accomplishments, the Bahá'ís in Ecuador did not perceive that heart-rending changes were on the horizon:

Little did any of the believers realize that this year would bring such sorrow to the hearts of the ardent lovers of Shoghi Effendi all over the world. Nor could anyone visualize that these Plans were the last ones he would outline for the Bahá'í World – for everyone was so accustomed to his guidance through his letters and messages. Often, his messages would lift the veil of obscurity little by little, so that glimmerings of greater horizons could gradually be discerned. This can be observed in his letter of welcome to the newly born Regional Spiritual Assembly of the Northern Countries of South America dated July 3, 1957 to which Gayle had been elected:[8]

Dear and Valued Co-Workers:

I welcome with feelings of exultation and pride, the formation of the Regional Spiritual

Assembly of the Bahá'ís residing in the Northern Republics of the South American continent – an event of enduring and far-reaching significance in the annals of the Faith of Bahá'u'lláh in Latin America. The emergence of this interim Regional Spiritual Assembly should be hailed as the fore-runner of the independent National Spiritual Assemblies which, in the course of the evolution of the Ten-Year Plan, are to be firmly established in these Republics, and which will signalize the triumphant termination of yet another epoch in the history of the evolution of the Administrative Order of that Faith in the South American continent.

That the Bahá'í Communities, laboring so devot-edly and so assiduously in these five Republics, should have, as a result of their steadfast exertions and whole-hearted response to the Message of the New Day, reached so swiftly so important a mile-stone on the high road of their glorious destiny, proclaims, in no uncertain terms, the high qual-ity of the faith which animates their members, and evokes in the hearts of all those who have, in recent years, watched the development of the institutions committed to their charge, feelings of unqualified admiration, and reinforces their con-fidence in the capacity of these rapidly advancing, steadily consolidating communities to achieve their ultimate objectives . . .[9]

Visiting Otavalo in the 1950s. Above: visiting Rufino Gualavisi; below: with Raúl Pavón

Marta Rosales Toromoreno at about 5 years old, when she first learned Bahá'í songs and prayers from Gayle

*National Regional Convention of the Bahá'is of South America, La Paz,
Bolivia, and the National Spiritual Assembly, 1955*

Serving on the first Auxiliary Board for the Americas: teaching in the Dominican Republic, 1956 . . .

. . . and in Baranquilla, Colombia

*First Regional Convention and National Spiritual Assembly for the
northern countries of South America: Brazil, Colombia, Ecuador, Peru
and Venezuela, in Lima, Peru, 1957, with Hand of the Cause Horace
Holley (back row, centre) representing the Guardian and the National
Spiritual Assembly of the United States*

The Guardian then gave specific guidance that later seemed prescient:

> The Six-Year Plan,[10] on which the attention of the members of these communities must be focused should be regarded by them as the chief and unfailing instrument for the execution of their high purpose.
>
> A supreme effort must be made to swell, as rapidly as possible, the number of the avowed supporters of the Faith in each of these Republics, and to multiply the isolated centers, groups and Local Assemblies constituting the foundations of the rising Bahá'í Administrative Order in these extensive territories. All firmly established Assemblies must, moreover, be incorporated in order to consolidate the foundations of this Administrative Structure. Recognition must, likewise, be secured from the authorities concerned for the Bahá'í Marriage Certificate as well as the Bahá'í Holy Days. The historic work initiated, so laboriously and auspiciously, in the newly opened territories, allocated to the Bahá'í communities of South America, must be zealously pursued, extended and reinforced. The translation, publication, and dissemination of Bahá'í literature in the Spanish, Portuguese and American Indian languages is yet another task which must be carried out with the utmost care, efficiency, vigor and vigilance. The increase in the number of summer schools, and the lending of a fresh impetus to the conversion of the American Indians and of other Minorities must henceforth receive the close and

uninterrupted attention of all those who are primarily responsible for the prosecution of this Plan. The Publishing Trust to be established in the capital city of Brazil, and constituting one of the foremost objectives of the Ten Year Plan, should be speedily and firmly established. And, last but not least, a site should be selected and purchased, in each of the four remaining Republics, for the purpose of the construction, at a future date, of a Mother Temple in each of these countries.[11]

He had outlined all they needed to know to have clear guidance through the remainder of the Plan. Soon, they would realize its value in ways they could not then imagine.

15

'What men lose they value much'

On 4 November 1957, an event occurred that would reverberate throughout the Baháʼí world: the unexpected passing of the Guardian, Shoghi Effendi. Not only did this bring the loss of one deeply loved, one relied upon as a constant source of guidance and inspiration. It also brought the loss of an expectation as to how the Faith and its institutions would unfold. Shoghi Effendi's passing and the events that then transpired had a life-changing effect, both individually and collectively, on the world-wide Baháʼí community. First-hand descriptions have preserved for posterity images of the shock, grief, love, and faith with which Rúḥíyyih Khánum, the other Hands of the Cause, National Assemblies, and the Baháʼí community arose to the challenge of those first hours and days of grief. Such accounts lend appreciation to the Hands' subsequent service on all continents, including the areas where Gayle was serving in South America. They lend weight to the determination with which the worldwide community strove to complete the Ten Year Plan, with its ultimate goal of establishing the Universal House of Justice.

In the dark days of November 1957, as the Hands gathered with others in London for the Guardian's funeral, many had never met each other, though they were bound together by a common faith and purpose. In retrospect, several remembered conversations in which the Guardian had seemed to indicate his passing was drawing nigh.[1] The same people said that until the moment came, they could not bear to let the idea penetrate their minds. Hand of the Cause Amelia (Milly) Collins was one.

Since the passing of 'Abdu'l-Bahá, Mrs Collins had dedicated her life to serving Shoghi Effendi, quietly providing funds as needed to accomplish goals around the world. (The Ecuadorian community had already experienced the impact of such generosity, which had enabled them to purchase both a national Ḥaẓíratu'l-Quds (centre) and endowment land for a House of Worship.) She had become like a mother to Rúḥíyyíh Khánum, especially after the unexpected passing of her own mother, May Maxwell, in Buenos Aires in 1940. Mrs Collins now spent several months each year in Haifa. When Rúḥíyyíh Khánum and the Guardian had left there in early summer, Shoghi Effendi had taken Milly Collins' hands in his and looked into her eyes.

He said: 'Don't be sad, Milly, don't be sad.' He had never said such words to her before. Those words were of great help to her during the sorrow and sadness of his passing and the turmoil and work of the Hands of the Cause; she tried, she said, to obey him and 'not be sad'.[2]

With that loving farewell to Milly Collins, the Guardian and Rúḥíyyih Khánum had left on what would be their last journey together to Europe. They followed the Guardian's inner wish to visit 'many of his favorite scenes in the mountains' of Switzerland,[3] a prompting that later caused Rúḥíyyih Khánum to wonder. They continued on to accomplish their mission of purchasing things for the Archives Building in London.[4]

While there, Rúḥíyyih Khánum and Shoghi Effendi both contracted the Asiatic flu that was sweeping through Europe.[5] They had seemed to be recovering, tended daily by their doctor, who would always stay at least a half hour to visit with the Guardian. On Saturday, 2 November, Shoghi Effendi stood for about three hours in front of a large table he had had brought into the room, striving to complete his map of the midpoint accomplishments of the Ten Year Plan. 'The table was strewn with pencils and files of papers which constituted the Guardian's lists of languages, tribes, countries, Temples, Ḥaẓíratu'l-Quds, work completed, work being carried out, and a tremendous amount of data. . . The beloved Guardian looked tired after working on his map that day. He went back to bed and continued reading the many reports he had received. He had only a mouthful to eat at lunch-time, and he refused to eat any dinner at all.' He talked with Rúḥíyyih Khánum about many of the things he planned to do upon return to Haifa.[6] On Sunday, he worked on correspondence for several hours. They talked longer than usual into the evening. Early on the morning of Monday, 4 November, he suffered a coronary thrombosis. Death must have come to him so gently and so suddenly that he died without even knowing he was ascending to another realm. When I went to his room in the morning to ask him how he was I did not recognize that he was dead . . . He lay as if he had wakened up and was thinking about something in a relaxed and comfortable position.[7]

On that morning of 4 November 1957, the previously unimaginable had become painfully real. Rúḥíyyih Khánum shared her own thoughts as she registered her shock and grief, while also preparing to inform the Bahá'í world:

It seemed to me, in the depths of my agony that black and terrible day, that I could not do to any Bahá'í what had been done to me. How could I cable the believers their Guardian had ascended? What of the old and the ill and the weak to whom this news would come as an insupportable blow, having the same effect on them which the news of the beloved Master's death had produced on Shoghi Effendi and on my own mother?[8]

But on 5 November, Rúḥíyyih Khánum knew she had to inform the Bahá'í world of what had transpired. As she later wrote, unable 'to deal the naked blow to the hearts of other Bahá'ís which she herself had received and had been forced to inflict on three of the Hands', she sent this first cable to Haifa, hoping to soften for the Bahá'ís

everywhere in the world the unacceptable news. Mr Ioas
carried out her wishes and dispatched this first message
to the Bahá'ís of the world early on 5 November from
Haifa:

WITH DEEP SADNESS ADVISE BELOVED GUARDIAN
DESPERATELY ILL ASIATIC FLU PLEASE IMMEDIATELY
INFORM ALL FRIENDS SUPPLICATE PRAYERS DIVINE
PROTECTION FAITH. LEROY IOAS.

Shortly afterwards, all Bahá'í institutions received the
second cablegram which also came from London via
Haifa:

SHOGHI EFFENDI BELOVED OF ALL HEARTS SACRED
TRUST GIVEN BELIEVERS BY MASTER PASSED AWAY
SUDDEN HEART ATTACK IN SLEEP FOLLOWING ASIATIC
FLU STOP URGE BELIEVERS REMAIN STEADFAST CLING
INSTITUTION HANDS LOVINGLY REARED RECENTLY
REINFORCED EMPHASIZED BY BELOVED GUARDIAN.
ONLY ONENESS HEART ONENESS PURPOSE CAN BEFIT-
TINGLY TESTIFY LOYALTY ALL NATIONAL ASSEMBLIES
BELIEVERS DEPARTED GUARDIAN WHO SACRIFICED
SELF UTTERLY FOR SERVICE FAITH. RUHIYYIH

During the morning of Saturday, 9 November, the day of
the funeral, Bahá'ís continued to gather from near and
far in a daze of disbelief that was yet pierced by stark
awareness of their immediate and sacred duty. A few
hours later, a cortège of sixty-five cars wound its way

from the Bahá'í National Centre at Rutland Gate out to North London Cemetery for the service and burial of the beloved Guardian, Shoghi Effendi. Of this time Rúḥíyyih Khánum wrote:

> We knew thee not beloved one
> Until thy soul took up its flight,
> Thy mortal journey done.
> We knew thee not beloved one
> Till we strew thy rooted grave
> With sacred flowers, and said, "Tis done".
>
> Gone from our gaze, our touch –
> We mourn deep, deep inside.
> What men lose they value much.
>   12 December, 1957[9]

For over two hours following the service, the Bahá'ís slowly passed by the casket, set upon a small rug from the innermost Shrine of Bahá'u'lláh, paying their last respects. Following this, Rúḥíyyih Khánum covered the green velvet that was over the casket with a blue and gold brocade from the same Shrine. Before the tomb was closed, she spread still fragrant jasmine Leroy Ioas had brought from 'Akká over the length of the whole brocade.[10]

The grief and renewed dedication born of these moments spread forth from London to touch the entire Bahá'í world. The National Spiritual Assembly of the northern countries of South America had received the

initial two telegrams one by one, as intended. The messages were similarly disseminated through the five
countries under the National Spiritual Assembly's jurisdiction. (Like dry autumn leaves falling from an ancient
oak, copies of these telegrams carpeted the Bahá'í world,
reaching the smallest communities. Even now, they may
be found in local archives – tucked away in folders of significant remembrance.) The Assembly cabled its support
to Rúḥíyyih Khánum, who rose above her own grief to
respond with the following, while also writing messages
to other institutions and individuals:

BAHAI LIMA
DEEPLY APPRECIATED NATIONAL ASSEMBLY'S MESSAGE
STOP HISTORY HOLY FAITH DEMONSTRATES GREATEST
CALAMITIES PRECEDED GREATEST VICTORIES STOP
EARTHQUAKE BELOVED GUARDIAN'S PASSING SHAKEN
ALL HEARTS BELIEVERS LIKE CHILDREN DEPRIVED
LOVING WISE FATHER MUST NOW ATTAIN MANHOOD
AND WITH MATURITY PROFOUND CONSECRATION
PURSUE ATTAINMENT GOALS HE SET CLINGING HEM
BAHAULLAHS MERCY KNOWING HIS LOVING PROTEC-
TION WILL NEVER FORSAKE US IF WE ARE STEADFAST
UNITED STOP TWENTYSIX HANDS VISITING MOST
HOLY TOMB MEMORIAL MEETING WILL JOIN THEIR
SUPPLICATIONS WITH THOSE BELIEVERS WORLD OVER
FULFILMENT PLANS HOPES PRECIOUS GUARDIAN
WHOSE LIFE WAS SACRIFICED PATH SERVICE.
RUHIYYIH
NOVEMBER 17, 1957[11]

Auxiliary Board members had been invited to attend the Guardian's funeral. Gayle's sister, Victoria, had contacted her upon learning of the Guardian's passing, offering to pay her way to London. With gratitude for such generosity, Gayle yet declined. Something kept her at her post, though in a note penned years later, she wrote of this decision, 'Another opportunity missed!'[12]

Marta Rosales Toromoreno, when in her 70s, remembered how Gayle helped the small community of Ecuador transcend its grief, though at the time she was a child of only six:

> When in 1957 our beloved Guardian died, Gayle became one of the strongest soldiers of the Cause of the Blessed Beauty. I remember that the people gathered to pray and cry bitterly over the passing of the Guardian. Gayle was a catalyst for the small community of Quito to overcome its grief and prove that the Bahá'í world was alive. After the ascension of our beloved Guardian the gatherings in the Historic District stopped. The community went through various tests and difficulties with various Covenant-breakers. All of this was in the 50s and the beginning of the 60s of the last century.[13]

Though she missed attending the funeral, Gayle would lose no chance to serve in South America in the challenging years ahead. Throughout her time there, as Hands of the Cause visited Ecuador, she assisted in making arrangements, hosting them, and most importantly, implementing their advice and guidance. As was the case for all Board members, her travel schedule was heavy, and many were the meetings, followed by reports to be typed and put in the post, all now on top of a full-time job. When one contemplates what the Hands had just endured with the Guardian's passing and their daunting task of strengthening communities and institutions throughout the world, one may catch a glimpse, perhaps, both of the sacrifices they made and also of what it meant to them to have steadfast Board members throughout the world to help carry out their work.

16

The Path Forward

As early as 5 November, a telegram had informed the Bahá'í world that the Hands of the Cause would meet in Haifa following the Guardian's funeral to consider the next steps in the development of the Faith. On 18 November, the Hands gathered for a memorial meeting, followed by what became known as their first Conclave.[1] As they climbed the narrow stairs to their meeting place in the upper chambers of the Mansion of Bahjí, how heavy their steps must have been with the weight of the unknowns they faced and the much-too-vivid memory of recent loss! Rúḥíyyih Khánum has written how every 'tree and pebble and flower' reminded them of the Guardian's passing,[2] of his absence from their midst.

All 27 living Hands of the Cause were present except for Corinne True, who remained in Wilmette, too frail to travel. From there, however, she followed the proceedings and participated in every decision, signing each by affidavit.[3]

According to Rúḥíyyih Khánum, it was the pen of Horace Holley, who came to Haifa despite his recent hospitalization and chronic pain, that captured the essence of the consultation of those fate-laden days from 18 to 25 November 1957: 'To me, it was here that Horace crowned his lifetime of service to the Cause of Bahá'u'lláh by

producing the finest fruit of his knowledge and understanding of its teachings – the Proclamation issued by
the Hands, the first draft of which and major portion,
we owe to his pen alone.'[4] That Proclamation, one of the
most moving documents to read even today, clarified the
way forward for the worldwide Bahá'í community com-
mensurate with the Sacred Text.

> The first effect of the realization that no successor to
> Shoghi Effendi could have been appointed by him was
> to plunge the Hands of the Cause into the very abyss
> of despair. What must happen to the world commu-
> nity of his devoted followers if the Leader, the Inspirer,
> the Planner of all Bahá'í activities in all countries and
> islands of the seas could no longer fulfil his unique
> mission?
>
> From this dark abyss, however, contemplation of
> the Guardian's own life of complete sacrifice and his
> peerless services gradually redeemed our anguished
> hearts. Shoghi Effendi himself, we knew, would have
> been the first to remind the Hands, and the wide-
> spread body of the believers, that the Dispensation of
> Bahá'u'lláh has quickened those powers and resources
> of faith within mankind which will achieve the unity
> of the peoples and the triumph of His World Order.
> In this new light of understanding the company of
> the Hands could perceive with heightened gratitude
> the existence of those innumerable blessings which
> Shoghi Effendi had created and left as his true legacy
> to all Bahá'ís.

Has not the World Centre, with its sacred Shrines and institutions, been firmly established? Has not the Message been established in 254 countries and dependencies? Have not the National and Regional Spiritual Assemblies, forerunners of the Universal House of Justice, been implanted in twenty-six great areas of all continents? Has not the Guardian left us not only his incomparable translations for English-reading Baháʼís, of the Baháʼí Sacred Literature but also his own master works of interpretation which disclose to us the unshatterable edifice of an evolving Baháʼí Order and world community? Has not the Guardian, building upon the enduring foundation of the Master's Tablets of the Divine Plan, created the World Crusade to guide our work until 1963?

Has not the Guardian, moreover, in his mysterious insight into the present and future needs of the Baháʼí community, called into being the International Baháʼí Council and the company of twenty-seven Hands with their Auxiliary Boards, whom, in his final communication to the Baháʼís, he designated 'Chief Stewards of the embryonic World Commonwealth of Baháʼu'lláh'?[5]

The Hands of the Cause called the Baháʼís all over the world to arise to the need of the hour:

Beloved friends! Is not the most precious legacy bequeathed to us all by Shoghi Effendi the privilege of constancy in the Faith of Baháʼu'lláh and devotion in teaching His Message? This is the heartfelt plea we direct to every Bahá'í: The hour has come, as it came with the passing of 'Abdu'l-Bahá, when true Bahá'ís will be distinguished by their firmness in the Covenant and their spiritual radiance while pressing forward the mighty work committed to every area of the world community – to every individual Bahá'í.[6]

Gayle and a now continent-wide group of Bahá'ís, scattered among fragile communities throughout Latin America, received that first Proclamation from the Hands of the Cause. She and her co-workers in Ecuador had already met or corresponded with several whose signatures were affixed to the document. They would become familiar with more in the coming years. Some Hands had come to South America as personal representatives of Shoghi Effendi at landmark formations of institutions. Both the Hands in the Holy Land and those for the Americas were in close, sustained correspondence with all communities through the Auxiliary Board members. Dr 'Alí-Muḥammad Várqá had been the first Hand to visit Ecuador in 1953, spending time in both Quito and Guayaquil. Paul Haney had been present at the election of the first National Spiritual Assembly of South America. Dorothy Baker had attended the second Convention the following year. In 1957, Horace Holley had attended the Convention in Lima, Peru, at which the election for the first National Assembly for the northern countries of South America was held. Among many services to Latin America, Amelia Collins provided funds towards the purchase of Ecuador's Ḥaẓíratu'l-Quds

(Centre) in Quito. In 1961, Hasan Balyuzi would represent the Hands for the first election of the National Assembly of Ecuador. In the 1960s, the Guardian's wish that a Hand might come to live in South America was fulfilled. Jalál Khazeh and his wife came to live in Brazil and served throughout the continent. Despite fragile health, Mr Khazeh made several trips to the high altitudes of Ecuador. His guidance to Gayle in how to work with many situations would become crucial to the community's protection. Raḥmatu'lláh Muhajir brought his teaching expertise to the country, serving intensively and often in the environs of Otavalo with Raúl Pavón, Rufino Gualavisi, and others. Dr Muhajir would later pass away while attending a conference in Quito. On a beautiful hillside overlooking that city, his luminous white gravestone can be found near that of his dear teaching companion, Rufino. It draws and inspires people even now.

Gayle also had ongoing correspondence with Hermann Grossmann and Abu'l-Qásim Faizi, who also made several visits – all responding to critical needs for fostering unity of understanding among the friends. Rúḥíyyih Khánum would come later, in 1968, and engrave the hearts with images of her presence and words, memories that would be mentioned for years to come. Even later, Enoch Olinga would inspire Ecuador with his presence.

After the Guardian's passing, it was realized that he had left the fledgling institutions of Latin America with guidance for next steps. On 3 July 1957 he had written to the National Spiritual Assembly of the northern countries of South America:

The Six-Year Plan, on which the attention of the members of these communities must be focused should be
regarded by them as the chief and unfailing instrument for the execution of their high purpose.[7]

When the regional Assemblies were formed, the as yet
unrealized objectives of the Ten Year Crusade remained
as goals, together with certain additions, now formulated
as a regional Six Year Plan (1957–1963). The Assembly
of the northern countries of South America joined other
regional and national communities in sending a pledge
of loyalty to the Hands of the Cause and therefore to the
Covenant, affirming unity of commitment in thought
and action. The work continued with a renewed sense of
urgency and significance.

Two years later, in 1959, from their third Conclave in
the Holy Land, the Hands of the Cause sent a message to
the Bahá'í world indicating progress made and outlining
the steps required to bring the World Crusade to a successful conclusion. They set the date for the election of the
Universal House of Justice in 1963, the date of the completion of the Guardian's Plan and the centenary of the
Declaration of Bahá'u'lláh. Referring to the Guardian's
Plan, the Conclave message stated, 'Alarmingly little time
is now left to us in which to accomplish his design.' Later
in the message, they discuss goals to be achieved internationally:

We call for the election in Riḍván 1961 of the twenty-
one National Spiritual Assemblies of Latin America

which will constitute some of the pillars of the Universal House of Justice in that region. This historic decision is based on the fact that we have every reason to hope and believe that the devoted band of the followers of Bahá'u'lláh in those countries will succeed during the Riḍván period of 1960 in forming those Spiritual Assemblies required of them by our beloved Guardian in the specific provision he laid down for them in the Ten Year Crusade . . .

We are also happy to announce . . . the election of the International Bahá'í Council during Riḍván, 1961. The embryonic institution . . . will thus enter its final stage preceding the election of the Universal House of Justice. The members of all the National and Regional Spiritual Assemblies of the Bahá'í world, duly constituted in Riḍván, 1960, will take part in a postal ballot to elect nine members to the International Council.[8] This International Bahá'í Council is to work under the direction and supervision of the Hands of the Cause residing in the Holy Land, serve a two year term of office, and cease to exist upon the occasion of the election of the Universal House of Justice. All the Bahá'ís of the world, men and women alike, are eligible for election . . . [A passage delineating its duties follows.]

At this turning-point in the Crusade when all our forces must be unitedly concentrated on winning its goals, the friends should not be deflected from the vital tasks confronting them by discussion of such subjects as can only be considered when the Universal House of Justice is established. Therefore we feel it necessary to recall the words in the Proclamation we sent out after the passing of the beloved Guardian: 'When that divinely-ordained Body comes into existence, all the conditions of the Faith can be examined anew and the measures necessary for its future operation determined in consultation with the Hands of the Cause.' This includes the subject of the Guardianship.

Aside from the pressing demands of the worldwide work of the Faith which must be met and administered from the Holy Land . . . plans are being formulated for the Hands to travel to various countries and lend the National Spiritual Assemblies their personal assistance during the months immediately ahead – and indeed until the end of the Crusade. These plans include visits to the Cradle of the Faith, where the vast majority of the followers of Bahá'u'lláh reside, to the Bahá'í communities in the United States and Canada, who constitute the chief prosecutors of the Divine Plan, to the Latin American countries where by 1961 so many National Assemblies must be formed, and to Europe, where another eleven of the future pillars of the Universal House of Justice must be erected by 1962.[9]

The visits of the Hands of the Cause to Latin America offer an example of the astounding love, vigilance, and consecration with which they carried out their responsibilities. In each centre, they met with individual believers and local assemblies, ascertaining the needs, answering questions, clarifying issues, and encouraging all to establish unity of thought and understanding. When it came time for the elections in 1961, Hands of the Cause were present at each Convention.

Gayle's work was focused in Ecuador, Peru, Bolivia, and Colombia, with the later addition of Venezuela. While her area involved much international travel, her place of residence offers an example of the challenges to be faced. In Ecuador at the beginning of 1960 there were only two local Assemblies and 58 believers in the whole country.[10] The goal was to have no less than four Assemblies as a foundation for the new National Spiritual Assembly. Quito and Guayaquil had Assemblies, but they were weak. The National Spiritual Assembly of the United States and its Inter-America Teaching Committee assured that pioneers were sent to assist in the two new areas, Cuenca and Otavalo. Auxiliary Board members Gayle Woolson and Rangveld Taetz made many visits to several communities and Hand of the Cause Hermann Grossmann (with his fluent Spanish and childhood spent in Argentina) gave special assistance.[11] Weekend schools were held to deepen believers and attract interested people.

In Ecuador as in other countries, much attention was necessarily focused on the adults who would soon shoulder responsibility for the development of communities and institutions. Even as intense discussions, study classes, informal conversations, and public presentations took place, something else was also happening whose effects would reach across generations. It was happening in small moments, sometimes outside in neighborhoods, sometimes in homes. A few Ecuadorian women have described what this was through remembrances reaching back 60 years. Through songs and games and stories, spiritual seeds were planted that grew and endured through the entire cycle of their lives. Sra Marta Rosales Toromoreno writes:

> Usually Gayle brought together the children of the neighborhood to play and sing. Many years later I understood that various of these songs and games had an important spiritual content, which brought me closer to the Faith, much more as a young adult.[12]

Dr Patricia Muñoz Naranjo de Dumet, then a child of about four, remembers the following both about the community and her own experience as a child:

> Yes, I had the privilege of meeting Gayle Woolson. My mother, Teresa Naranjo, accepted the Bahá'í Faith in 1960 in Quito, Ecuador. At that time, we had two pioneers in Quito: Mrs Gayle Woolson and Ms Dorothy Campbell, who was the spiritual mother of my mother. They both arrived in Ecuador during the late 50s, but I believe Gayle got to Quito a few years before Dorothy. The Bahá'í community in Quito was very small, and I heard that Gayle was the only woman among a group of maybe 5 or 6 men. They used to say that initially these men were attracted by the beauty of Gayle, who at that time was still a young and beautiful woman. Later, the wife of one of these

men also became a Bahá'í, and I believe there is a photograph of this group that we keep in the Archives
of the Local Assembly, where you can see only two
women. Other photographs show Gayle and a group
of men. Some of those first Bahá'ís were Luis Arguello,
Alberto Carbo, Mr Peñaherrera, Mr Sotomayor, Raúl
Pavón (who years later became a Counsellor) and a
few more whose names I can't remember. During the
early 60s, a few more Ecuadorian women declared as
Bahá'ís. Some of those names I still remember: Célida
Leiva, Mrs Gallegos, Teresa Jara, Isabel Pavón de
Calderón (also a future Counsellor), Clemencia Pavón
(Raúl and Isabel Pavón's mother), Teresa Naranjo (my
mother), and a few more . . .

Gayle was an officer at 'Punto Cuarto', a USA
Government Agency, which later changed its name to
USAID. I remember Gayle as a very fine lady who was
always motivating the community to participate in the
Bahá'í activities, which were mainly the 19-day Feasts
and firesides that were frequently hosted at her home.
She had an apartment on the second floor of a house
located in the Pinzón St. I was around 4 years old
when my mother first learned about the Bahá'í Faith.
We used to live in La Florista neighborhood, at my
grandma's house, not too far away from Gayle's apartment. My mother used to take me to the firesides, and
I can say that most of my knowledge about the Faith
comes from that time. I listened to the prayers, the
readings and the enlightened discussions this small
group of Bahá'ís used to have. Sometimes I fell asleep.

For a few years, I was the only child in the community, so there were no children's classes that I could attend, but Gayle used to prepare some materials (I believe she translated them from English) that I could read, memorize and also paint or draw. A few years later, during the mid 60s, others declared as Bahá'ís, including the Dávila family. Their daughter was my age, and now I had a partner. Then Gayle started a children's class. For awhile, we were the only participants. I remember she was a great and loving teacher.

Gayle Woolson and Dorothy Campbell[13] were very close. The current development of the Ecuadorian community is the result of the commitment and sacrifice of these two women. They had several tests but could guide those few early believers to establish a community that still survives. During 1961–1963, we had a group of Covenant-breakers, as in other countries. This was a very hard test and some of those few believers left the community.

Gayle left the country around 1967. Although she didn't have the opportunity to see the results of her sacrificial work, I have witnessed it. If those two courageous women had not come during the Ten Year Crusade, we wouldn't have the community we have now.

My mother used to keep in touch with Gayle until my mother passed away. I visited her once during her last years in Wilmette. My daughter also visited her. It was amazing that she could still remember the years she lived in Ecuador, as well as the names of some of the friends . . .[14]

In the stories of childhood they relate, both Sra Marta Rosales Toromoreno and Dr Patricia Muñoz Naranjo de Dumet speak of the Covenant-breaking in Ecuador. This problem became acute in 1961 and involved people who espoused the claim of Mason Remey to be the rightful successor of the Guardian, Shoghi Effendi. Mr Remey had been among the truly veteran Bahá'ís from the first group of Western believers in Paris; he had served with distinction for many years, was himself a Hand of the Cause and had signed the Proclamation of the Hands just a few years earlier. This shows how great was his fall and how great the challenge to Bahá'ís of the time who had known him for years as one of the most eminent teachers.

The Hands prayerfully struggled with this defection which became flagrant right in their midst during the Conclaves at Bahji. Ultimately, it became clear that Mr Remey was intent upon his ambition. It fell to the body of the Hands of the Cause to declare him a Covenant-breaker in 1960.

Gayle, Dorothy, and their co-workers were directly affected by these developments. As previously described, following the Convention in Wilmette in 1944,[15] Mason Remey had offered to travel to every centre in South America, followed by Emeric and Rosemary Sala. He therefore had come to know Bahá'ís throughout the continent personally, had collected names and addresses, had established correspondence and had distributed literature. Several in both the Quito and Guayaquil communities, with whom Gayle Woolson and Dorothy

Campbell served, received and were influenced by his material. Over several years, Dorothy, as Secretary of the National Spiritual Assembly, and Gayle as an NSA member and Board member, would collaborate in carrying out the instructions of the Hands to ascertain conditions, seek to illumine understanding, and report findings back to the Hands of the Cause. Helen Hornby writes:

> As it happened, it was Professor Moyses Mosquera, the first believer of the Galapagos Islands, who alerted the Regional Teaching Committee to difficulties in Quito. Very lonely in his isolated location, he would visit the believers when he traveled to the mainland on vacation. He attended a gathering in Quito one night and wrote the following:

>> The Community of Quito, with . . . as its head, has decided and has recognized Mason Remey as the Guardian, and . . . has written to Mason Remey and offered to spread his claim and form a community and to be a pioneer, with subsistence, and offered to travel to the United States and to all of South America.

> They showed him circulars from Mr Remey which they stated they had kept hidden from Gayle Woolson. According to this account, it seemed that the community had lined up with a majority in support of Mr Remey.[16]

Quito, at this time, was Gayle's home base; her apartment and employment were here. The people involved were Bahá'ís she knew and with whom she served, people who had often been in her home. The correspondence back and forth and over time between her as an Auxiliary Board member and the Hands of the Cause reflects careful, immediate, and specific guidance from the Hands; wise and precise implementation of every detail of that guidance on her part; and precise reporting of the process, including both concerns and possibilities for healing.

In her papers, Gayle kept a long letter from Mr Faizi that gives an example of the guidance received, though this was written later, in 1962. It gives her detailed instructions on how to respond to claims in Mr Remey's literature regarding the Guardianship and the evolution of the International Council. First, he shows a diagram of the four stages of its development as initially envisioned by the Guardian. He tells her to draw that and review the stages. He then gives a list of questions to bring up and explain, showing how and why the International Court envisioned as one step did not come into being. With each question, she is to explain why Mr Remey's reasoning about each question is not in accord with the Guardian. Mr Faizi then has questions for her to clarify about the relationship of the Council as an embryonic form of the Universal House of Justice and the Guardianship, from which its development is entirely distinct. Part of the confusion was that Mr Remey claimed that his status on the Council justified his claim to Guardianship after

Shoghi Effendi's passing. This approach of the Hands guiding their Board members and through them the believers always provided an opportunity for the person(s) involved to fully explore and understand the truth, in the hope and prayer that clarity would be gained and unity restored. At the same time, Gayle, as a Board member, was to observe carefully, remain vigilant and offer a written report regarding possibilities for healing and any fixed motives that directed a person's actions and views, lest he/she be intent on striking at the root of the Cause. Every chance would be given to independently investigate the truth and restore unified understanding.[17]

Later, when Gayle was serving as Board member for Mr Khazeh for several years, there is a volume of similarly specific correspondence regarding every visit, project, and community their work together involved.

In 1961, two months before the election of the 21 new National Spiritual Assemblies, the Hands of the Faith in the Western Hemisphere wrote a 15-page, single-spaced letter to 'The heroic lovers of Bahá'u'lláh who are holding fast the vital fortresses in every local Assembly in Latin America.'

> In just over two short months, the eyes of the followers of Bahá'u'lláh in nearly 6,000 centers around the world will be turned toward 21 cities in Latin America, where, during a Riḍván period unique in our Administrative history, 21 new National Spiritual Assemblies, pillars of the Universal House of Justice, will come into being . . . [18]

This letter was based upon the questions which the members of National and Local Assemblies had asked the different Hands of the Faith during their several visits to the 21 countries. Thus, the letter responded to the specific needs and questions expressed in each community. The Bahá'ís were asked to read the letter aloud in their Assembly meetings, to consult on it, and to ensure that all the friends became familiar with its contents. The Hands pointed out that these new Assemblies had the opportunity to take advantage of all that had been learned and to establish their institutions on a stronger footing, more consciously aligned with the teachings, than ever before.

As these preparations went forward, the Hands had also arranged for all present National or Regional Assembly members to elect the International Council. This represented a further step in its evolution, as outlined by the beloved Guardian, from an appointed body to an elected one. Previously, five Hands of the Cause had been appointed to serve on it. Now that it would no longer be appointed, the Hands asked that they not be considered for election, due to the distinction between appointed and elected institutions. On 20 March 1961, the Hands of the Cause in the Holy Land sent a letter indicating that the ballots from Ecuador had been received.

Meanwhile, there continued to be difficulty in the Quito community. Less than a month before the new National Spiritual Assemblies were to be elected, on 24 March 1961, the Hands of the Faith in Haifa sent the following telegram to Gayle, who was at that time in St Paul, Minnesota, recovering for two months from a major surgery. It was also sent to the Regional Assembly in Lima:

REPORTED LARGE PROPORTION QUITO COMMUNITY SUPPORTING REMEY PROMPT ACTION NECESSARY REMEDY SITUATION URGING WOOLSON RETURN IMME-DIATELY ADVISE CLOSE COOPERATION HANDS AMERICAN NSA DETERMINE MEASURES REQUIRED STOP IF NECESSARY AMERICAN OR OTHER PIONEERS CAN ASSURE FIRM ASSEMBLY STOP WILL DEFINITELY HOLD CONVENTION KEEP US INFORMED PRAYING SHRINES VICTORY ADVISING AMERICAN HANDS NSA AS ABOVE[19]

A return cable from Gayle stated 'RETURNING NEXT THURSDAY'. She arrived on Thursday morning and met with the friends in the afternoon. A letter dated 5 April 1961 offers the Hands a detailed report of her findings. This is followed by a cable from Gayle and two other believers asking that action not be taken until the Hand of the Cause Mr Grossmann could come and assess the situation. His report is dated 16 April 1961, from Quito, Ecuador.[20]

It was under such conditions that the days passed leading up to the Conventions that would elect the first National Spiritual Assembly of Ecuador and of 20 other countries in the western hemisphere. Their formation a primary goal of the Ten Year Plan, these institutions became pillars for the establishment of the Universal House of Justice, increasing the breadth of representation to include all of Latin America.[21]

The First National Convention of Ecuador took place from 24 to 26 April 1961, simultaneously with that of the 20 other new National Spiritual Assemblies in Latin America. Ecuador was privileged to have Hasan Balyuzi as the representative of the Hands of the Faith. He was well aware of the 'smouldering enmity and the raging fury' affecting those influenced by Mr Remey's literature. For this reason, he asked all nine delegates (from Cuenca, Guyaquil, Otavalo, and Quito) to 'sign a document declaring their loyalty to the Cause and to the Hands of the Faith'.[22]

The Convention was opened with prayers for John Pope Stearns, the first pioneer to Ecuador, and for three Hands of the Cause who had recently passed away: Horace Holley, Clara Dunn, and Corinne True. Sr Juan Luis Aguirre served as Chairman and Gayle Woolson as Secretary. The following were elected to the first National Spiritual Assembly of Ecuador: Fereydoun Monadjem (Chairman), Guillermo Sotomayor, Dorothy Campbell (Secretary), David Beckett, Patricia Conger, Juan Luis Aguirre, Raúl Pavón (Recording Secretary), Khalilu'lláh Bihjati (Treasurer), and Gayle Woolson. Significantly, the Convention sent the following cable to the Hands of the Faith in the Holy Land on 24 April 1961:

DELEGATES VISITORS FIRST HISTORIC CONVENTION
ECUADOR EXPRESS DEEPEST GRATITUDE MOMENTOUS
MESSAGES REJOICED GREAT TRIUMPHS DETERMINED
INCREASE EFFORTS ACHIEVE ASSIGNED TASKS DEEPLY
APPRECIATE GENEROUS CONTRIBUTIONS HANDSFAITH

AND AMELIA COLLINS. DELEGATES UNANIMOUSLY
PLEDGE UNRESERVED LOYALTY HANDSFAITH. CON-
VENTION

The following reply was received:

OVERJOYED LOYALTY DETERMINATION ECUADOR
BELIEVERS PRAYING SHRINES UNPRECEDENTED VIC-
TORIES HANDSFAITH

All the National Spiritual Assemblies were asked to send
greetings to one another, increasing conscious celebration of the unified web of international relationships
being woven through these Conventions. (Even after she
returned to the United States in later years, Gayle continued this practice of sending annual Riḍván greetings
to the National Conventions of countries where she had
served.)

The Ecuador Convention was also blessed by people
newly arrived to ensure the victory of the Plan. Pacora
Blue Mountain, whom Shoghi Effendi considered the
first of Inca descent to become a Bahá'í, had returned to
South America from several years in the United States,
during which time he, a brilliant pianist, had learned of
the Teachings through Vafa and Saffa Kinney in New York
City. He would now play a significant role in teaching in
indigenous areas. (Shoghi Effendi placed his photograph
in the Mansion of Bahjí, in honor of the Inca people.) Mr
and Mrs Fred Schechter[23] and Mr and Mrs William Sears
Jr. had been asked to come to assist in weak Assembly

areas. Mrs Florence Mayberry[24] and Hand of the Cause
Dr Grossmann, as well as several other Hands, would
make later visits. They would offer strength, wisdom, and
understanding as the Ecuadorian institutions and community struggled for some time until they attained full
victory and unity of understanding.

Just a couple of months later, on 25 June 1961, the
Hands of the Cause in the Holy Land sent the following
cable to 'Bahá'í Wilmette' and through this address to all
Hands and National Assemblies regarding preparations
for the establishment of the Universal House of Justice
in 1963:

REJOICE ANNOUNCE FIRST MOMENTOUS MEETING
HANDS HOLY LAND ALL MEMBERS NEWLY ELECTED
INTERNATIONAL COUNCIL HELD PRECINCTS HOLY
SHRINE BAHA'U'LLAH CONSULTED MEASURES NECES-
SARY DISCHARGE HISTORIC DUTIES DESTINED FULFIL
HIGH HOPES BELOVED GUARDIAN PAVE WAY ELECTION
SUPREME HOUSE JUSTICE OCCASION MOST GREAT
JUBILEE STOP SHARE MESSAGE HANDS NATIONAL
ASSEMBLIES. HANDSFAITH[25]

Two years later, in 1963, Rúḥíyyih Khánum would offer
this tribute to the Hands of the Cause regarding their
service during the five and a half years leading up to this
culminating event, the election of the Universal House
of Justice:

No testimony to the truth and strength of the Cause

could have been greater than the triumphal conclusion of the Guardian's World Crusade which the believers achieved. It had been a hard, an overwhelming task to begin with. That the Bahá'ís achieved it, that for over five years they worked and sacrificed to a greater degree than ever before in their history without his leadership, without those appeals, those reports, those marvellous word-pictures he painted for them in his messages, without the knowledge that he was there at the helm, their so dearly-loved captain steering them to victory and safety, is little short of a miracle and testifies not only to how well he builded, but to those words of the Master: 'there is a mysterious power in the Cause, far above the ken of men and angels.'[26]

17

The Election of the Universal House of Justice

In April of 1963, one hundred years after Baháʼuʼlláh had declared His mission to His followers in the Garden of Riḍván, the time had finally arrived for the election of the Universal House of Justice. Gayle Woolson, Dorothy Campbell, and three others from Ecuador were among the 288 delegates (of 504 electors), all members of Regional and National Spiritual Assemblies from around the world, who travelled to Haifa for this momentous event. They were guests of the World Centre while in the Holy Land, though responsible for their own travel expenses. Some National Spiritual Assemblies had ensured that all members could attend, regardless of financial concerns. Others ensured at least one representative. Ecuador had five. Three National Assemblies could not send representatives due to travel restrictions.

The election took place on Sunday morning, 21 April 1963, at the House of ʻAbduʼl-Bahá, 7 Haparsim Street, Haifa. Rúḥíyyih Khánum has described how months before, while having dinner with Ian Semple, she had said that the election should take place in the house of

'Abdu'l-Bahá. He agreed that it would be possible if they took off all of the doors to enlarge the hall. With the help of her father's architectural tape measure, they figured out how to seat all who would be there.[1]

Hand of the Cause Zikrullah Khadem recalled that 'Abdu'l-Bahá had once said: 'This very hall will witness the election of the House of Justice.'[2] Now the doors had been removed and seats for all arranged.

Anita Ioas Chapman described the voting process beautifully:

This sacred event would 'cast its sacred and protective shadow down through the ages' in the words of the Hands of the Cause. To prepare the electors for their role, the Hands in the Holy Land, when sending out election ballots in November of the previous year, had emphasized the spiritual atmosphere in which those who could not attend must vote. It should be done in the presence of their fellow members: 'Because of the sacred nature of this historic occasion, and in order that those voting by mail may also partake of the spiritual atmosphere which surrounds this unique and unprecedented election, we urge each National and Regional Assembly to make every effort to meet together in a body on this occasion; not as a part of a National Assembly session, but as a separate and distinct electoral session for the purpose of casting their ballots for the Universal House of Justice.'

To ensure the sacred atmosphere of the International Convention itself, the delegates were invited to arrive on April 18th and to use the three days before the election in spiritual preparation for their unique responsibility. The Shrines of the Báb and Bahá'u'lláh were closed to the public for five days so that the delegates could pray and meditate there at any hour and as often as they wished. The Hands had carefully scheduled periods of time for the delegates to spend in the Shrines and at the Holy Places. On each of the three evenings, designated groups of delegates – this was the greatest mass pilgrimage ever to have been made to the World Centre – would be taken to the International Archives to view the documents and sacred relics preserved there.

On the morning of April 21 the delegates gathered outside the house of 'Abdu'l-Bahá and silently entered the main hall. At 9:30 Rúḥíyyih Khánum briefly welcomed them and explained the procedure to be followed. There were prayers, after which the delegates voted in utter silence. The roll call began by country in alphabetical order, Alaska, Arabia, Argentina, Austria . . . to the last, Venezuela. The Universal House of Justice had been elected.[3]

That afternoon, the Riḍván celebration was held at Bahji, in the gardens surrounding the Shrine of Bahá'u'lláh.

The eighteen tellers worked through the night. The results of the election were announced at the end of the next morning's session, at Beth Harofe Auditorium, 2 Wingate Avenue, Haifa.[4] Rúḥíyyih Khánum introduced the new members, emphasizing the diversity of those elected: Charles Wolcott, Borrah Kavelin, Hugh Chance, Amoz Gibson, Hushmand Fatheazam, Ali Nakhjáváni, Lotfullah Hakim, David Hofman, and Ian Semple.[5]

Following this occasion, those gathered in Haifa joined about 6,000 people in London at the Royal Albert Hall for the Bahá'í World Congress, 28 April–2 May 1963. At this gathering, Gayle's sister, Vicki Abas, joined her. (They did not miss this opportunity!) Each person present has told precious stories of the event as seen through their own eyes, including such aspects as witnessing the most diverse gathering of humanity ever assembled, hearing talks by the Hands of the Cause, forming new friendships, and most powerful of all, offering a standing ovation as the new Universal House of Justice was presented.

Nearly 60 years later, one Bahá'í who was present recalled his emotions on that occasion:

Closing my eyes, even after all the years, I can easily feel standing inside the Albert Hall on one of the balconies left of the one that's directly across from the Hall's podium. All of us on this and other balconies as well as the rest of the Bahá'ís down in the hall are looking at the podium as we're clapping and silently crying. There the nine members of the first Universal House Justice, elected a few days before, stand in a row with that, now familiar, profound dignity and humility. The thankfulness of reaching to this historic point are the unstoppable clapping and shedding of silent tears of more than 6,000 Bahá'ís from around the world standing in the Albert Hall. When it finally subsides, the

Universal House member at the very right reads that Prayer of Bahá'u'lláh about praise and gratitude that begins: 'All praise, O my God, be to Thee . . .'[6]

Similar descriptions are scattered among pilgrim notes and biographies now allowing readers to draw near to this historic occasion. Near the close of five days of inspiring talks, music, and prayer, Rúḥíyyih Khánum put forth a call to further action:

> Friends, do not fail Shoghi Effendi. You have not fin-
> ished with him and he has not finished with you. It is
> the time to put your step on new trails, to make new
> vows, to go out and please Shoghi Effendi and make
> him happier than he ever was in this world . . . Let us
> all carry on the work of our beloved Lord, Bahá'u'lláh,
> every day of our lives, because we are His people and
> we are blessed far beyond our deserts.[7]

Shortly after the Congress ended, the Universal House of Justice sent out a message to the National Conventions all over the world:

> The Universal House of Justice wishes to reaffirm at
> this time the tribute which it felt moved to pay to the
> Hands of the Cause of God at the World Congress,
> those precious souls who have brought the Cause safely
> to victory in the name of Shoghi Effendi. We wish
> also to remember the devoted work of their Auxiliary
> Board members, as well as the services of the Knights

of Bahá'u'lláh, of the army of pioneers, the members of the National and Regional Spiritual Assemblies, the services and prayers and sacrifices of the believers everywhere, all of which in the sum total have attracted such bounties and favors from Bahá'u'lláh . . .

Beloved friends, we enter the second epoch of the Divine Plan blessed beyond compare, riding the crest of a great wave of victory produced for us by our beloved Guardian. The Cause of God is now firmly rooted in the world. Forward then, confident in the power and protection of the Lord of Hosts, Who will, through storm and trial, toil and jubilee, use His devoted followers to bring to a despairing humanity the life-giving waters of His Supreme Revelation.[8]

A letter from Mr Faizi

Even with Rúḥíyyíh Khánum's call to action, one might imagine that the Hands would take at least a little time to rest after the five and a half years of intense labour just completed. They might take time to absorb all that had changed in their personal, professional, and family lives. A few months after returning to Ecuador, Gayle received a letter from Mr Faizi that indicated this was not so. The letter is shared here as one instance of how the Hands arose instantaneously to serve the Universal House of Justice and the new Nine Year Plan. By example, they stimulated their co-workers throughout the world to do the same. They used tired moments to share not only instructions and guidance but vivid descriptions of meaningful events. Through his letters, Mr Faizi bound the hearts of East and West in a deep and personal sense of their oneness as members of a new-emerging world-wide community. With shorter notes, he would often add his own artwork in the form of beautiful flowers at one edge.[9] In this letter sent to Gayle, his description of seeing Persian youth he had once taught as children fostered awareness that Gayle would later express in her Children's Public Speaking Project. (She kept this letter in her brown envelope of treasured mementoes.) More than anything, one feels the love of the Faith expressed in action and sent through words.

Dearly beloved Friend,

I am so late in answering your very kind communications that I do not really know how to start this letter. I hope that you are still as kind as ever before and that you will overlook this horrible delay.

It is about a month that I am back in the Holy Land after my world tour which took me to the International Convention, to the London Congress and eventually to Iran where I sojourned for about 45 days.

The story of this one month and a half is simply wonderful. Though the friends were requested not to arrange extensive programmes for me, after two or three days experience showed that it was utterly beyond my power or that of any committee to control the many demands of the dearly beloved friends of Tehran. They were so eager to ask and so longing to know!

My daily programme would start in the early

morning and ended at midnight. The moment I opened my eyes, there were people who had gathered in the hall and who desired to confer with me on different subjects. This done, I usually went to the houses of the veteran teachers, valiant pioneers, the sick and the poor, who, due to illness or long distances, could not possibly attend any meeting. The gatherings were held in the houses of the friends and I had to go from one to another. In all such assemblages of the friends I encouraged them to ask questions. This proved very delightful and profitable both to me and to them. By such questions I would understand the nature of the community, their difficulties, problems and shortcomings, and they in turn would receive news of the world and the progress of our Faith in many different countries. The only thing which caused me a little trouble was the terrible cold of the winter and the heavy snow which had covered all roads. Having lived for fifteen years in Arabia, I was not accustomed to such terrific cold. I was never warm enough, especially my feet. But the waves of love and enthusiasm which encircled me everywhere compensated for this physical coldness which did not really matter very much.

The youth in Iran are especially interested in any problem concerning our Faith. They proved to be so eager to attend the meetings that if the committee had invited, for example, a hundred, there would be at least five hundred present. If there were not enough chairs, the incomers would just stand in rows, sometimes for hours. The Youth Committees everywhere in Iran have many subsidiary committees, such as Public Speaking, Teacher Training Classes, Publications, etc. Though confronted with many, many difficulties, they have had wonderful achievements in all lines of their activities.

Let me describe to you one of their classes: On a special day parents and friends were invited to observe the final examination of the Public Speaking Class. There were two groups, each group consisting of more than thirty boys and girls under the supervision and guidance of three teachers. The members of each class had taken many teaching tours from Teheran to many different parts of Persia, especially to villages. Each one had committed to memory more than 75 quotations from our Sacred Writings. Thus they get ready to use the proper sayings in their speeches or when they talk to some contacts. Each knew by heart at least five long Tablets in Persian or in Arabic. Though the means of transport are not adequately comfortable, available, or cheap, scarcely any of the students had been even late to any of the classes. When they made speeches or recited the Tablets or quoted the Writings, their pronunciation and delivery were clear and penetrating. At the end of the meeting we had the pleasure to look at the many different books that the students had copied and the different books to which they had referred during the whole year. When they asked me to tell them something, I was so thrilled that I could hardly talk. At the end of the day they promised to continue their studies to get ready for their future services. With tears in their eyes they expressed homage, respect and loyalty to this House of Justice and conveyed the message that they would be ready to participate in the Nine Year Plan arranged by that exalted Body.

Having in mind the many obstacles that our young and old people have in Iran, what they achieve approach[es] miracles. This proves that no obstacle is unsurmountable if we rely wholeheartedly upon the Grace of God and the strength we receive from Him.

From Teheran I went to Isphahan [sic.] where I spent five nights. One of these nights I went to a nearby village called Najaf-Abad, the friends of which are renowned for their bravery and steadfastness. As it was winter and the friends could not use their Bahá'í Hall, they had taken the trouble of pitching a huge tent in one of the houses. The floor was covered with many colourful carpets. More than a thousand Bahá'ís sat on the floor and as the ladies had covered themselves with coloured cloths the whole gathering seemed to me like a beautiful garden of many different flowers.

The friends who were sitting there were the ones who suffered the most during the year 1955 when the cruel waves of persecution covered all lands in Iran. For many months they were not allowed to purchase provisions from the market and could not even gather their own crops, most of which had already been devastated and plundered by the angry mobs. The enemies paid errand boys to go on bicycles round and round the lanes and unfrequented passages to see whoever dared to help the Bahá'ís. These brave souls managed to hold on with what they had previously stored in their houses, but eventually many of them were forced to leave their villages for other places in search of other ways of earning their living. As the drivers did not accept them in their buses or taxis, many took their way to their unknown destinations on foot. None of these tribulations could ever loosen their hold on the hem of Bahá'u'lláh's Grace and Faith. Standing there in the midst of these wonderful Bahá'ís whom I loved and adored I could not utter a word.

Besides that I knew them from before. Many of them as children had been sitting on my lap, when more than 25 years ago I lived about five years in their village and was immersed in the ocean of their love, care and consideration.

My struggle for words proved useless. Love and devotion and the memories of the past and the remembrance of their sufferings were too strong for feeble words to express anything. I continued looking at them, and from every row of friends I received strength and inspiration and then at last I started to talk to them about the beloved friends of Bolivia, the rapid progress of the Cause in India and Africa and I told them some stories which I had gathered throughout my one year trip round the world. The description of the International Convention and the World Congress brought tears to their eyes. I could see visibly in their faces that they were praising Bahá'u'lláh and said that if their feet are in fetters and they cannot take the torch of God freely round the countries, their brothers and sisters in other parts of the world with their sacrificial services take the light of the Cause even to the very dark and obscure corners of the world.

After 25 years I found my dear ones close to myself, and it proved very hard to me to depart again.

In Shiraz I spent five nights. There I had the honor to visit the House of the Báb and the very same room where Mulla Hossein [sic.] sat face to face with the Báb and heard His melodious voice when He declared His mission.

Something really miraculous took place for me in Shiraz. I sent a cable to the Hands in Haifa and begged them to appoint a certain date and hour when they would gather in the Shrine of the Báb and I in the Báb's room, for the purpose of a simultaneous prayer. Thus a spiritual magnetic chain would be stretched between the starting point and the final one – His house in Shiraz and His Resting Place on Mount Carmel.

I received the answer to this cable in Teheran, but let me tell you this. One day I was drawn as if by mysterious forces to the House and I walked in in tears and full of supplications. There . . . I remembered all my dear ones in the countries where I had passed through, and prayed and supplicated for every one of them. The illumined faces of the dear friends were just in front of me when I was in that very small room. It was a feeling which permanently stays with me and forever remains undescribable. What affected me the most was the very small size of the House, the rooms and the little pond in the court-yard. To compare this smallness with the grandeur of the message which covered the whole earth, makes us comprehend the mysterious ways by which the Cause of God makes progress in different countries of the world under so much hardships [sic.], difficulties and plights. How great! How very great is the plan of God! That very tiny room, by His decree and desire became the fountain-head of all the blessings, the springtide of the spiritual revival of mankind and the Primal Point from which powers are constantly released for the spiritual conquest of the globe!

When in Teheran I received the Hands' cable which I expected from Haifa, I came to know that on the very same day and hour that the friends gathered in the Shrine of the Báb, I went to His House in Shiraz.

Since my return from all these trips, especially in Iran, I felt so exhausted and tired that I could not possibly do any serious work. I hope that by prayers and spending more time in the Shrines I will regain my strength.

These days are the wonderful days of the early weeks of the year 121. I hope and pray that you will be ushered into this year with fresh powers and ample energy and be ready to do your part in this glorious Nine Year Plan of our beloved House of Justice. We all remember vividly the Guardian's words when he gave us his World Crusade. He said that the Ten Year Plan was a preliminary step or an introduction for the future world plans which would be initiated by the House of Justice. We see how this plan is made and how the members of the House of Justice spend days and nights in preparing the different stages, so much so that we are worried about their health. They work from early morning until about midnight. We are sure that the results will be great and full of powers, chances and potentialities which will enable every Bahá'í to perform heroic feats. Fresh forces and ample resources will be at the disposal of the beloved friends and I am certain that the Bahá'ís will once more mount their steeds and render their sacrificial services to the Cause with such terrific speed and enthusiasm that the eyes of the whole world will be amazed at the rapid consummation of the Plan. Any substantial help and assistance given by the friends to fulfill the goals of this divine plan will surely and abundantly attract many blessings from On High [sic.] for themselves, their friends, relatives and their homelands.

Dearly beloved friend, I assure you once more of my ardent and continued prayers in the Shrine. I write this hurried note to you from Bahjí and I hope that this letter will bring you the fragrance, the tranquility and assurance which prevail in the atmosphere surrounding the Resting Place of the Supreme Manifestation of God in this Age.

Yours humbly in the beloved's servitude,
A. Q. Faizi [signed in his hand]

It was in this spirit that the believers stepped forth with a new consciousness of themselves as a world community, now to serve the Universal House of Justice in its first global Nine Year Plan.

18

'Steps on New Trails' in Ecuador and El Salvador

As people returned home from London, the Universal House of Justice, assisted by preparations already made by the Hands of the Cause, prepared to launch the new global Nine Year Plan. Each Regional and National Spiritual Assembly would have specific goals. There were some institutional changes. Up until this time, some Hands of the Cause and Auxiliary Board members, if elected to a Regional or National Spiritual Assembly, had served on both the appointed and elected institution. This was true for Gayle. On 27 June 1963, the Hands of the Cause Jalal Khazeh and Zikrullah Khadem wrote a letter to the Board members of the Western Hemisphere, informing them of the following:

> Since, with the formation of the Universal House of Justice the responsibilities of the individual as well as all Bahá'í Institutions everywhere have increased immensely, the Hands thought it advisable to pave the way for those dearly loved friends who are serv-ing in both institutions of the Hands and the National Spiritual Assemblies to serve with all their energies and hearts in either one of these two Institutions, so

that the Cause of God may benefit best from their meritorious achievements, and in the meantime that other Bahá'ís may find opportunities to serve these two Institutions. Hence the decision was taken, some of the Hands who were formerly members in the National Spiritual Assemblies requested to be excused from the membership of the NSAs.

The Hands urge those dear members of the Auxiliary Board who have been elected in some of the NSAs to consider prayerfully this point and choose the membership to whichever one of these two Institutions that their hearts tell them and would enable them to serve the Cause the best.[1]

Similar letters were sent to Auxiliary Board members in other parts of the world by the Hands of the Cause responsible for those regions. On 10 July 1963, Gayle replied:

Thank you very kindly for the letters which you have sent me since our glorious World Convention and Congress. I wish to refer especially to your letter of June 27th in which you request the members of the Auxiliary Board who are also members of N.S.A.'s to choose just one institution of these two which they can best serve. As an Auxiliary Board member and also as a member of the N.S.A. of Ecuador, I would prefer to remain as a member of the Auxiliary Board and resign from the N.S.A. This I will do at a forth-coming meeting this week-end of the N.S.A.

I pray to Bahá'u'lláh to help me and guide me to

serve to the best of my ability as a Board member. Although my time is relatively limited for much travel due to my job, I will make as many trips as I possibly can on week-ends, holidays and vacations. I feel unworthy to be a Board member but I will sincerely try to do the best I can.

I just returned from the United States after spending two months there. I underwent major surgery on May 10th and spent the two months convalescing. I am feeling quite well now and was glad to return to Ecuador on July 6th. I had the pleasure of participating in several firesides in St. Paul and Minneapolis while I was in the States.[2]

In another significant change, Hand of the Cause Mr Khazeh and his wife came to live in Campinas, Sao Paulo State, Brazil on 27 September 1963, fulfilling a wish of the Guardian to have a Hand[3] in Latin America. The Board members now served directly under him. Mr Khazeh immediately made plans to visit all of the centres in all of the countries under his jurisdiction. The focus of the Universal House of Justice and therefore of the Hands of the Cause was now on strengthening and protecting communities, while also spreading the teachings to a wider audience, with particular emphasis on indigenous communities.

Gayle's work situation was also approaching a time of flux. USAID employees had tours of duty with fixed time limits in a given location, followed by transition to another country. Aware that she would soon have a required transfer, Gayle felt drawn to serving in the Middle East, which would offer a new context for service and immersion in Arabic, the language of her childhood. As always, seeking institutional guidance, she shared this idea with the Hands of the Cause for the Americas as 1964 came to a close.

On 10 January 1965, Mr Faizí sent her the following:

Your decisions about your future places of service are so vital and important to the interest of our beloved Faith that I can't possibly answer them by myself; therefore with your permission I take them up with the House and Hands. This will be done after my heartfelt supplications at the shrine of Bahá'u'lláh in Bahjí – the place we both adore because of the wonderful memories.

. . . It is two days after my return from Bahjí. I discussed it with the Hands and then in our joint meeting with the most beloved members of the House of Justice. Here is the summary: She is a rare individual with so many excellent qualities and especially with the two most essential languages needed in Latin America. These countries need the greatest help in these days and a person like you who has so much knowledge of all these countries and so much loved and respected by all should continue to serve in these areas. If Ecuador is not possible, please do your utmost to take a job in some of the countries of C. or S. America. You will be wasted in N. E. Countries. In Arabia, you can't teach. The same thing is true of Iraq.

The conditions of the Cause in Syria and Lebanon and the Bahá'ís there are under control. No activities and no services as yet. We are hoping that by the grace of God and the constant supervision of the Hands, the people in these countries will gradually be raised to serve the Faith the name of which gives them so much credit. Do you remember I asked you to try to write about your dear father Abbass [sic.] and the family? I think it will be very useful for the N.E., N.S.A. to be formed in the future. By the N.E., N.S.A. I mean the N.S.A. of the Near East, the seat of which will be Beirut.

The Hands in the Holy Land responded to Gayle's inquiry with the following communication to the Hands of the Cause in the Americas on 23 January 1965:

It has come to our attention that Mrs Gayle Woolson probably will not be able to remain in Ecuador after the conclusion of her present tour of duty there in a few months, owing to the policy of rotation of the U S. Government in the case of employees in foreign posts.

Mrs Woolson will be given an opportunity to express a preference for her next assignment, and we understand that she is considering the possibility of the Middle East.

The view of the House of Justice and of ourselves is that a person of such outstanding qualifications for service in Latin America as Mrs Woolson should remain in Central or South America. Her long and glorious record of service in these countries, and her knowledge of Spanish and English certainly are a great asset to the work of the Cause in Latin America, and to that of the Institution of the Hands in her capacity as a Board Member.

We suggest that you may wish to write to her and encourage her to remain in a South American country in order that her special qualifications, so needed there, may be fully utilized in the Nine Year Plan.

With warmest loving greetings,
In the service of the Beloved Guardian,
HANDS OF THE CAUSE IN THE HOLY LAND
Signed by Leroy Ioas, Paul S. Haney, A. Furútan,
A.Q. Faizi[4]

As it happened, the office in Quito extended Gayle's work in Ecuador beyond the normal tour of duty. In response to the Hands' guidance, she remained at her post and, when USAID required a transfer, accepted a post in El Salvador.

During the mid- and late 1960s, the education and protection of the believers in relationship to the Covenant continued to present a challenge in communities where Gayle lived and served, as the influence of Mason Remey's claims, literature, and correspondence still lingered in the minds of some in Quito and Guayaquil. Over time, these ideas receded and the communities became united in vision and thought.

This was a period, worldwide, of concentration on teaching large populations. In Ecuador, this effort was focused on the Quechua area, a mountainous region of widely scattered villages, often inaccessible by car. There were religious and political prejudices, which resulted in the Faith being often misconstrued. It was to meet these challenges that, with the inspiration and perseverance of Raúl Pavón and others, the first radio station of the Baháʾí world came into being as an effective and transformative institution. With participatory programming in both Spanish and Quechua, local people shared music, announcements, questions, and educational discussions reflecting the needs and culture of their community. An institute was established in Otavalo for training teachers. A family gave land for a cemetery, as the Catholic Church would not allow Baháʾís to be buried on its property. Hand of the Cause Dr Muhájir came several times to Ecuador to lend his expertise to the process, collaborating with the community, with Mr Khazeh and with the other Hands who visited.

In 1968, USAID decided to transfer Gayle to El Salvador. Helen Hornby writes:

January 1968 brought regrettable news which dismayed all the Baháʾís and many non-Baháʾís of Ecuador; it was that their dear loved one, Auxiliary Board member Gayle Woolson was being transferred by her employer, USAID, to another country. She had served Ecuador with distinction since the early 1940's. She was privileged and honored to host Rúḥíyyih Khánum before she left.[5]

Rúḥíyyih Khánum and her devoted travelling companion,

Violette Nakhjavani, arrived in Quito on 20 March 1968, greeted at the airport by Bahá'ís from eleven communities. It is interesting to contrast the community's own awareness of its struggles with that same community as seen through the eyes of Rúḥíyyih Khánum. The very evening of her arrival, she gave a talk at the Náw-Rúz celebration in Quito. A transcription made from a tape recording of the talk includes the following:

> There must be some significance in how this journey of mine in South America started and ended. It started in La Paz, Bolivia, which was in the Inca Empire, and ended in Quito, which was also of the Inca Empire. Most of you here know something of the history of the Incas. The Incas were the greatest empire of South America and one of the greatest which the world has seen. In many ways, the Inca Empire was superior to the Roman Empire. It had a very high standard. I was surprised to learn that the greeting of the Incas was: 'Don't lie, don't steal, don't be lazy.' It would be a very good greeting for everybody in the world . . .
>
> I believe that as we teach the descendants of the Incas, we should always tell them the reason why we are bringing the Message of Bahá'u'lláh to them. It is not because we pity them, not because we look down upon them; it is because it is the duty of every Bahá'í to give the Message to all of humanity, but especially to the Indians of the Americas because of the wonderful prophecy in the Faith which is unique. It says that if the Indians[6] of America will accept the Message of

Bahá'u'lláh they will become like a previous people who, in another epoch, accepted the Prophet Muhammad and illumined the world. We must believe that because this prophecy is in our books, it has a great significance and we must also believe that this power is in the Indian people. There is something inside of them. If they will accept the Message of Bahá'u'lláh, it will release this great power which is latent within them.

I must say something tonight because this is my last visit in South America. I believe the Indian people are the people who are going to have to teach their own people the Faith. There are hundreds of thousands of Indians all the way from the north of Canada right to the end of South America in the peninsula of Chile and Argentina, Tierra del Fuego. There are hundreds and hundreds of tribes. They have suffered an injustice that I don't think is equalled in history. But men are always unjust to each other, and what occurred hundreds of years ago cannot be changed now. Now we must cling to the prophecy of Bahá'u'lláh about the future of the Indians.

The only people who are going to have the strength and who are sufficient in number as Bahá'ís are the Indians. That does not mean other people will not help them. There are many people and some right here in this room, who have dedicated years and much effort to teaching this Message to the Indians. But we are not sufficient; there are not enough of us, nor do we have the strength to go out among the Indians. All the advantage is with the Indians themselves. It is their language, their

country, their people. The Indian knows his own environment; he knows his people better than we do; he has
good legs which many of us from North America don't
have. Because of these things he is the ideal person to
take this Message to his own people. We must teach
the Indians in South, Central, and North America to
become the great teachers of their own people . . .

There is an important thing in Latin America,
which is a bounty of God – it is the common language,
the Spanish. If a Quechua Indian from Ecuador who
knows Spanish should go to Mexico, he could communicate with them, not through Quechua, but
through Spanish. We should expect wonderful things
in the future from the Indians.[7]

While in Quito, Ruḥíyyíh Khánum also addressed over
300 students and 15 teachers at the Colegio Simon
Bolivar, delivered a radio address, and spoke to about
130 people at a hotel.

She then set off with Violette Nakhjavani, Raúl Pavón,
Gayle and others, to accomplish her primary goal: visiting the indigenous believers in the area around Otavalo.
They visited 17 villages, most of which were not acces-
sible by car. The trips therefore involved driving, then
walking, and sometimes climbing.

Ruhiyyih Khanum was charmed with the beautiful
scenery and the many wild flowers, and one day she
sat down on the road to make a crown of those she
had picked for her hat.

[*From the report to the Universal House of Justice*]: Her spontaneous love for the Indians and the sincere appreciation she unfailingly showed them won their hearts immediately and they lost all of their shyness. In most of the villages a meal had been prepared for her. On one occasion it was hot milk followed by soup, potatoes and beans. Most often it was a filling soup of grains . . . Often they gave her eggs or coins for the Fund . . .

In many of the villages, Ruhiyyih Khanum drew a map of the world on the ground with a stick, using it to teach them the history of their own people and telling them of their own glorious past. Then she told them how she had always wished she were an Indian and how happy she was to be with them; she related the wonderful promises in the Bahá'í Writings about the Indians of the Americas – that when they have become illumined by the Teachings of Bahá'u'lláh they will in turn illumine the whole world. She told them how difficult it is to teach the Cause in the cities but that they who live in the midst of such great natural beauty are more receptive spiritually, and when they have learned the Teachings they will be able to go and teach the Faith to the people in the cities. She stressed everywhere that they should not think of themselves as being ignorant because many cannot read and write . . .

She told them to teach the Bahá'í prayers to the children as they would protect them from bad dreams. She told us [the believers who were travelling with her] to teach the children about all of the Manifestations of

God so that they will become firm believers . . .

She was impressed by the work being done in the Teaching Institute in Otavalo . . . but suggested that we also use a mobile institute to go out and teach in the communities, as this would reach whole families instead of just one member. She found many capable and receptive souls among the women and said that with the mobile institute we could train many of them to go out as teachers . . .[8]

Upon her return from Otavalo, despite exhaustion and a high fever, Rúḥíyyih Khánum arose to consult with the National Spiritual Assembly, emphasizing the importance of the indigenous peoples and their capacity to arise, become educated and teach others. To accompany Rúḥíyyih Khánum and Violette Nakhjavani on this journey was indeed a wonderful farewell gift for Gayle in this country whose people she loved so deeply and to whom she had given so much.

Days in El Salvador

Helen Hornby writes:

On 24 May 1968 the National Assembly met with Mrs Gayle Woolson in order to express formally and officially their thanks and gratitude for her many years of noteworthy service to the Faith in Ecuador. In 1968, the time had arrived for her departure to her new full-time professional post with USAID in El

Salvador. Prayers were said that she would have a safe journey and achieve continuous success in her new endeavors and that one day she would return to them. Before leaving she contributed many tangible articles to both the national community and local community of Quito as well as an ample donation to the National Spiritual Assembly for the construction and furnishing of the Teaching Institute in Otavalo.[9]

Charles Hornby, later joined by his wife, moved to Ecuador from Colombia to carry out the services Gayle had been rendering as an Auxiliary Board Member.

Once in El Salvador, despite her full-time position for USAID at the Embassy, Gayle maintained an intense teaching schedule in her free time, opening several communities to the Faith and eventually serving on the National Spiritual Assembly of the Bahá'ís of El Salvador.

Six months after she arrived, she received an invitation to apply for and subsequently to serve as a Spanish/English bilingual translator at the Bahá'í World Centre in Haifa, Israel. However, when she explained that she would lose all of her benefits if she resigned at this point in her two-year tour of duty, the Universal House of Justice advised her to complete it. She offered to do translations for the World Centre while still in Central America. She would receive them by post and work on them in the evenings.[10] Additionally, knowing she would be going to the World Centre, she got the second printing of her book, *Divina Sinfonia* (The Divine Symphony), accomplished, as well as producing her second book, *Rumbo Hacia el*

Futuro (The Direction Toward the Future). She said she hoped the books could teach for her in her absence.

In contrast to the survival of her written words, her friends Quentin and Jeanne Ferrand wrote to her in 1986 that the building where she lived had fallen during the recent earthquake. They also reported that the Embassy where she had worked had been demolished due to severe damage in the same event.[11] As it happened, Gayle's literary work survived and continued to teach. Even as late as 1998, the Director of 'Concultura' in El Salvador requested 135 copies of her first book, *Divina Sinfonia,* and distributed them to all the Houses of Culture.[12] This was after Gayle's period of service in the Holy Land, and after her return to the United States, when she was 85 years old.

19

In the Shadow of the Shrines

Gayle arrived in Haifa for her period of service at the World Centre on 21 October 1970. On 7 November 1970, she wrote a general letter to friends and family about her first days there:

. . . I arrived at 9 p.m. on October 21st in Tel Aviv and was met by a dear Baháʼí who works at the World Centre. The drive to Haifa is about two hours so during that time I was briefed about many things and you can imagine how many questions I asked! I was told that the next day I would be received by the Universal House of Justice at 3:30 p.m. together with Mr and Mrs Ben Guhrki, pioneers from Alaska, who had also come here to work and who had just arrived . . . When we arrived in Haifa, my heart swelled with emotion and joy upon seeing the Shrine of the Báb towering majestically over the city. I was taken to the Shrine and permitted to go in to pray even though it was already about 11 p.m. I brought all of you with me in my heart and prayed for all . . .

The atmosphere of the Shrine is heavenly and powerful and my experience of going in alone was beautiful. I seemed to come in contact with the realms on high and it truly was overwhelming. I was told that the next day the members of the Universal House of Justice would be praying in the Shrine and would be leaving it at 8:30 a.m. and that if I wanted to, I could wait in the outer gardens and greet them after their prayers. I waited by the Pilgrim House and met several other Bahá'ís in the gardens – then the members of the UHJ came down the stone path: David Ruhe, Borrah Kavelin, Ali Nakhjavani, Hooshmand Fatheazam, Ian Semple, Amos Gibson and David Hofman. (Hugh Chance and Charles Wolcott were not in the country at that time.) They were so loving, kind and radiant, and they all embraced me and graciously welcomed me, and said they had been waiting for me for a long time.

The Guhrkis and I were truly welcomed into the World Centre on a 'magic carpet'! That morning was spent in the Shrines and gardens, which are more beautiful than ever, then were taken to the building where the World Centre office is to meet the staff – all wonderful Bahá'ís. The offices are on two floors and the building is surrounded by lovely gardens. I have an office by myself with two windows, both of which look off to gardens, and if I want to walk around in a larger one, all I have to do is go across the street! . . .

The meeting with the Universal House of Justice was a beautiful experience. They have a general meeting room and this is where we were received. The impact of being in their presence was tremendous and very impressive. I was struck by their spiritual power and by their sweetness, humility, and kindness. It was a brief meeting in which they expressed words of loving welcome.

That evening we were invited to Ian Semple's for a welcome dinner, a couple of nights later to the Ruhes and last night to Amos Gibson's. In each case, there were some members of the UHJ and some Hands as well as other Bahá'ís, so you can imagine what kind of gatherings they have been.

The second day we were taken to Akka by House member Hooshmand Fatheazam . . . and spent the whole morning in the Shrine of Bahá'u'lláh and the Mansion of Bahji, as well as in the gardens. The gardens have been extended and their magnificence is very impressive. The holy atmosphere of the Shrine of Bahá'u'lláh and its beauty is very elevating, to say the least, and there we prayed together, each one, in turn, saying a prayer.

In the office we frequently see members of the UHJ and the Hands. Every Tuesday morning we all have a devotional period together from 8:30 a.m. to 9 a.m. and we take turns choosing the material and the readers. Everyone sounds like a professional reader and the chants are glorious. Wouldn't it be wonderful if in every office the executives and the staff would get together for prayer occasionally. The work week here begins on Sunday and ends on Friday noon according to the Israeli custom.

Every two weeks, starting on a Monday, a group of

National Spiritual Assembly for the northern countries of South America, 1960, with Dr Hermann Grossmann. Front row, left to right: Mercedes Sanchez, Margot Worley, Dr Grossmann, Gayle Woolson, Dorothy Campbell. Back row, left to right: Henrique Sanchez, Cyrus Monadjem, Rangvald Taetz, Edmund Miessler, Jamshed Megrot

First National Spiritual Assembly of Ecuador, 1961

*Hand of the Cause Jalál Kházeh in Ecuador
at the 1964 National Convention*

*Visit of Hand of the Cause Raḥmat'u'lláh Muhájir
to Otavalo, 1965*

Growth of
the Colombia
Bahá'í
community,
Bucaramanga,
1965

*Members of the Pavón family: Clementina
(Mother Pavón) and Segundo Pavón (seated),
with Raul and Isabel Pavón de Calderón (both
later members of the Continental Board of
Counsellors) in the back row*

*Amatu'l-Bahá Rúḥíyyih Khánum with the
Pavón family and Rufino Gualavisi, 1968*

*Visit of Hand of the Cause Rúḥíyyih Khánum and
Mrs Violette Nakhjavani to Ecuador, 1968*

With Hand of the Cause Raḥmatu'lláh Muhájir at the Central American Baháʼí Teaching Conference, El Salvador, 1969

Accompanying Hand of the Cause Enoch Olinga and Elizabeth Olinga to Kingston, Jamaica, 1977

*Returning to
Costa Rica, 1978*

pilgrims comes for nine days. A wonderful schedule is worked out for them and there are frequent occasions when we can meet with them. In the last group, which was the first group for this nine month period, there was Eda Rae Peterson and her husband, an ex-pioneer of Ecuador.

David Hofman told me that the latest statistic is 43,000 localities in the world. This morning (today is the Sabbath) I guided at the Shrine with two other Bahá'ís. The visitors and tourists stream in from 9 a.m. to 12 noon. These are the visiting hours each day at the Shrine of the Báb only. The non-Bahá'ís cannot enter the Shrine of 'Abdu'l-Bahá nor the Archives Building. They can enter in Bahá'u'lláh's Shrine on Friday, Saturday and Sunday mornings. There were only 300 this morning, which is a small number. Sometimes as many as 700 come in those three hours, in the normal times, and up to 1,800 in peak tourist periods . . .

I am going to start studying Hebrew in a class. It is really necessary to know it here in order to communicate with the people. At the World Centre I am also exposed to Persian, Arabic, and French. As I hear Arabic I am recalling many words I used to know – that is, spoken Arabic, which is quite different from the classical Arabic (which I can't understand at all). I have met a few people who speak Spanish so, of course, I am delighted to speak with them . . .

When my shipment comes in from El Salvador, I will start using my tape recorder and will be able to say many things on the cassettes. I am very grateful for this precious gift from the dear friends in El Salvador and I will put it to good use.

Every other Saturday there is a group of Bahá'ís that get together to study 'Epistle to the Son of the Wolf' by Bahá'u'lláh. They take turns having it at different homes and it starts out with a luncheon. The study is led by Mr 'Abdu'lláh Mesbah who works in the 'Research Department' at the World Centre and who is very well versed in the Bahá'í Writings in Persian and Arabic. He speaks very good English. Every other Sunday night there is a class given by the Hand Mr Furutan when he is in Haifa. There are also social get-togethers frequently among the Bahá'ís in different groups . . .

I was always aware that it would be a great bounty to be here at the World Centre but to imagine it, as I did before, and to actually experience it are two different things! You will all always be with me spiritually and always remembered in my prayers in the sacred Shrines.[1]

Gayle offers little further documentation of her life during this period, perhaps out of respect for the agreement employees make with the World Centre not to create personal publications regarding one's time of service there. The time was filled with service in Spanish/English translation, with opportunities to welcome friends from Latin America who came on pilgrimage, and with daily efforts to keep up her own worldwide correspondence. She also participated actively in the classes for children of Bahá'ís serving at the World Centre, training them to stand up and speak in public, wearing their best clothes. Years later, when she had returned to the United States, she would develop this into the Children's Speaking Project described in Chapter 22.

At the World Centre, several significant events took place during her time of service there. In 1973, she had the privilege of participating in the celebration of the 100th Anniversary of the Revelation of the Kitáb-i-Aqdas. She had the privilege of witnessing the establishment of the International Teaching Centre, which comprised, at that time, all living Hands of the Cause of God and the following three Counsellors: Hooper Dunbar, Florence Mayberry, and ʿAzíz Yazdí. This was also the year of the Third International Convention in Haifa to elect the Universal House of Justice.

From 2 June – 18 June 1972, she made a trip to Spain, during which she visited several communities, including Madrid, Seville, Málaga, Granada, Murcia, Valencia, and Catalonia.[2]

In 1974, she received unexpected and upsetting news from home. Her younger brother, Julian, had drowned in a boating accident near his home in Casper, Wyoming. It was hard to be far away and unable to be with her family at such a time. In light of this tragedy, she may have found a blessing in the suggestion of the Universal House of Justice some months later in 1975, that she consider a transition back to the field of teaching. In a letter to Mr Nakhjaváni (1979), she relates how the committee of three (Mr Nakhjaváni, Mr Kavelin, and Mr Hofman) met with her and ʿexpressed, after such beautiful remarks about my services to the Faith, that the House felt I could render more valuable services in the teaching field than in translation at the World Centre, and I was consulted as to my own feeling and was given a choice. The thoughtfulness, delicacy, and loving consideration of the Universal House of Justice expressed through you . . . three . . . have always stood out in my mind as emanations of the great light, love and wisdom of our Supreme Body.'³

On 24 September 1975, the Universal House of Justice sent her a gracious and loving letter, including the following:

> The members of the House of Justice who met with you on our behalf stressed, in their report to us, the very spiritual nature of the meeting and we are sure that your own radiant dedication to the needs of the Cause contributed very largely to this.
>
> We confirm by this letter that you should leave the World Centre by the end of October 1975. The time between now and the date of your departure is entirely your own to complete all your arrangements . . . You will doubtless wish to spend as much time as you can in the sacred Shrines.
>
> . . . We feel sure that you will devote the whole of your energy and love for Bahá'u'lláh to the promotion of His Cause and thereby add further distinction to your already splendid record.⁴

She describes being deeply moved by her farewell meeting with the Universal House of Justice, during which the members gave her a small rug hanging with the Greatest Name woven into it, carefully kept with her most treasured gifts.

20

Reflections on a Weaving Partway Done

Gayle's return to the United States in 1975 was both a dramatic transition in service and a poignant personal homecoming. First, she would spend time in Wyoming with the wife and children of her late brother, Julian, and then with family members in and near St Paul. As she moved from visiting one part of her family to another, she realized it was the first time in 35 years that such visits would not lead to another departure for an international post. She may have mused on trips now past – to Costa Rica in 1940 and, over time, throughout Latin America.

She may have recalled visits to the indigenous villages of Ecuador, high in the Andes Mountains. There, in Otavalo, near a famous market with brightly coloured woven wares, she had seen women in flowing skirts among flowering trees, weaving at blanket-sized looms. In similar fashion, Gayle now mentally gathered together the strands of memories from those times, surveyed the work already done, and intuitively perceived the next steps towards completing the unfinished design. This last part of the weaving would take almost 36 years, though she would always say she felt 'in a race against time'. It would echo earlier motifs, creating a symmetry in which images of her early life found reflection in its final years.

She may have mused that even the meeting with the House of Justice committee had contained such a reflection of themes, where past, present and future seem to merge. Back in 1934, when Gayle had first consciously embraced the Bahá'í teachings, the St Paul Minutes had the following entry:

Sunday, June 3, 1934 – 8 p.m.

Meeting held in Bahá'í Room – 322. Opening prayer by Morris Abas. Visiting speaker Mrs Schopflocher of Montreal, Canada, sent by Shoghi Effendi to show moving pictures of the Holy Land and tell the Assemblies of the United States and Canada to prepare themselves for the New World Order. Accompanying Mrs Schopflocher was a young man named Mr Hofman of England who also gave a talk on The Administration. Thirteen members were present.[1]

This visit occurred at a time when Gayle and her older sisters and brothers were all participating regularly in the gatherings in St Paul. The presentations would have been among the first Gayle heard on Bahá'í administration, shortly before she began to serve on the Local Spiritual Assembly. Then, 41 years later, Mr Hofman had lovingly served on the committee to guide her return to the teaching field. The young man who had passed through St Paul when she was 21 had become one of the first members of the Universal House of Justice!

Although Gayle would still make some trips abroad and would continue her international correspondence, she would eventually settle in Evanston, near her beloved House of Worship. She would have few administrative duties. Having been out of the country for so long, yet engaged in government employment in Ecuador and El Salvador, she had a small federal pension. Uncomplaining, resourceful and well-schooled in simplicity, she would find ways to live and serve that accomplished remarkable goals with fewness of means.

As always, the strands of her service were intricately interwoven. She would continue daily habits of prayer, study, teaching, and service. Grateful to compensate for the long years away from St Paul, she would keep closely in touch with family members, sending cards at birthdays, calling family members by phone, and attending reunions, always with her camera and cassette recorder at the ready to capture the moment for history. The time together with her siblings would be fast-fleeting. One by one, over the next 30 years, they would pass away, eventually leaving her as the last survivor of the nine sisters and brothers who had peopled the home in St Paul.

She would travel both internationally and domestically as much and as long as possible, responding to invitations to attend milestone anniversaries of the founding of Bahá'í communities and of National Spiritual Assemblies in countries where she had pioneered. She would guide at the House of Worship in Wilmette; help with publicity and devotions; prepare children to speak at public programmes, and give introductions to the Faith in

Spanish. Always prepared with slides of her travels and the history they represented, she would be a frequent public speaker in outlying communities, particularly at Spanish-speaking gatherings.

A way with words

During her later years, Gayle would complete a variety of writing projects related to the early history of the Faith in the Americas. She would also continue to give talks in both Spanish and English, translating for others as needed.

Her early work had been done in the days of mimeograph machines, typewriters, carbon copies, and physical cutting and pasting, when each change could require retyping large sections; when accuracy and forethought saved time, and when editing involved months of correspondence with publishers, back and forth from one country to another. It is hard for us now to remember or, if too young to remember, to grasp both the painstaking work and the skills this involved. One learned to conceptualize paragraphs and chapters with an almost musical sense of theme, development, and conclusion. Literary awareness and attention to detail developed through the laborious process of editing multiple drafts until the final one was complete.

Gayle realized the historical significance of the developments unfolding through the Plans of the Guardian and the Universal House of Justice. She would continue to research and document the history in which she and others she knew had participated, realizing, as she did, the significance of the implementation of the Tablets of the Divine Plan through the Guardian's Plans. Conscious of how quickly accurate remembrance yields to innocent imagination and distortion in the telling of events, she would encourage pioneers and early believers to write down their experiences. She was a natural historian who was painstaking in backing up statements with primary source documentation. She interviewed early believers in person or through correspondence to encourage the first-hand documentation of their lives and remembrances. Those who knew her in her Evanston days remember her arriving early in Foundation Hall at the House of Worship for every presentation, sitting front and centre, with either her notebook or her cassette recorder. She interviewed and taped people incessantly, to a degree that tried the patience of some. Following lectures, she typed out notable talks she had recorded for study. In the days before cassette recorders, she took down lectures and meeting consultations in shorthand with word-for-word precision. This practice, together with her translation experience, trained her mind and memory to perceive both thematic principle and detail. This kind of care informed her every report and the contents of her correspondence.

In these later years, she researched and wrote biographical accounts of early Bahá'í residents of Evanston, Illinois for its newsletter, *The Eagle*. She was often asked to write obituaries for 'In Memoriam' articles for *The Bahá'í World*, as those she knew passed away. She contributed stories to the biography of Dorothy Baker and to that of Eve Nicklin. She wrote the obituaries for almost all of her siblings. She documented the history of her own life with care.

Examples of her speaking engagements in both Spanish and English are scattered through other chapters of this book. Talks she gave in 1998, now preserved in the Cedar Rapids Archive, show how her eloquence and distillation of thought remained present even then.

When first preparing to go abroad, Gayle had obeyed the instructions in *Tablets of the Divine Plan* for those going to Latin America to learn the language of the country where they would reside. This bore fruit in more ways than she first imagined. As a child, she had already developed an ear for language, absorbing both English and Arabic in her bilingual home. Remarkably, her four years in Costa Rica rendered her sufficiently expert in Spanish to offer simultaneous translation at the 1944 Inter-American Conference and at other times. She assisted with the translation of Bahá'í books; wrote in Spanish; and translated voluminous messages and letters for the work in Central and South America. When her subsidy as an itinerant teacher in South America ended and she needed employment, she took an entry-level position with USAID in Ecuador, where the director needed a bilingual secretary. Her proficiency in Spanish resulted in several promotions, so she was well able to support herself. Later, her five years at the Bahá'í World Centre in Haifa were spent doing translation related to Spanish-speaking countries including Latin America.

Before leaving for Costa Rica in 1940, Gayle had already begun gathering material on comparative religions for what later emerged as her first book, *La Divina Sinfonia* (Divine Symphony). In Latin America, she found that most people were Christian, the majority being Catholic, and that they had little exposure to other traditions. She wrote this book for the Latin American people, to show the relationships among the lives and teachings of the Founders of many of the great religions.

The first edition was written in Spanish and printed in Quito in 1968, with a cover collaboratively designed by Gayle and Counsellor Raúl Pavón. The second was produced in El Salvador in 1970 as her way of leaving something that could continue to teach on her behalf when she left to serve in Haifa. Later, at Dr Muhajir's suggestion, an English version was published in India and subsequently in Australia. Gayle often gave copies to people she met. After leaving Latin America, she asked that her royalties be used to provide free copies to communities and people of capacity, especially in Latin America.

In this book, we find evidence of Gayle's ability to express profound ideas in a few simple words. With an image from a talk in *'Abdu'l-Bahá on Divine Philosophy*, she invites the reader into her book:

> Let us listen to a symphony which will confer life on man . . . then we shall receive a new spirit; then we shall become illumined . . . and will develop the inner potentialities of life.[2]

She translated a teaching book first written in India, *The New Garden,* into Spanish. Additionally, she wrote a second book, *Rumbo Hacia el Futuro* (Direction Toward the Future). In 1967, as part of the national teaching programme, every secondary school in Ecuador received a copy. Later, while in El Salvador, she produced more copies, in order to leave something that could teach on her behalf after she left for service in Haifa. Years later, in 1998, she received word from El Salvador that 135 copies had been placed in the Houses of Culture throughout the country.

As an itinerant teacher and later as an Auxiliary Board Member, her responsibilities included maintaining a widespread correspondence, as a way to nurture individuals and communities throughout Latin America. In response to requests, correspondence courses were also developed to allow people to continue learning from a distance. Writing letters became a lifelong habit. In 1978, she wrote on her calendar that her goal was to write two letters each day, one long and one short. Each evening, her two typewriters would have fresh paper in them, ready for the letters to be composed in the morning.

Even in the 1980s and 1990s, she made final revisions to her books. However, her correspondence with the publishing trusts reflects how as the years passed, the process became harder. Collaboration also became unwieldy, as she remained bound to her typewriter and to mail by post in a world overtaken with the speed of word processing and electronic communication.

* * * * *

Given all of this, it is remarkable that in 1980 she found herself impelled to further develop her Children's Public Speaking Project. This work would engage her attention for almost 20 years. It brought her full circle to where she had begun to serve so long ago, learning about holistic psychology from her husband, Clement Woolson, then offering the children's class in St Paul.

In 1992, twelve years after starting the children's project, she would respond to the invitation of the Universal House of Justice and attend the 100th Anniversary of the Ascension of Bahá'u'lláh in Haifa, when the scroll with the names of the Knights of Bahá'u'lláh would be deposited at the entrance of the inner sanctuary of His Most Holy Shrine.

Her service in Evanston and its environs, with its extension worldwide through correspondence and her promotion of the children's project, would continue until almost 2005. It was then that her physical needs would narrow the scope of her life, as the last rows of weaving were done.

21

Seeing Both Sides of the Coin

When she moved to St Paul on 15 May 1976,[1] following the visit to family in Montana, Gayle gave formalized
expression to her understanding of a theme she termed
'Spiritual Psychology'. When she left the World Centre,
the Universal House of Justice had introduced her by
letter to Dr Samuel McClellan, a well-known psychiatrist
and Auxiliary Board member, that she might discuss her
ideas with him. Instead of travelling to the McClellan
home as initially envisaged, she made a cassette tape
addressed to Dr McClellan between 6 and 18 June 1976.[2]

In this carefully prepared presentation, she grounds
her thought in the Bahá'í Writings, describes her research
in the professional world, and then explains insights she
says were received through 'dreams', 'visions', or thoughts
'upon waking'. If one returns briefly to the image of
weaving, the convictions she expressed are like the vertical warp on which the design of her life was woven.
(It was these convictions and the desire to hand down
to children the best of what she had gleaned from life
that would inspire her to dedicate the next 20 years to
her Children's Public Speaking Project. The following
thoughts and quotations come from the tape.

Gayle was convinced that much disease, especially on the mental and emotional levels, has a spiritual and moral base. She cited the Bahá'í teaching that human life has three phases: one in the womb of the mother; one in this physical world; and one in a dimension beyond this earthly realm. She said that to truly address physical, mental, and spiritual health, one must consider each in the context of these three phases and of spiritual law.

She summarized to Dr McClellan material explored both in Bahá'í scripture and in current professional thought. Regarding the latter, she sought to ascertain the degree to which concepts of moral law and spirituality informed psychologists' practice and teaching. She interviewed more than ten professors at the University of Illinois and at Hamline University, St Paul, Minnesota. She was struck by how the professors with whom she spoke in 1975 and 1976 consistently affirmed a separation between psychology and religion, and between spirituality and a defined moral structure. She later visited several schools in the Evanston area to observe and interview teachers about how they envisioned the moral training of children. From these interviews and other reading, she concluded that the science of psychology was lagging because it had become too compartmentalized. This field of psychology, she noted, had been separated from its very definition: the 'knowledge of the psyche, soul, mind', and therefore from its relationship to a coherent moral structure. She then quoted a letter from the Universal House of Justice dated 6 February 1973 regarding obedience to spiritual law:

Just as there are laws governing our physical lives . . . so also there are laws governing our spiritual lives . . . and obedience to them is of vital importance if each human being, and mankind in general, is to develop properly and harmoniously. Moreover, these various aspects are interdependent. If an individual violates the spiritual laws for his own development he will cause injury not only to himself but to the society in which he lives. Similarly, the condition of society has a direct effect on the individuals who must live within it.

. . . Life in this world is a succession of tests and achievements, of falling short and of making new spiritual advances. Sometimes the course seems very hard, but one can witness, again and again, that the soul who steadfastly obeys the law of Bahá'u'lláh, however hard it may seem, grows spiritually, while the one who compromises the law for the sake of his own apparent happiness is seen to have been following a chimera: he does not attain the happiness he sought, he retards his spiritual advance and often brings new problems upon himself. Thus, by upholding Bahá'í law, we both strengthen our own character and influence those around us.[3]

Relating spiritual law to the three phases of life, she stated that 'a vital relationship . . . exists between this life and the next'. They could not be 'considered as two unconnected, unrelated aspects', as indicated in the following passage which she underlined in her copy of Rúḥíyyih Khánum's *Prescription for Living*:[4]

Death is always with us, and yet we almost never think of it unless it is forced on our attention. Death is implicit in life; the two are partners. The throbbing of our arteries, so full of vitality and strength, should remind us that that swift beat may suddenly stop. The transition is so light, but the break so complete and irrevocable. If people thought just a little more of what death is, its purpose, the nature of the change it brings about, they would not only live differently but with far more conscious direction to their lives, with more poise and more assurance than they do at present. Life should be viewed always in the perspective of death. To separate one from the other is to produce a great disequilibrium. Life is a road which leads to a door, that door is death. Life is a flowering and a planting; beyond the gates of death the harvest will be drawn in. Life, with all its beauty and all its richness and varie-gated experiences, is only the womb-world of the soul; death is the real life into which we are born.[5]

On the tape, Gayle concludes that psychology is 'still a very young and inexact science, inasmuch as most current thought in the field does not consider this life in the light of the next'. She continues, relating psychology to character development:

The structure of the human being is harmed by diso-bedience; a natural disturbance sets in. The soul is a gift from God. You cannot mistreat it and get away from it. Through disobedience, one's highest, true destiny is diminished. Actions, words, attitudes and thoughts form patterns in our character structure. Each of these forms vibrations, like the notes of a piano. With disobedience, a false note is introduced into the soul. Punishment has begun.

She then widens the vision:

The purpose of the life of the individual is to evolve to the highest possible level of character and of service. Whatever diminishes that possibility will ultimately affect the individual, who fails to reach his true destiny.

Ultimately this idea leads to how noble qualities may be instilled in children:

The Teachings . . . form the structure of the Kingdom of God in the human character . . . Divine civilization will unfold gradually as those elements become more and more the constituents of our character structure.

Gayle then tells Dr McClellan of her visit to the family in Montana and how Julian's passing had evoked contemplation:

A new perspective of life is gained; it is like the two sides of a coin. In this life, we see one side only. In the next, we see both sides of the coin. One side's significance can't be fully known without the other.

Here, we live our life from day to day; there we see the consequences of every act. Even every split second is significant in the sight of God. The whole life of the individual in the next world is structured upon his life in this world. Obedience to the divine laws of God is like the umbilical cord.

She then explains how these principles of Spiritual Psychology relate to character development in children:

Teaching the children at an early age about the structure is important, so that they don't become dislodged from their high destiny. The children of today should be protected and not content themselves with a lesser destiny. Children are the kings and queens of the earth. We must keep them this way, giving them a great vision with all the wonders of the world, which are the greatest achievement of history. What are the great factors that make life worth living and fascinating? What are the wonders of nature? We should help them explore the major professions and trades through every means to give them an early orientation to future careers. All children should have insight into all the greatness the world has thus far achieved in the various fields of culture. Through devotion to God, they may achieve spiritual distinction. Parents need support, as many are also still immature. The atmosphere may be insufficient and incapable of supplying that for which the children yearn.

Gayle then relates to Dr McClellan how her father taught the youth in St Paul, back in 1930, that the young people are the ones who will build the new world civilization. She says it was in this spirit that their participation in the community was embraced. Furthermore, relating development in this world to that in the next, she continued:

When a person passes away, a person gains a new perspective on creation, the world, and his or her role in the great symphony of life . . . In the next world there are rewards and punishments for obedience and violations of the divine laws . . . The importance of the principle of making up for a wrong committed is that it frees the soul from its burden that it would have to carry in the other world until God ordained it otherwise. Our life here in this world is the beginning of an eternal journey. Whatever we do or say we take with us. Whatever was done that was wrong should be made up for before passing on . . .

She concluded:

The ideal code of life is written in *The Hidden Words*, Part Two, #44, that part that reads, 'Live then the days of thy life, that are less than a fleeting moment, with thy mind stainless, they heart unsullied, thy thoughts pure and thy nature sanctified, so that, free and content, thou mayest put away this mortal frame, and repair unto the mystic paradise and abide in the eternal kingdom for evermore.'

Distilling these ideas for Dr McClellan put into words themes that became increasingly central to Gayle's own life and service to others. Her attunement to every thought and act as significant brought with it an unusual attentiveness to the value of time, word, and deed. She sought to serve in ways that would give lasting expression to important lessons learned during her lifetime. Keenly aware that deeds done in the memory of others have an effect on the progress of their souls in the next world, she began to dedicate specific efforts to family and friends who had passed on.

22

'. . . speak forth with wisdom and eloquence'[1]

It was in 1980, four years after her communication with Dr McClellan, that Gayle systematically implemented her Children's Public Speaking Project. She had already been teaching children to present speeches while in Haifa and possibly before then. Now she continued that service through the Child Education Committee in Evanston and expanded its reach from there. The project embodied principles Gayle outlined in her discussion of spiritual psychology. Key to this is the idea that a child needs to learn and gradually internalize those principles that guide one to be true to and attain one's highest destiny. The Creative Word and highest teachings of humankind embody these truths. Memorizing the sacred verses is one means of shaping the internal structure of thought and attitude that determines in great part how a person may utilize and direct his/her gifts and capacities. The Bahá'í Writings define one's purpose as to know and love God and to carry forward an ever-advancing civilization. Therefore true learning will result not only in inner knowledge and love but in its translation into service to humanity. The Public Speaking Project was carefully designed as a template for attaining excellence in this inner learning that would then be channelled into presentations as a service to the wider community. Most important, Gayle saw that the process planted seeds of nobility within the children that would remain in their hearts and become a means of attracting them towards service to all.

Gayle brought a lifetime of experience to the project. She had a natural affinity for children, first helping to raise her own siblings, then starting a children's class in St Paul, and always being mindful to plan activities for the youngest in the community at all her pioneering posts. As a youth, she and her friends had been encouraged to memorize prayers and passages from the Writings. She still had the letter Shoghi Effendi had written her in St Paul, encouraging her to see her children's class as a stepping stone that could lead to public speaking. He had always encouraged her (and others) to see each step of service as leading to an increased expression of capacity in a wider field. It would be natural for her to perceive this principle as it applied, not only to her own life, but to those of children. She spoke frequently of her father's oft-repeated conviction that young people have a very important role to play in building a new world spiritual civilization. She dedicated the project to her father, her mother, and one she considered a spiritual mentor, Dorothy Baker.

Dorothy Baker had encouraged Gayle to overcome her timidity about speaking in public by memorizing a talk of 'Abdu'l-Bahá and then presenting it. It had worked. Marguerite Reimer (Sears) had shared with Gayle what she learned as a public speaking student at the Curry

School of Expression and then as a teacher of this subject at Green Acre. Gayle also brought with her decades of her own experience giving talks and interviews in Central and South America. Now she would hand down her own learning by providing a pathway for children to memorize and present eloquent speeches, knowing that one such step could lead to a thousand. As she formulated publicity about the new project, she emphasized the following quotations from 'Abdu'l-Bahá about children:

Encourage ye the school children, from their earliest years, to deliver speeches of high quality, so that in their leisure time they will engage in giving cogent and effective talks, expressing themselves with clarity and eloquence.[2]

Take the utmost care to give them high ideals and goals . . .[3]

Among the greatest services . . . to Almighty God is the education and training of children . . .[4]

She compiled passages related to memorizing, including the following:

The sanctified souls should ponder and meditate in their hearts regarding the methods of teaching. From the texts of the wondrous, heavenly Scriptures they should memorize phrases and passages bearing on various instances, so that in the course of their speech they may recite divine verses whenever the occasion demandeth it, inasmuch as these holy verses are the most potent elixir, the greatest and mightiest talisman.[5]

The Master used to attach much importance to the learning by heart of the Tablets of Bahá'u'lláh and the Báb. During His days it was a usual work of the children of the household to learn Tablets by heart... the practice is most useful to implant the ideas and spirit those words contain into the minds of the children.[6]

The learning process in action

Gayle gathered quotations appropriate for various age groups and framed them into speeches. She consulted with various families and, with their support, began to work with three students: Tarissa Mitchell (4), Jian Khodadad (7), and Arya Czerniejewski (8). After careful preparation, Jian and Arya presented speeches at the Green Lake Conference. Gayle described it thus:

About a thousand people had gathered to attend the Green Lake Annual Bahá'í Conference in September of 1981. It is a popular conference and generally has that many persons each year. That conference was particularly special for me because two of my only three public speaking students were on the program for the plenary session of the popular Saturday evening event. They were Jian Khodadad, age 7, and Arya Czerniejewski, 8. The student who was not present was Tarissa Mitchell, 4 years old. She, too, would have amazed the audience.

When their turn was announced and those two small children went to the stage, the audience gasped expectantly at the thought of hearing 'Bahá'í speeches' given by them. They looked so beautiful on the stage which was adorned with floral arrangements. Jian spoke first on the topic: 'A Golden Age – Golden Character', then Arya on: 'What is the Bahá'í Faith?' They were very poised and delivered their talks wonderfully, projecting their sweet voices, pausing at the right places, pronouncing with perfection. There was a standing ovation from the astonished audience. It was a great moment for all. Then I was introduced as their instructor, and I was overjoyed at their success.

The speaker who was next on the program was Angus Cowan from Canada. His opening remark was: 'What can I say after that!' Then he commented beautifully about the excellence of the presentations of Arya and Jian . . .[7]

As word got around, more families in the Chicago North Shore area were attracted to what Gayle was doing. There were challenges as the group became enlarged. She didn't have a car, and the children had varying schedules. Getting together was not always easy. As always, using the resources at hand, Gayle developed a system to meet the limitations and possibilities of circumstance.

She wrote out instructions for children and for tutors, or 'volunteers', as she called them, so that others could duplicate what she was doing. She developed a process for memorization and defined simple principles of oratory. She typed and xeroxed speeches appropriate to children of each age, adding to them over time. She kept track, in spiral notebooks, of each child, each practice. She realized that much time would be saved if she rehearsed daily with each child by phone, rather than relying on times they could get together in person. It worked. Harry Murray Sr. recalled that Gayle would call his two children every single day. They would talk with her just as with their other friends, for about ten minutes each, going over and over the talk being learned. She did the same for 6 to 12 children at a time, each with a different speech.

As soon as the group was ready, she would arrange a venue for the group to make a presentation. Local gatherings, such as the Feasts and Holy Days were wonderful places to begin. Universal Children's Day at the House of Worship offered participation in a larger venue. She then found that Rotary Clubs, Kiwanis Clubs, and other civic organizations were eager to host her project. People were moved and delighted to hear young people voicing such lofty and all-embracing thoughts with eloquence and poise. Summer schools, conferences, and other gatherings offered additional opportunities. A high point was a Conference held in San Francisco, where the twins Allen and Mark Eghrari stunned the crowded auditorium with their delivery.

She always had a set of materials ready to give or send to any new person who showed interest. She shared the idea, and materials if requested, with all with whom she corresponded and with family members. There were those as far afield as Africa and Australia and South America who put them to good use. A letter written to Diana Werle's mother, Tarasieh Werle Vahdat, of Ecuador, offers an example of Gayle's loving encouragement:

Dearly-beloved Tarasieh, sweet angel of Heaven,

It was such a great joy to receive your wonderful letter of September 30. Thank you for the various efforts you made in regard to my 'encargos' and I deeply appreciate them.

How delighted I am to know that precious Shirin knows 'O Dios, guíame . . .' by heart. It gives me pleasure to include a typewritten copy of Diana's speech. I hope she will continue practicing it so that she will not forget it. How nice that you have talked to Diana by telephone and thank you for giving her my greetings. It seems that our working together on her speech has established a special bond between us. At least, that is the way I feel. It was like bringing into creation something new. A Bahá'í talk memorized by a child, as His Holiness 'Abdu'l-Bahá has advised, is like a beautiful dress of light and of gold which is a great adornment for that soul, and it gives light to so many others as it is so deeply impressive. Please encourage her not to forget it. She can use this for the rest of her life. She must never tire of it or get bored. Its meaning is very great and when she gives it, it is like planting seeds of light in the minds.

Thank you for your wonderful kindness in saying

that you hope to have me back again in Ecuador. I, too, desire this, but I must complete some important writing here before I can think of going back. However, maybe Bahá'u'lláh will give me the bounty of another visit sometime, before I am finished with my work here. That also would make me very happy. I feel that Ecuador, too, is my home . . .

May I suggest that you keep a cassette for Shirin's recitations and some conversation at the different stages of her infancy. It will be rewarding later.

My prayers at the Temple are with you.

Love, Gayle[8]

Violette Eghrari wrote the following regarding the experience of her twins with Gayle Woolson:

'. . . ye needs must deck the tree of being with fruits such as **knowledge, wisdom, spiritual perception and eloquent speech.**' ~Bahá'u'lláh

When my children were still very young, I began searching, thinking and planning how to help my children develop these skills when I heard about Mrs Gayle Woolson's program . . . I called [her] and she invited us to . . . visit her.

It was such a joy and blessing for us to have her as a teacher for my children.

They were five and a half years old. They were very happy to memorize through encouragement. In a week, they were ready to practice on the phone.

- Starting at a young age was a blessing, because they did not know fear and anxiety. Standing in front of an audience of 10 or 100 or 1,500 was the same for them. Their first talk took place at the Green Lake Bahá'í Conference in front of an audience of about 1,500 people.
- Practicing memorizing the Writings at a young age was another blessing in that it assisted the children to follow the Word of God with regards to memorization and increased their capacity for learning.
- Shaping and forming the mind and the heart of the child, which was like a blank slate. It stayed with them and guided their steps.
- One of the most important aspects of it was teaching the Faith of God before starting school. They gave talks at Kiwanis Clubs, Rotary Clubs, in conferences, senior citizen centers, and later in their school for their fellow classmates.
- It gave them confidence and positive attitudes towards learning, giving presentations, and receiving positive feedbacks.
- Human contact, modeling, and positive emotional reinforcement are additional important aspects to this development.

Mrs Woolson contacted different organizations and arranged for the children to give presentations. Then she gave us copies of the correspondence that she received from them, which provided encouragement and confirmations of their work.

Mrs Woolson was an angel with a bright, and happy face, with a kind, calm, patient and sweet voice. She worked to develop all the good qualities that characterize good speech, such as content (the tact, wisdom and sweetness of His Words), intonation, volume, style, calmness, and enthusiasm. As for more effectiveness, it was delivered by young children who showed natural purity of heart, sincerity, enthusiasm, and unity practiced in the Faith.

- The qualities and character which developed through memorization of the Writings, and practice with an angelic teacher, Mrs Woolson, became deep rooted in their heart and mind.
- It guided their thoughts and endeavors, formed their attitudes towards the life and the purpose of living, service and teaching the faith.
- It was a blessing for us to see her. I asked her about meeting the Guardian and her services, but she was such a radiant and humble soul that she did not talk about herself. She was focused on her students and their progress.

This is a program that can be copied and continued for young children.

We can see how Ruhi books can help the development of a new culture which is Bahá'í Global Culture, which never existed before.[9]

In Evanston, Mary Louise Suhm of the Bahá'í National

Center in Wilmette invited Gayle to attend training programmes for people going to serve abroad, introducing
her project, accompanied by children who would each
recite a memorized speech. In a letter written to Mary
Louise Suhm on 28 August 1992, Gayle wrote:

> Often I recall the wonderful support you gave the
> children's public speaking project, when you were the
> head of the Pioneering Office, in the early days of the
> development of the project. You have my eternal grati-
> tude. In those days when I was struggling to promote
> the highly-creative concept of 'Abdu'l-Bahá about chil-
> dren giving speeches, the doors you opened for the
> effort through the Pioneering Institutes were of invalu-
> able assistance. To this day, persons who attended one
> or another of those institutes mention the enjoyment
> they derived from hearing the children speak. So I am
> greatly indebted to you always and admire your percep-
> tion and vision as to the importance of promoting the
> concept. I am continuing with that effort.[10]

The impact of such presentations is conveyed in a letter
Kathy Cornyn wrote to Gayle from her post in China:

> Dear Gayle Woolson,
>   Today I am thinking of you. This seems to happen
> a lot. I have taught the children here to memorize
> English dialogues and songs using your methods. I am
> also very inspired by your patience and persistence. It
> was good to know a person with these qualities and so

to have an example to follow . . . These people are very special. I am learning to be relaxed, calm, diligent and gentle/strong from them.

I hope that some of the people who will come here will have an opportunity to know you because it has helped me so much to know you and learn from you.

Among the civic organizations that invited the children to speak was the Rotary Club in Evanston:

A Rotary Club of Evanston . . . accepted my offer to present a children's public speaking program at one of their luncheon meetings. Our theme was 'The Promise of World Peace'. Four children participated, and I made the opening and closing remarks. About 100 men and women were present. Many of them were professionals of various fields. Copies of the statement of The Universal House of Justice, 'The Promise of World Peace' were made available to the audience.

The child speakers presented their talks in this order: Errol Doris, Jr., age 11 – 'Looking into the Future'. Allen and Mark Eghrari, (twins), age 6 – 'Humanity is One Family', each giving one half of the text. Saba Firoozi, age 13 – 'Children Can Help Build a Better World'.

Prior to the speeches, one of the children, Errol Doris, presented a violin selection, accompanied on the piano by Dr Rosamond Brenner.

In a thank-you letter to me from the Rotary Club expressing gratitude for what they termed 'an outstanding program', it stated, among other remarks:

'The "promise of world peace" seems much more promising when young children who are imbued with a deep religious commitment are able to speak so convincingly.'[11]

The following weekly newsletter of the club gave this eloquent summary of the message conveyed in the project:

UNITY PEACE STRESSED BY BAHAI SPEAKERS

Four children, including twins age six, delivered short but wide-ranging summaries of the Bahá'í Faith in which human brotherhood, peace and unity were stressed. They declared that peace on earth and peace of mind and heart were inevitable, particularly in this era which appears so stressful and full of nationalistic animosities. According to the Bahá'í Faith, this kind of conflict among men is the 'dying gasp' of a world that is becoming increasingly a planetary family. Advances in technology and knowledge, instead of leading to world destruction, will direct mankind eventually to unity based on a world-wide consensus that all men were created by the same God and, in that sense, share a common destiny. According to Mrs Woolson, who introduced the children and who formerly worked in Latin America for the Agency for International Development (AID), all major religions have prophesied the inevitability of peace among men. These principles are implicit in the Hindu, Zoroastrian, Judaic, Islamic and Christian faiths, she said.[12]

Gayle also invited the children to reflect about their experience with the project.

Maya Ashby (8) wrote:

> When I give my speech in front of an audience, it makes me happy . . . After I finish speaking, my happiness makes me feel like I want to cry because the people stand up to clap.

Jenna Burton (9) said:

> It makes my life more important by learning to say a speech of high quality. It is a nice way to learn about the . . . principles that are in the speech. It makes me happy and I understand that I am helping to build a better world.

Camille Henderson (10) explained:

> It makes me feel like I am doing something great. If more people were doing this, it would be very important for the world, and more people would learn about the high ideals of the Bahá'í Faith which aim at uniting mankind as one family.

Jian Khodadad (11) offered this:

> It is a very exciting process in your life and makes you feel that you have an important role to play. You

become inspired by the beautiful words and concepts, and you learn something that you never knew before. You learn the meanings of words and learn to memorize. You are teaching and inspiring adults instead of adults teaching you. It makes me feel close to the Faith.

Shani Eftekhari (13) mentioned both the learning and doing involved:

It is a wonderful project because it helps a child to develop and to have a better understanding of the important teachings of Bahá'u'lláh. It makes me happy to see the enthusiastic response of the audience after I give my speech.

Saba Firoozi (12) emphasized these thoughts:

I feel it is very important for me to be able to give a Bahá'í speech in front of large or small audiences. It is wonderful to speak the words of Bahá'u'lláh, 'Abdu'l-Bahá, and Shoghi Effendi, and of some important persons of the Bahá'í Faith. It makes me feel inspired when I see how people react with amazement when they hear me give a talk because they think it extremely difficult for a child to memorize and speak eloquently. The best part of it, though, is that I am teaching the Bahá'í Faith.

Errol Doris, Jr. (11) wrote:

> Giving a Bahá'í speech before an audience makes me
> very happy. It helps me to learn more about the Bahá'í
> Writings. When I finish saying my speeches, I always
> feel like I have done something special. Before I give
> my talks, I say prayers so that when I am speaking,
> Bahá'u'lláh will inspire me and help me to speak pow-
> erfully and shine like a brilliant star.

Arya Czerniejewski (who started public speaking training at age 7; the following comment was expressed when
she was 15 years old) reflected:

> I think that the children's public speaking project
> broadened my knowledge of the Faith and it is a great
> preparation to further teach the Faith. It gave me con-
> fidence to speak in public and I developed confidence
> in myself. My memorization capacity increased. There
> are so many things that it did which I cannot express
> in words.

Sia Abu (12) added:

> I like giving Bahá'í speeches because it makes me
> feel like I am doing something for God. It shows the
> audience how much we children can learn and how
> we can teach them more about the Bahá'í Faith. Also
> it encourages them to investigate further the Bahá'í
> Teachings. Public speaking has helped to build my

self-confidence. May my efforts to work at memorizing, thinking, and expressing myself help to encourage adults and youth to realize that they also have potential to teach the Faith in the same manner.

Erin Bodan (10) echoed other thoughts:

It is very exciting for me to see the people in front of me listening and watching attentively and it is an inspiration and joy to have the opportunity to speak to them about the beautiful Bahá'í teachings.

Barissa Kumsa (10):

The development of the ability to give a Bahá'í talk has made me feel more confident about myself. Before I started the public speaking training, I didn't go up in front of any gathering because I was shy about speaking. The opportunity to learn a speech and present it on programs has raised me to another level. The more I gave my talk the more confident I became, and it made me happy to present such great words of Bahá'u'lláh and 'Abdu'l-Bahá.

Joseph Senchuck (13):

Learning, practicing and presenting a Bahá'í speech was a worthwhile experience. It is a great idea to get children to speak about Bahá'í subjects because it makes a convincing impression regarding the points contained in the speeches. It is a good exercise for the children's ability and guides them to turn more to the Bahá'í Writings. My memory improved and I even got better at remembering ordinary things. I also became used to getting up in front of large audiences. It increased my courage. Before this experience, I was timid about speaking in front of a group of people.

Syda Segovia (11):

It was fun to learn speeches and give them on programs. I felt that I was doing something important and helping people to understand about the Bahá'í Faith. After I learned the words, I became self-confident. Even though I would be nervous before I would speak, once I started, the nervousness would leave me and I knew that God was right there with me, reinforcing me. I feel that children can play an important part. If they put their minds to it, they can render a good service to the Faith through learning to speak.[13]

Reflections on the process

The project began with Gayle's awareness of how memorizing the Creative Word had affected the development of her own character. Knowing that 'Abdu'l-Bahá confirmed this idea, she tried her ideas first with a small group of children. Choosing appropriate quotations, she established a pattern of individual learning followed by a group presentation in which each child recited a different passage. Over time, she chose quotations and fashioned them into speeches appropriate for each age level. She developed relationships with a number of organizations such as the Rotary and Kiwanis Clubs that were eager to invite the children to speak. She developed a system of frequent phone calls to each child to allow practice without the difficulty of travel. Her greatest challenge in expanding and sustaining the project lay in finding others willing to put in the time and dedication to make the project sustainable in other communities. However, through correspondence, the project came to be used in several countries, if only with individual families. The importance of teaching children, having them memorize prayers and passages, and encouraging them to express what they learn in service are all elements now given a different form of expression in the Institute Process current in the Bahá'í community. In many ways, early believers like Gayle gave form to the very process of learning and practice that is now finding systematized expression in the worldwide community.

23

Desire of the Nations

In September 1991, the Universal House of Justice invited all living Knights of Bahá'u'lláh, together with 19 representatives from each country, as guests of the World Centre for the upcoming observance of the Centenary of the Ascension of Bahá'u'lláh to be held in Haifa in May 1992. This would include a reception at the Seat of the Universal House of Justice; a ceremony at Bahjí for the placement of the Roll of Honour of the Knights of Bahá'u'lláh at the entrance of the Most Holy Shrine; a devotional programme at night in commemoration of the Ascension of Bahá'u'lláh; the ascent to and circumambulation of the Shrine of the Báb and a viewing of the portrait of Bahá'u'lláh at the Seat of the Universal House of Justice.

As the time of the commemoration drew near, the Universal House of Justice wrote in its Riḍván Message to the Bahá'ís of the World:

> Only a few weeks from now, in the sacred precincts of the Shrine of Bahá'u'lláh, a gathering of solemn purpose will take place to mark the one hundredth anniversary of the Ascension of the Desire of the Nations. The scroll bearing the Roll of Honour of the Knights of Bahá'u'lláh will, on the previous morning,

28 May, have been deposited, as indicated by our beloved Guardian, at the entrance door of the inner Sanctuary of the Most Holy Shrine, there to remain a symbol of the historic victory that rewarded the unswerving determination of the lovers of the Blessed Beauty who, in response to the call of the mighty Ten Year Crusade, planted the banner of His Faith in virgin territories throughout the world.[1]

Guests were allowed to spend six nights in Haifa and several additional days in other parts of Israel, especially to help people adjust to the time when travelling long distances. Three thousand people came from 200 countries.

Still blessed with good health, though one month shy of her 80th birthday, Gayle made the journey and attended all the events. In her own words,

The night of the transcendental program to commemorate the Centenary of the Ascension of Bahá'u'lláh on May 29, 1992, the many Bahá'ís lodging at hotels were picked up by buses about 1 a.m. to be driven to Bahjí. Arriving approximately at 1:45 a.m., the process of the seating took place efficiently on those exquisite extensive grounds. The program was scheduled to start at 2:30 a.m. While waiting, we could bask in silence in the beauty and impressiveness of the setting. Even though hundreds of believers were gathered, the silence of reverence, devotion and awe was striking. We sat spellbound by the majesty of the event. Each person felt completely alone under the star-lit sky, with no sound to distract during those precious medi-tative moments. If the ground had been a floor, one could rightfully say, figuratively speaking, that if a pin should drop, it could be heard.

The place where I was seated in that spacious garden which surrounded the holy Shrine of Bahá'u'lláh was the side where there are terraces. Rows of seats were placed on those terraces. From where I sat, there was a good view of the entrance area of the Shrine. Candles of a special kind lined the edges of the landing or path of each terrace. The candles were thick and short, of long duration, and each was contained in a low, thick glass, like a drinking glass. All the grounds had rows of these candles, six thousand of them, placed sym-metrically in radial form – like wide-apart spokes of a wheel extending from the Shrine.

The attractive entrance of the Shrine was brightly lit. In addition to its own chandelier and a light at each side of the door, there were spot lights placed in a nearby tree that shone upon it. It was a beautiful sight to behold, together with the illumination of the grounds by means of those numerous candles.

. . . As soon as the chanting and readings from the holy writings of Bahá'u'lláh and 'Abdu'l-Bahá started, it seemed as though the beautiful resonance of the words was vibrating throughout the world. The beauty and power of the voices, and the marked perfection and potency of the microphone system were extraor-dinary. Each word was clear as a bell reaching easily that large audience.

. . . Those indelible moments of the program were also reminiscent of what had occurred a hundred years before, following the passing of Bahá'u'lláh and His appointment of 'Abdu'l-Bahá as His successor. It is wonderfully described by Shoghi Effendi in these words:

The cloud of despondency that had momentarily settled on the disconsolate lovers of the Cause of Baha'u'llah was lifted. The continuity of that unerring guidance vouchsafed to it since its birth was now assured. The significance of the solemn affirmation that this is 'the day which shall not be followed by night' was now clearly apprehended. An orphan community had recognized in 'Abdu'l-Bahá, in its hour of desperate need, its Solace, its Guide, its Mainstay and Champion . . . the Covenant that was to perpetuate the influence of that Faith, insure its integrity, safeguard it from schism, and stimulate its world-wide expansion, had been fixed on an inviolable basis. (*God Passes By*, pp. 245, 244–5)

Following the recitation of the Tablet of Visitation of Bahá'u'lláh, which closed this part of the program, we circumambulated His Shrine on a wide path. That same reverential silence and solemnity that reigned during the program was also prevalent on this occasion of the procession. Soon the light of the dawn was beginning to appear and we could enjoy even more fully the paradise-like gardens on one side of the path and luscious trees and bushes on the other. The sweet singing of the birds accompanied us.[2]

She continues:

The Universal House of Justice magnificently describes the events that transpired in the Holy Land in this moving and inspiring message written shortly after the conclusion of that unforgettable occasion.

To the Baháʼís of the World

As we reflect on the events which a few days ago marked the commemoration in the Holy Land of the Centenary of the Ascension of Baháʼuʼlláh, we feel impelled to express to the Baháʼí world our sense of wonderment at the exalted character of what transpired. The nature of the Anniversary was in itself awe-inspiring and evocative of profound emotion. But the gathering of some 3,000 Baháʼís, including 113 Knights of Baháʼuʼlláh, representing no less than 200 countries and dependent territories – the widest diversity of human beings ever to have assembled on a Baháʼí occasion – filled the eyes with the vision of a garden of humanity that overwhelmed the senses, inducing a spirit of beauty, joy and splendor. Bahji was never more resplendent. And we offer prayers of thanksgiving to our beloved Lord that so fitting an assemblage could have been realized on this special Anniversary, indicating the amazing extent to which the pervasive power of His influence has triumphed throughout the world.

May the evident blessings flowing from this heavenly experience infuse the dear friends everywhere with new strength and fresh encouragement, emboldening their efforts and enlarging their capacity to proclaim the Name and promote the Cause of Bahá'u'lláh during the course of the Holy Year so auspiciously begun.

The Universal House of Justice

7 June 1992

24

'Oneness with this Infinite Life'

To the end of her days, Gayle kept the notebook entitled '1940' that she had carried to Costa Rica.[1] In her late 80s and 90s, she still found meaning in words such as these, copied then, as a young woman in her 20s:

> The great central fact in human life, in your life and in mine, is the coming into a conscious, vital realization of our oneness with this Infinite Life, and the opening of ourselves fully to this Divine Inflow.[2]

She remained open to that same inflow as she navigated the final six years of her life. In 2005, Gayle went to live at a skilled care facility, ManorCare Wilmette. A bequest from her sister, Victoria, covered the cost of a private room for a period of time. Gayle had originally hoped to use these funds to return to South America, as she had expressed in a letter to the Universal House of Justice written when she was almost 90 years old. Victoria had hoped to pioneer to Fiji but passed away before realizing this wish. Gayle wanted to pioneer in her name. In the mysterious way that things sometimes work out differently than we imagine, Gayle, with quiet grace, turned

With Allen and Mark Eghrari (both 5 years old) for the Children's Public Speaking Project, September 1988

Diane (15) and Shirin (9) Werle learned speeches for a conference in Ecuador, 17 April 1989

At the Rotary Club, Skokie, Illinois, 28 August 1990. Front row, left to right: Allen Eghrari (7), Jhontia Williams (7), Mark Eghrari (7). Back row, left to right: Gayle Woolson, Errol Doris Jr. (13), Saba Firoozi (14), with Peter Butler, the Rotary member who introduced the presentation

Knights of Bahá'u'lláh view the Roll of Honour bearing their names

Amatu'l-Bahá Rúḥíyyih Khánum places the Roll of Honour at the threshold of the Shrine of Bahá'u'lláh

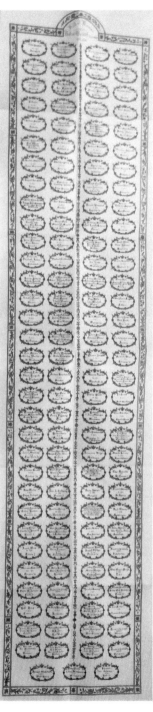

Knights of Baháʼuʼlláh gathered in the Holy Land, May 1992

Gayle, her niece Trudy Abas, and her sister-in-law Marge Abas

Dancing at Trudy's wedding, and surrounded by her family, 2000

her time at the nursing home into her last pioneering post.

For any of us, navigating later stages of life involves hard transitions. Although Gayle made the necessary adjustments with grace, they were not always easy. While in a private room, she still had a place to offer hospitality to her friends. She had control over her time and could continue her pattern of staying up late at night. She had several places where familiar pictures and books could offer a sense of beauty that was familiar. As time went by, her funds were depleted and she moved to a room shared with others. Now her space was more limited, her view not only of the pictures and books that fitted in the new space, but of roommates behind curtains that tried to offer a degree of privacy. At the head of her bed, the Regional Council hung a beautiful portrait of 'Abdu'l-Bahá. A member of the Wilmette Assembly brought a lovely photograph of the terraces leading to the Shrine of the Báb to set on a table at its foot. Lights out came promptly at 8:00 p.m. She did not complain, nor did she harbour the negative. When not in bed, Gayle could always be found with a ready smile and greeting in the visiting area or wherever activities were taking place. To any staff member offering help, she would say, 'You are an angel!' And to friends visiting: 'You are all angels! How did you get here?'

To find Gayle, one would come up a slow and creaky elevator to the third floor and walk across the hall past the nurse's station to the dining room, where she would usually be sitting in her chair by the table where she ate meals. She would greet both long-time friends and new-comers with a delighted smile, asking, 'How did you get here, dear? Thank you for coming . . .' If it happened to be meal time and she had a tray, she would take a dish of food and offer it to you, saying, 'This is for you, dear.' She would say, 'I wish I did not need to eat.' For several years, she would take only a few bites, despite the encouragement of friends and staff, unless sweet cake or chocolate ice cream appeared, which she always enjoyed. Sometimes, when a friend shared songs the residents could sing together, Gayle would conduct from her chair, following every note with delight. Her niece, Trudy, came often. For as long as possible, she would take Gayle out to lunch or even home for the weekend.

As the details of this evanescent life became less salient for Gayle, what remained was the essence of a character forged over many decades of loving humanity with heart and soul. In her first years at ManorCare, a small group of residents became friends and sat together for meals. They were people of capacity, all now living with various limitations of age. They appreciated each one's stories of times past, while sharing a quiet understanding of how it felt to have the scope of an adventurous life narrow to the circumference of a table or the area of a few rooms. One friend was a man who had spent time in the Galápagos Islands! He invited Gayle to read at the weekly Shabbat services given at ManorCare, which she did for several years. Her friend's brother said that he learned to read the service with renewed spirit from hearing the reverence and expression in Gayle's voice as she read (without glasses!). As had happened with Gayle's siblings, one by one this circle of friends slipped away.

However, Gayle kept on making connections with each person who crossed her path. She attended resident council meetings, pen in hand, though it's hard to know if her mind was most attuned to current planning or to Plans of the past. Other religious visitors found in her a gentle welcome and willingness to participate in their ministrations, whatever their spiritual path and practice. One resident in a wheelchair reported that she had spilled her popcorn and Gayle picked it all up for her. She would converse in fluent Spanish with a Cuban woman whose sister suffered from severe dementia. The woman's grandfather had been significant in Cuba's history; she herself was now a professor. Gayle knew her homeland because of visits to Cuba in the 1940s. Another woman came to help a relative with her meals. While doing that, she would converse with Gayle in Arabic and learned the names of Gayle's eight siblings. Gayle's younger brother, Edward, would call weekly. When friends visited from countries where she had lived, it would spark alive the memory of people known and experiences shared. Even in the last years, Gayle would at times get a very wise look in her eyes and respond to questions with brief but profound thought. The staff became her friends. One staff member, Ms Dotson, informally but consistently became her personal attendant, fed her dinner, protected her things, and helped her get ready for bed each night for several years. Ms Dotson's radiance and spirit of service were similar to Gayle's.

Aspects of her character that had shone years ago in the Galápagos Islands were still operative at ManorCare. When she went to those inhospitable islands, Gayle had demonstrated an unusual capacity to see that no matter how tattered the envelope of a person's life might appear, there was a letter inside of inestimable potential, of value divine. When one contrasts her own descriptions of that difficult island post with other accounts, one is struck by how she hardly seemed to see what others described as a depressing and morally degraded environment, deprived of all but the rudiments of survival. Although realistic and street-smart about the conditions, Gayle's experience was of a virgin territory that would become part of a new spiritual civilization, of a 'paradise because reached in time' in response to the Guardian's call.

Before moving to ManorCare, she had reckoned in writing with what such a move would represent for her. Once having defined and accepted this possibility, when the time came, she drew upon a wellspring of strength she had earlier articulated to friends in Cedar Rapids (1998): 'We have a tremendous faith. We are given courage by these statements (of the Bahá'í Writings). That is exactly what promoted the pioneers of all times, from the time of the early Dawnbreakers . . . We don't strive with our own energy. We strive with the energy of God.'

One day in the late spring of 2011, the ManorCare staff sent Gayle to the hospital emergency room with abnormal fluctuations of her heart. She was then admitted to the hospital, with friends taking turns staying by her side.

At one point, as witnessed by a friend, Gayle shook her head to decline food and drink and attempted to take off her oxygen tube. Attuned to the moment, her friend and companion of the moment asked if she felt ready to go. Her eyes lit up. Resting her head against a pillow, her fragile face broke into a smile. She slowly raised her friend's hand to kiss it, lowered it down, and then gently clapped. Softly, she said, 'Oh yes!' Later, as witness, another was asked to repeat the question. Gayle responded with the same illumined smile, the same words, confirming her wish.

With her conscious agreement, she was then transferred to Midwest Palliative & Hospice CareCenter in Skokie, where she had a peaceful, light-filled room with large windows and plenty of room for visitors. For her last eleven days, by her own insistence, she had no food, only enough water to moisten her mouth, and no medicine except a few doses slipped in by nurses who could not believe she meant what she said.[3]

When one entered her room, she would take one's hand, kiss it, and, in the first days, say 'Thank you!' The doctor, nurses, and nurses' assistants were touched by her serenity and heartfelt love for each person. One day, her door was closed for a long time while nursing assistants were helping her. Upon opening the door, they explained that they had been singing to her in Spanish because she loved to hear that language sung. The chaplain would sit and read prayers from Gayle's prayer book. Two harpists, trained to attune their music to the breath and pulse of the patient to bring relaxation and peace, came several times, moved by Gayle's response. Gayle would offer a welcoming smile and then relax ever more deeply, her breathing becoming open and deep, a smile on her face.

Friends and family came, including children, singing songs and reciting prayers, evoking impressions of the work she had done for so many years. The staff from ManorCare came to bid her farewell. One later commented to this writer, 'You have to understand. This is the closest we will come to being with Mother Teresa.'

In the final days, friends accompanied her day and night. On 30 May 2011, a few days shy of her 98th birthday, she peacefully breathed her last and 'put away this mortal frame'.

25

Tributes and a Loving Farewell

Eighty-one people gathered at Scott Funeral Home in Wilmette for the funeral service of Knight of Bahá'u'lláh Gayle Woolson, followed by a graveside service at Skokie Memorial Gardens, where the Prayer for the Dead was read. This was followed later by a reception.

The service included tributes from the Universal House of Justice, the National Spiritual Assembly of the United States, the Local Spiritual Assemblies of Evanston and of Wilmette, and from the family.

The message from the Universal House of Justice read as follows:

> We were grieved to learn of the passing of handmaiden of Bahá'u'lláh Gayle Woolson, who won the immortal distinction of being designated by the beloved Guardian as a Knight of Bahá'u'lláh for the Galapagos Islands during the Ten Year Global Crusade. Her many decades of service, distinguished by the historic efforts to advance the Cause of God in those islands and throughout Latin America, are remembered with loving admiration and respect. Also recalled with grateful appreciation are the devoted services Mrs Woolson rendered at the Bahá'í

World Centre. We offer our fervent supplications at the Sacred Threshold for the progress of her noble soul throughout the heavenly realms.

The National Spiritual Assembly of the Bahá'ís of the United States sent the following to Gayle's family:

The National Spiritual Assembly was saddened to learn of the passing on Monday of dearly loved Gayle Woolson, a devoted Bahá'í whose wholehearted, energetic, and distinguished services to the Faith we hold sacred will long be warmly and gratefully remembered. While mourning the loss of her gentle, kind, and endearing personality, we join you in celebrating her nearly a century of life exceedingly well spent.

Active in efforts to further the progress of its vision of a peaceful and just World Order from her first embrace of the Faith while still barely out of her teens, Gayle was early drawn to pioneering service on the international stage and participated in efforts spanning some three decades – and several Teaching Plans – to launch Bahá'í communities in numerous countries throughout Latin America. An adept speaker and writer in Spanish, she was later in her life invited to the Bahá'í World Centre, where she engaged in translation work. An author in her own right, Gayle's *Divine Symphony*, originally published in Spanish, was for years a popular introduction to the central Bahá'í principle of the oneness of religious truth progressively revealed, down the ages, by a series of divine Manifestations.

Valuable though all these assiduous efforts were and are, it was Gayle's brave decision to settle in the Galapagos Islands – in response to the beloved Guardian, Shoghi Effendi's, 1953 call for pioneers to open to the Faith's unifying teachings the vast number of countries in the world that were still wholly unacquainted with them – that earned her the appellation 'Knight of Bahá'u'lláh' and the everlasting esteem and respect of the worldwide Bahá'í community. We honor the intrepid spirit that enabled her to undertake such a service, as we recall with great fondness the loving heart that impelled her to reach out to countless children, patiently teaching them the value of memorizing and reciting with developed oratory skill excerpts from the Bahá'í sacred writings.

We extend to you, her dear family – as well as to her legion of friends and admirers – our deepest sympathies on the loss you have sustained, assuring you that Gayle's name will be affectionately mentioned in our prayers beneath the lofty dome of the majestic Bahá'í House of Worship, where we will offer supplications for the eternal progress of her generous and luminous soul.

With tender Bahá'í love,
Kenneth E. Bowers
Secretary

The Spiritual Assembly of Evanston, Illinois, where Gayle had resided for almost 30 years, sent the following 'To the family and loved ones of Gayle Woolson':

For a number of years the Evanston Baháʼí community had the special honor of being the home of one of the few Knights of Baháʼuʼlláh, those intrepid souls who pushed back the veil of darkness and illuminated new lands with the light of Baháʼuʼlláh, and whose names are forever inscribed on the Roll of Honor at the Threshold of the Shrine of Baháʼuʼlláh.

Our beloved Gayle Woolson was known to the world as the pioneer who only a year after the launching of the Ten Year Crusade opened the Galapagos Islands to the Faith. But what many forget is that she had already been pioneering for fourteen years, having responded in 1940 to the Guardian's call for pioneers to Latin America. Her time in Latin America included election to four different National Spiritual Assemblies, and appointment by the Hands of the Cause of God to the first Auxiliary Board of the Western Hemisphere, serving in that capacity until 1968.

Gayle was also known in many countries as the author of the book *The Divine Symphony*, which helped many come to understand progressive revelation, to love the Messengers of the past, and to recognize Baháʼuʼlláh. First published in Spanish, the book was subsequently published in English and other languages, and for as long as she was able she continued to work on revisions.

But to the Baháʼís of Evanston, her long-time community, she was known as an angel of unlimited courtesy and graciousness, of humility and service. Many among us will forever be grateful for her efforts and patience in the many hours she spent training our children to give 'speeches of high quality', laying a foundation for their spiritual certitude and self-confidence that has served them well in academia and life.

And when she moved from our community to Wilmette, members of our community continued to visit her and to witness how her sweetness and love captured the hearts of the residents and staff at Manor Care, as the trappings of the world faded away leaving only the unveiled light of her pure soul to attract the hearts of those around her.

Today, on the anniversary of her 98th birthday, we gather to celebrate the life of Gayle Woolson, and with our prayers to wish her well she is accompanied by the messenger of Joy on her continuing journey of service to Bahá'u'lláh. May we each in some small way take our lessons from her life, and through our services in her memory contribute to the progress of her soul.

With loving Bahá'í greetings,
The Spiritual Assembly of the Bahá'ís of Evanston

From the Spiritual Assembly of Wilmette, under whose guidance Gayle lived for her last six years, the family received the following:

The Spiritual Assembly of the Bahá'ís of Wilmette shares with you its deep sense of loss, and at the same time, its profound joy for Mrs Gayle Woolson, Knight of Bahá'u'lláh, who is continuing her journey of service in the spiritual world. Among her countless other ways of serving around the world, we witnessed first-hand her teaching the children.

Gayle's passion and ability to teach children how to speak publicly with confidence and how to carry themselves with grace of movement was deep and true. She made lasting impressions on the lives of many of the young adults that we see in our communities who are now themselves active teachers in the faith, exhibiting a confidence in their speech and a grace in their movement that can largely be attributed to her influence.

Gayle was precise in the instructions she provided the children, telling them how to stand erectly and enunciate clearly, thus helping them to become confident and capable speakers. She was patient without limit, always with a smile of encouragement on her face, which at the same time carried a message of her high expectations and belief in their capacity. When children were speakers at Bahá'í gatherings or at House of Worship programs, one could always identify those who had the Gayle Woolson experience.

We are so grateful to have witnessed so great a treasure, one that is present to us whenever we see and hear her students, her living legacy.

With loving regards,
The Spiritual Assembly of the Bahá'ís of Wilmette
Lorelei McClure
Secretary

Gayle was survived by eleven nieces, five nephews, and two sisters-in-law. Trudy and Hans Osvoll, and Moira and Daniel Moser (having driven many hours to attend) represented the family at the service. Moira later wrote:

> . . . there were about 100 people in attendance . . . We were greeted with so much love and introduced to those who were most involved. Everyone was so gracious and happy to meet us. Those who were near or with Gayle during her last days/hours wanted to share with us how peaceful she was and how aware up until about the last 24 hours or so. She just slept peacefully away with no struggle at all even up to her last breath.
>
> She was highly respected and loved by those who cared for her, both at Manor Home and the hospice facility where she was for the last 12 days before she expired.
>
> There was a harpist who had come to her room almost daily and played for her. This same harpist was near the closed casket and played her harp before and during some parts of the service.
>
> The service was opened by a very soft-spoken man who had met Gayle back when she first fell. The family befriended her and she was visiting at his home when he was alerted to the fact that she really should not be living alone. So that is what got things started.
>
> Trudy had been involved with the moves and very involved with the people who subsequently ended up taking care of Gayle's affairs. The two most involved were Juliet and Ellen – delightful, caring women who were totally devoted to Gayle. They both did short tributes to Gayle. There were readings and a song was sung.

. . . Trudy did a wonderful job with her eulogy for Gayle . . . She was able to bring a little humor to the room, as everyone appreciated how fitting it was to Gayle and who she was. Right up to the end, she was holding the hands of her visitors, kissing their hands, and calling them 'dear'. All attending could relate.

The service lasted an hour and then the guests filed out past the closed casket, paying their last respects. We went out last and waited out by the hearse for the pall bearers to bring the casket out. Daniel and Hans were asked to be pall bearers and helped move the casket to the hearse – and then from the hearse to the gravesite.

I am so very, very glad I went . . . I was totally honored and humbled to have been a part of Gayle's send off. She was a very special lady and touched many, many lives – she will live on in many hearts and be remembered for a long time.

In her eulogy, Trudy shared reminiscences sent by several family members:

I am not sure where to start, so I will begin by saying, 'Hello Dear.'

When I was asked if I wanted to speak at my Aunt Gayle's funeral, I wasn't quite sure what to say. There is so much to remember. So I sent a message to my sisters, brother, and cousins and asked if they had any memories to share. Here is what I received:

Sharon Abas writes:

. . . I didn't even have to think about this one. The one thing I remember that I learned from Aunt Gayle is she always said 'You should learn at least one new thing every day.' I still try to follow that advice to this day and I tried to pass that on to my son as well, but I don't know if it stuck in his head as it did in mine all these years.

Dawn Moore writes:

I found her to be a very nice lady, and she always had respect for everyone. She was very caring of her family; she wrote my mother many, many letters from El Salvador. And of course, she was very dedicated to the Bahá'í Faith. She was great at public speaking and said the Eulogy at my mother's funeral. She got a lot of joy teaching Bahá'í children public speaking. This was only one of her children's projects that kept her busy. I wish I had known her better; our times together were not many.

Moira Moser writes:

Aunt Gayle was such a dear, sweet, kind person; I recall her saying in her very soft-spoken voice and in a very non-threatening manner 'if you cannot say something nice about someone, do not say anything at all'. She certainly lived by that and it really is very good advice to follow. I am sure that she never hurt anyone in her entire life. It seems she died very peacefully, which is the way she lived.

Lisa Rebeck writes:

When I think of Aunt Gayle the first word that comes to mind is 'Dear'. Everybody was 'Dear'. She was always so sweet and I am thankful to have had the opportunity with my mom to say goodbye just a couple of days before she died. She was a 'Dear' sweet aunt. Even in her dying day, she took my hand and so tenderly brought it to her mouth, and kissed it. In her face I could see her saying, 'Thank you, Dear, for coming so far to see me. It was so nice of you, Dear.'

Ron Hick, who some of you may know, writes:

I will always remember my Aunt Gayle as the woman in my family who traveled and lived in exotic places like the Galápagos Islands, Panama, Ecuador, and the Holy Land. I also knew her as the woman in my family who travelled and lived in these places because of her passion for her faith and the desire to spread the word about the Bahá'í Faith so that others in these remote and exotic places might learn about and join in her passion.

I later found out how effective she was in spreading her passion. In 1992, after the Bahá'í World Congress in New York, my wife and I had the privilege to meet with and provide hospitality to some Bahá'ís from Panama who were members of the Guaymi Tribe, one of the indigenous peoples of that country. I gained instant credibility with them when they found out I was Gayle

Woolson's nephew. They knew the history of the Bahá'í Faith in that area and knew of Gayle who, because of her passion, was the first Bahá'í who traveled to the province where they lived to let people know about the Faith.

. . . and from me (Trudy Osvoll)

I found her to be exotic. She lived in these far off places. To me as a young girl I thought that was so cool. That may be part of why I chose the travel industry for a career. She loved to take pictures. She loved to write. She was devoted to her faith.

I moved to Illinois in the fall of 1983. My Aunt Gayle was already living here in Evanston. I lived farther out in the suburbs. But we connected periodically. I would pick her up and take her to lunch or bring her out to the suburbs for a weekend or take her shopping. I got married 11 years ago. She danced at my wedding.

She invited me to join her at some of her events. The Children's program for one. As I heard each one of the children speak, I could only smile, as they sounded exactly like her . . . word for word.

I always knew where to find her. Every time I had guests in town, I would take them on a tour, which included a drive along the lake taking us by the Bahá'í House of Worship. We would stop in and there would be Gayle.

Then about 6½ years ago, I received a phone call from my mom. She said she had gotten a phone call from someone saying that Gayle had fallen and could I go and check in on her. I got to her apartment and for the first time I watched as she struggled with her keys, which she had marked so she could remember which one was for which door. She struggled as she made her way up the stairs. She told me when she was out she looked for the 2 bushes so she could remember where she lived. I knew she was getting meals on wheels, but I wasn't sure she knew how to use the microwave and was concerned that she might turn the oven on and forget. I knew she had a roommate, Eve, but she worked longer than usual hours and wasn't always there.

I invited a couple of my cousins to come into town and help me start cleaning up her apartment. We started to go through things and found bills piling up among other things making it apparent that she shouldn't be alone any more. Back at my home we started researching options for assisted living facilities. I wasn't sure if I should take her back to Minnesota, bring her out to the suburbs, or keep her near her beloved Temple and local community of friends. Then my cousins left. I felt this was going to be a very challenging task.

Then one wintry eve, Gayle was invited by friends to attend an event. She ended up spending the night and it was these friends who made known to others that she really could not be alone any more. Her community stepped up. Within very little time, care workers were assigned to take care of her. She was moved to Manor Care and the rest is history.

So now as I look around this room today, I can only say . . . Wow! I am overwhelmed at the people who are here today. Words cannot express the appreciation I feel for all of you taking such good care of my aunt.

Thank you to those from Manor Care that include her in all the activities. When I saw pictures of her at a Cub's game or dancing the hula at a luau, I could only smile. My goodness, she was in her 90s. I was told she attended all the religious services.

Thank you to the gentleman who found her on the sidewalk when she fell and stopped to assist her.

Thank you to the people who brought her to their home for an event in inclement weather and recognized that she really could no longer live alone.

Thank you to those who spent countless hours visiting and spending time with her, not only at Manor Care, but also the last 2 weeks in Hospice.

Thank you to . . . [those] who initially stepped up to the challenge to make sure that both her financial and medical affairs were in order and taken care of. This was a task that I knew I would not have been able to do on my own. I was so grateful for their support.

. . . and dear Juliet who has remained consistently by Gayle's side throughout this entire time.

I am so glad I had the opportunity to get to know you through all of this and I hope we will remain friends.

I know there are many other stories here to tell. Stories of how Gayle touched your lives in one way or another. I am glad now that this is her final resting place. This area truly was her home. Here is where her friends were. Here so close to her beloved Bahá'í Temple. Here she is at peace.

Thank you all for everything. Your support, your prayers, your care and devotion.

I know my Aunt Gayle would find this 'lovely' and I know her final words would be, 'Thank you, Dear.'

* * * * *

It seemed that the weaving, now removed from the loom, was complete. The last strands woven mirrored the beginning of the design, completing a life given to words such as these:

We must be like the fountain or spring
that is continually emptying itself of all that it has
and is continually being refilled from an invisible source.
To be continually giving out for the good of our fellows
Undeterred by the fear of poverty
and reliant on the unfailing bounty
of the Source of all wealth and all good –
this is the secret of right living.
Shoghi Effendi[1]

Bibliography

BOOKS AND PRINTED ARTICLES

'Abdu'l-Bahá. *Abdul Baha on Divine Philosophy*. Comp. I. F. Chamberlain. Boston: The Tudor Press, 1918.

— *Paris Talks: Addresses given by 'Abdu'l-Bahá in 1911* (1912). London: Bahá'í Publishing Trust, 12th ed.1995.

— *Selections from the Writings of 'Abdu'l-Bahá*. Comp. Research Department of the Universal House of Justice. Haifa: Bahá'í World Centre, 1978.

— *Tablets of the Divine Plan*. Wilmette, IL: Bahá'í Publishing Trust, rev. ed. 1977.

The Bahá'í World: An International Record. Vol. IV (1930–1932), Wilmette, IL: Bahá'í Publishing Committee, 1934; vol. VI (1934–1936), Wilmette, IL: Bahá'í Publishing Trust, 1937; vol. VII (1936–1938), Wilmette, IL: Bahá'í Publishing Trust, 1940; vol. IX (1940–1944), Wilmette, Bahá'í Publishing Trust, 1945; vol. X (1944–1946), Wilmette, IL: Bahá'í Publishing Trust, 1949; vol. XI (1946–1950), Wilmette, IL: Bahá'í Publishing Trust, 1953; vol. XII (1950–1954), Wilmette, IL: Bahá'í Publishing Trust, 1956; vol. XIII (1954–1963), Haifa, The Universal House of Justice, 1970; vol. XIV (1963–1968), Haifa: The Universal House of Justice, 1974; vol. XV (1968–1973), Haifa: Bahá'í World Centre, 1976; vol. XVIII (1979–1983), Haifa: Bahá'í World Centre, 1986.

Bahá'u'lláh. *The Hidden Words of Bahá'u'lláh*. Trans. Shoghi Effendi. Wilmette, IL: Bahá'í Publishing Trust, 1970; New Delhi: Bahá'í Publishing Trust, 1987.

— *Tablets of Bahá'u'lláh Revealed After the Kitáb-i-Aqdas*. Comp. Research Department of the Universal House of Justice. Haifa: Bahá'í World Centre, 1978.

Balyuzi, H. M. *'Abdu'l-Bahá*. Oxford: George Ronald, 1971.

Chapman, Anita Ioas. *Leroy Ioas: Hand of the Cause*. Oxford: George Ronald, 1998.

The Compilation of Compilations. Prepared by the Universal House of Justice 1963–1990. 2 vols. Sydney: Bahá'í Publications Australia, 1991.

Cornbleth, Hascle. 'Ilusiones', in *The Bahá'í World*, vol. XI (1946–1950), p. 757.

Dahl, Roger M. 'Three teaching methods used during North America's First Seven-Year Plan', in *Journal of Bahá'í Studies*, vol. 5 (1993), no. 3 (Association for Bahá'í Studies).

The Dawn-Breakers: Nabíl's Narrative of the Early Days of the Bahá'í Revelation. Trans. Shoghi Effendi. Wilmette, IL: Bahá'í Publishing Trust, 1932, 1999.

Degeberg, Gary. *The History of the Kadrie Family*, in USBNA, The Kadrie Family Papers.

Esslemont, J. E. *Bahá'u'lláh and the New Era* (1923). Wilmette IL: Bahá'í Publishing Trust, 1980.

Gilstrap, Dorothy Freeman. *From Copper to Gold*. Wilmette: Bahá'í Publishing Trust, 1999.

Ginés, Eugenio. 'The story of the Bahá'í Faith in Cuba', in *The Bahá'í World*, vol. IX (1940–1944), pp. 916–17.

Handal, Boris. *Eve Nicklin: She of the Brave Heart*. Self-published 2011.

Hein, Kurt. *Radio Bahá'í Ecuador: A Bahá'í Development Project.* Oxford: George Ronald, 1988.

Heller, Wendy. *Lidia: The Life of Lidia Zamenhof, Daughter of Esperanto.* Oxford: George Ronald, 1985.

Holley, Horace. 'International survey of current Bahá'í activites the the East and West', in *The Bahá'í World,* vol. XI (1946–1950).

Holmquist, June. *They Chose Minnesota: A Survey of the State's Ethnic Groups.* Minnesota Historical Society Press, 1992.

Hornby, Helen B. *Heroes of God: History of the Bahá'í Faith in Ecuador 1940–1979.* Quito: Arqtelier, 1984.

— (comp). *Lights of Guidance:A Bahá'í Reference File.* New Delhi: Bahá'í Publishing Trust, 1983.

Ives, Howard Colby. *Portals to Freedom.* Oxford: George Ronald, 1943.

Mathews, Loulie. 'Preface', in USBNA, *First Four Latin American Sessions Teaching Notes, International School Temerity Ranch, The Bahá'í One Hundredth Anniversary, 1844–1944.*

Miessler, Muriel. *Pioneering in Brazil: Our Glorious Spiritual Adventure: Memoirs of Muriel Miessler.* Rio de Janeiro: Editora Bahá'í-Brasil, 1986.

Merriam-Webster. *Collegiate Dictionary.* Springfield, Mass., 10th ed.1998.

The Ministry of the Custodians 1957–1963: An Account of the Stewardship of the Hands of the Cause. Haifa: Bahá'í World Centre, 1992.

Morrison, Gayle. *To Move the World: Louis Gregory and the Advancement of Racial Unity in America.* Wilmette, IL: Bahá'í Publishing Trust, 1982.

Newhall, Muriel Ives Barrow. *Mother's Stories: Recollections of Abdu'l-Baha.* Bahá'í Library Online, 1998, first published in 1970.

Perry, Anne Gordon, et al. *Green Acre on the Piscataqua.* Wilmette, IL: Bahá'í Publishing Trust, 2012.

Pfaff-Grossmann, Susanne. *Hermann Grossmann, Hand of the Cause of God: A Life for the Faith.* Oxford: George Ronald, 2009.

Rabbani, Rúḥíyyíh. *Poems of the Passing.* Oxford: George Ronald, 1996.

— *Prescription for Living.* Oxford: George Ronald, 1950.

— *The Priceless Pearl.* London: Bahá'í Publishing Trust, 1969.

Sears, Marguerite. *Marguerite . . . and More About Bill.* Eloy AZ: Desert Rose Publishing, 2003.

Shoghi Effendi. *The Advent of Divine Justice* (1939). Wilmette, IL: Bahá'í Publishing Trust, 1984, 1990.

— *Afire With the Vision.* Wilmette, IL: Bahá'í Publishing Trust, 2018.

— *God Passes By* (1944). Wilmette, IL: Bahá'í Publishing Trust, rev. ed. 1974.

— *Letters from the Guardian to Australia and New Zealand, 1923–1957.* Sydney: Australian Bahá'í Publishing, 1971.

— *Messages to the Bahá'í World, 1950–1957.* Wilmette, IL: Bahá'í Publishing Trust, 2nd ed. 1971.

— *This Decisive Hour.* Wilmette, IL: Bahá'í Publishing Trust, 1992, 2002.

Trine, Ralph Waldo. *In Tune with the Infinite.* Richmond: The Oaklea Press, 2002.

True, Edna, M. 'Progress in Latin America', in *The Bahá'í World*, vol. X (1944–1946), pp. 698–699.

Universal House of Justice, The. *A Wider Horizon: Selected Messages of the Universal House of Justice, 1983–1992.* Riviera Beach, FL: Palabra Publications, 1992.

— *Century of Light.* New Delhi: Bahá'í Publishing Trust, 2001.

— *Messages from the Universal House of Justice, 1963–1986: The Third Epoch of the Formative Age.* Comp. Geoffry W. Marks. Wilmette, IL: Bahá'í Publishing Trust, 1996.

Woolson, Gayle. *The Divine Symphony.* Buenos Aires: Ebila, Bahá'í Publishing Trust, 1992.

— *Rumbo Hacia el Futuro.* El Salvador: National Spiritual Assembly of El Salvador, 1970.

— *Taking the Bahá'í Message to the Galapagos Islands in the Bahá'í Ten-Year World Spiritual Crusade, 1953–1963.* USBNA, Gayle Woolson Papers.

Youtube. *Election First Universal House of Justice.* Available at: https://www.youtube.com/watch?v=ksl8qgr8TVs.

ARCHIVAL COLLECTIONS

United States Bahá'í National Archives (USBNA):

Dr Homer Harper Papers
Dr Clement Woolson Papers
Gayle Woolson Papers
Inter-America Committee Papers
The Kadrie Family Papers

National Spiritual Assembly of South America Papers

Cedar Rapids Archives of the Spiritual Assembly of the Bahá'ís of Cedar Rapids (Cedar Rapids LSA Archives).

NEWSPAPERS

www.newspapers.com.

PERIODICALS

Bahá'í News Archive online

Star of the West: The Bahai Magazine. Periodical, 25 vols. 1910–1935. Vols. 1–14 RP Oxford: George Ronald, 1978. Complete CD-ROM version: Talisman Educational Software/Special Ideas, 2001.

World Order. Magazine, September 1942.

INTERNET WEBSITES

www.ancestry.com.

Notes and References

Prelude

1 USBNA, Gayle Woolson Papers. Letter from Shoghi Effendi written in 1942 to Mrs Gayle Woolson and Mrs Amalia Ford while they were in Costa Rica.

2 Bahá'u'lláh, *Hidden Words*, Persian no. 44.

1. Coming to America and Making a Discovery

1 Alice Abas was born on 2 June 1913 (USBNA, Gayle Woolson Papers). In this chapter, biographical information regarding Gayle Woolson's parents and grandparents is taken from typed accounts Gayle herself researched, verified, and documented in her later years. Her personal experiences with the Kadrie family are from her papers. Further Kadrie family information is taken from *The History of the Kadrie Family* available in USBNA, The Kadrie Family Papers. Gary Degeberg wrote this account, based on stories told by his mother, Voroth Kadrie, a daughter of Mel and Sarah Kadrie. Degeberg's work also refers to Holmquist, *They Chose Minnesota: A Survey of The State's Ethnic Groups*, the primary source of information on immigration from Syria to Minnesota at this time.

2 Tapes made at the 60th Anniversary of the founding of the Faith in Cedar Rapids, in Cedar Rapids LSA Archives, Gayle Woolson Papers.

3 USBNA, Gayle Woolson Papers. Details regarding the family and household are taken from typewritten descriptions by Gayle Woolson.

4 Gary Degeberg's *The History of the Kadrie Family* (USBNA, The Kadrie Family Papers) is the source for all information in this section regarding the Kadrie family, with the exception of items identified as coming from Gayle Woolson's typewritten accounts.

5 Balyuzi, *'Abdu'l-Bahá*, p. 277.
6 Degeberg, *The History of the Kadrie Family*, p. 23, in USBNA, The Kadrie Family Papers.
7 Talk by Gayle Woolson given in Cedar Rapids at the 60th Anniversary of the founding of the Faith in Cedar Rapids, in Cedar Rapids LSA Archives, Gayle Woolson Papers. The story is told according to Mrs Woolson; a few details differ from Degeberg's text.
8 Degeberg, *The History of the Kadrie Family,* p. 13.
9 ibid. p. 17.
10 Details are taken from Degeberg, *The History of the Kadrie Family.*
11 USBNA, Gayle Woolson Papers, typed account.

2. A Spiritual Change in the Family

1 USBNA, Gayle Woolson Papers: Woolson, Biographical information.
2 Talk by Gayle Woolson given in Cedar Rapids at the 60th Anniversary of the founding of the Faith in Cedar Rapids, in Cedar Rapids LSA Archives, Gayle Woolson Papers.
3 ibid.
4 USBNA, Gayle Woolson Papers: Woolson, Gayle, biographical information on Mrs Hider.
5 *The Bahá'í World*, vol. IV.
6 The Bahá'í calendar is organized into nineteen months of nineteen days, each of which begins with a Feast, or service, that includes devotional, administrative, and social portions. The Holy Days commemorate significant events in Bahá'í history.
7 *St. Paul Record of Activities*, in USBNA, Gayle Woolson Papers.
8 Lidia Zamenhof, the founder's daughter, was a Bahá'í. In 1937, she gave lectures on Esperanto in many communities in the United States, before having to return to Poland in 1938, unable to extend her visa. Her courageous life is beautifully depicted by author Wendy Heller in *Lidia: The Life of Lidia Zamenhof, Daughter of Esperanto.*
9 'Abdu'l-Bahá, born 'Abbás, was the eldest son of Bahá'u'lláh and served as head of the Bahá'í Faith from 1892 until 1921. He is also known to Bahá'is as the 'Master'.

10 *St. Paul Record of Various Activities*, in USBNA, Gayle Woolson Papers.

11 ibid.

12 ibid.

13 Farhad was the son of Clement and Orrol (Leona) Woolson.

14 This is the day, time, and date listed in the *St. Paul Record of Activities*, though the actual time for this annual commemoration was on the evening of 22 May.

15 The National Teaching Committee later arranged for Gayle to accompany Mabel Ives and Marguerite Reimer in travel teaching; see Chapter 5 below.

16 Dahl, 'Three teaching methods used during North America's First Seven Year Plan'.

17 These topics represent ideas current at the time, though not specific Bahá'í teachings, showing how Bahá'ís of each generation were influenced both by the teachings of Bahá'u'lláh and by the milieu in which they lived.

18 Mrs Rexford encouraged several early Bahá'ís to adopt the name 'Lorol'. Mrs Leona Harper Woolson became first 'Lorol', then 'Orrol', as she was commonly known in St Paul, and then 'Nagene'.

19 This statement was offered in 1997 or 1998 as part of a programme at the Bahá'í House of Worship in Wilmette, Illinois on the occasion of the Birth of Bahá'u'lláh. Gayle later read it in an interview conducted at the Bahá'í National Center in 1998.

20 USBNA, Gayle Woolson Papers, typed statement, no date.

3. The Woolson Family

1 USBNA, Gayle Woolson Papers, letter from Voroth Kadrie, 18 February 1976.

2 ibid., undated letter from Bertha Kadrie to Gayle Woolson.

3 ibid., typed account from the individual, given to Gayle Woolson.

4 Dr Harper's letter to Martha Root may be found in his papers at the National Bahá'í Archives of the United States (USBNA). Balyuzi also speaks of this visit to the Woolson home in his book, *'Abdu'l-Bahá*, pp. 274, 277.

5 No information has been found regarding whether Mrs Woolson and Farhad came to live in Chicago or stayed in St Paul during this time, nor how long she continued her medical practice.

6 USBNA, Gayle Woolson Papers. According to Gayle's documentation this 'came through Mirza Assad'ulláh to "His Honor Mr. Woolson"'. It was translated by Ali Kuli Khan on 21 January 1918.'

Dr Woolson became known in his practice for his prayerful approach and healing touch. Either by coincidence or perhaps through direct influence, Dr Julian Abas, who received medical and spiritual guidance as a young person from Dr Woolson, also developed and was known for this gift of prayerful healing touch as a chiropractor. Gerald Abas, the youngest in the family, became a reflexologist, also healing through his hands. Even when in her nineties, people visiting Gayle would comment on the feather-light touch of her hands, and how she would gently stroke one's hand or forearm, as though instilling a healing influence.

7 Morrison, *To Move the World*, p. 118.

8 According to Gary Degeberg, the author of the *History of the Kadrie Family*, Voroth Kadrie, the daughter of Sarah and Mel Kadrie, was the source of this information. She was active in the community at the time that the changes took place.

9 If the Kadrie account is accurate, it would offer a possible explanation for the lack of information. At the time, mental institution policies left historians in difficulty in locating individuals. Institutions often had their own cemeteries where they would bury patients with a number rather than a name. This could also offer an explanation for why Farhad stayed with his father and then with the Abas family rather than with his mother; why the author has been unable to find further information or a death certificate; and why no grave location has as yet been found. Leona Harper Woolson (also Lorol and Nagene) disappears abruptly from the *St. Paul Record of Activities* about a month before the wedding that united Clement with Alice (Gayle). In

later years, Gayle Woolson wrote up what information she could find, including in her search a visit to the Minnesota Historical Association. To date, this writer has found no further verification of what happened.

4. Marriage

1 The material in the Gayle Woolson Papers regarding this time includes biographical information Gayle wrote in later years about both the Woolson and Abas families; entries from the *St. Paul Record of Various Activities;* and publicly available historical records she researched and/ or verified.

2 USBNA, Gayle Woolson Papers, typed biographical information on Khalud Hider and letter to the Universal House of Justice. Gayle even wrote to the Universal House of Justice to ask whether her grandmother's experience would constitute recognition of the Faith and therefore identity as part of the community. A letter on behalf of the House of Justice did not answer the question directly but encouraged her to write the story of her parents and grandparents for inclusion in the St Paul Archives.

3 It was not unusual for Bahá'ís at that time to be married by a Justice of the Peace, as most Assemblies were not yet incorporated and therefore ineligible to apply to officiate at weddings.

4 *The Bahá'í World*, vol. VI, p. 82.

5 A symbolic term denoting the next world.

6 Gayle maintained her friendship with Rose Washick; their last visit was in 1986, when Rose was 80 years old.

7 *St. Paul Records of Various Activities,* p. 255. Farhad is listed at 235 Fuller on 12 January 1937.

8 Letter from Shoghi Effendi to Clement Woolson, 9 February 1933, photocopy in USBNA, Gayle Woolson Papers.

5. From Children's Classes to Teaching Teams

1 Letter from Shoghi Effendi to the Bahá'í communities in North America, 10 January 1936, in Shoghi Effendi, *This Decisive Hour*, no. 19, p. 11.

2 Minutes of St. Paul Assembly, 5 April 1936.

3 Shoghi Effendi, Message to 1936 Convention, in *This Decisive Hour*, pp. 11–12. The 'glorious century' mentioned by the Guardian refers to the first century of the Bahá'í Era, ending 22 May 1944.

4 Letter from Shoghi Effendi to Gayle Woolson, 21 May 1936, photocopy in USBNA, Gayle Woolson Papers.

5 Quoted in Rabbani, *The Priceless Pearl*, p. 215.

6 ibid. For a further description of the significance and impact of this work, see ibid. pp. 214–19.

7 A message on behalf of the Guardian to the National Spiritual Assembly of the Bahá'ís of Australia and New Zealand dated 3 January 1936 states:

> Miss Effie Baker is leaving for Australia with the consent and full approval of the Guardian. As you know for over ten years she has been devotedly working for the Cause in Haifa, as keeper of the Western Pilgrim House and also as the custodian of the International Bahá'í Archives. During this long period of service she has accomplished much for our beloved Cause, and she is now in need of some rest after so many years of strenuous labours (Shoghi Effendi, *Messages to Australia and New Zealand*).

8 For an account of the life and service of Emogene Hoagg, please see *The Bahá'í World*, vol. X, pp. 520–26.

9 Shoghi Effendi, cable to the North American believers, 30 July 1936, in *This Decisive Hour*, p. 13.

10 Merriam-Webster, *Collegiate Dictionary*, 10th ed.

11 This followed the communication below: August 28, 1936:

> A copy of Shoghi Effendi's most urgent Cablegram was given to each believer: Dated July 30, 1936, it reads as follows: (I) entreat (the) American believers (to) ponder afresh (the) urgency (to) rededicate themselves (to the) task (of the) complete fulfilment (of the) Divine Plan. (The) National Assembly's energetic leadership (and careful planning (are) ineffectual unless supplemented by vigorous action by every

believer, however humble, however inexperienced. Time is short. (The) sands (of a) chaotic, despairing civilization (are steadily running out. Founded on (the) unity (and) understanding so steadily achieved, functioning within (the) framework (of the) Administrative Order (so) laboriously erected, inspired (by the) vision of the Temple edifice so nobly reared, galvanized into action (by the) realization (of the) rapidly-deteriorating world situation, (the) American Bahai Community should rise as never before, (to the) height (of the) opportunity now confronting it. Audacity resolution (and) self abnegation (are) imperatively demanded. Impatiently and prayerfully waiting. Shoghi

Mrs. Gayle Woolson, Sec'y

A copy of this cable without the additional words added is published in Shoghi Effendi, *This Decisive Hour*, p. 13.

12 The *St. Paul Records of Various Activities* note that a letter was written to the National Teaching Committee inquiring about making such a trip. Gayle was then invited to accompany Mabel Ives, a more experienced teacher.

13 USBNA, Gayle Woolson Papers, *The First Bahá'í of the State of North Dakota: Mr. Hassen Abas*, p. 2.

14 Among these teachers were the following: including but not limited to Dorothy Baker, Louis Gregory, Ruth Moffett, Orcella Rexford, and Mamie Seto; see Dahl, 'Three teaching methods used during North America's First Seven-Year Plan'.

15 Mabel Ives (1878–1943) and Howard Colby Ives (1867–1941). See McKay, In Memoriam article for Howard Colby Ives, in *Bahá'í World*, vol. IX, pp. 608–13; also Newhall, *Mother's Stories: Recollections of Abdu'l-Baha*.

16 *The Bahá'í World*, vol. IX, p. 611.

17 The gift becomes especially meaningful when we consider the circumstances in which he wrote it:

It was in Knoxville, in 1934, that Howard began to write – at sixty-seven. He was employed to write articles about the great dam project there, the T.V.A.

Suddenly he found the knack of writing vivid prose. In the late spring and summer he sat four hours each day at his typewriter in the unaccustomed heat of Tennessee. One morning he fell unconscious on the floor by his bed – his first attack of angina. He had found a gift which might have resulted in a relief from economic stress only to lose the use of it almost at once. His health, always precarious, was now undeniably gone, also his eyesight and hearing began rapidly to go, and he now, already facing an end that might come at any moment, began to struggle for time. Time to put down in his newfound style the spiritual memoirs we have referred to as 'Portals to Freedom.' Forbidden to use his eyes, he learned the touch system on the typewriter and completed the book, which was published by Dutton and Co. in 1937 (ibid. p. 612).

18 Born on 23 November 1912, Marguerite Reimer later married the future Hand of the Cause, William Sears.

19 Mary Maxwell, the daughter of Sutherland and May Maxwell, and the future wife of the Guardian, Shoghi Effendi.

20 Sears, *Marguerite . . . and More About Bill,* p. 136.

21 *The Bahá'í World,* vol. VII, p. 49.

22 *Bahá'í News,* no.114 (February 1938).

6. Preparing for International Service

1 Rabbani, *The Priceless Pearl,* p. 381.

2 The Universal House of Justice, Message to the Bahá'ís of the World acting under the Mandate of 'Abdu'l-Bahá, 26 March 2016, available at: https://www.bahai.org/library/authoritative-texts/the-universal-house-of-justice/messages/20160326_001/1#749196100.

3 For a description of this event, see *Star of the West,* vol .10, 1919, various issues.

4 Shoghi Effendi, Message to 1939 Convention, in Shoghi Effendi, *This Decisive Hour,* p. 32.

5 Letter from Sara Kenny on behalf of the Inter-America Committee to Gayle Woolson, 7 August 1939, in USBNA, Inter-America Committee Correspondence.

6 Letter from Gayle Woolson to Sara Kenny, 20 August 1939, ibid.

7 Letter from Gayle Woolson to Sara Kenny, 28 August 1939, ibid.

8 Letter from Sara Kenny on behalf of the Inter-America Committee to Gayle Woolson, 20 August 1939, ibid.

9 Letter from Leroy Ioas on behalf of the Inter-America Committee to Gayle Woolson, 11 September 1939, ibid.

10 USBNA, Gayle Woolson Papers, handwritten on a piece of paper.

11 *Bahá'í News*, no. 132 (January 1940).

12 Cedar Rapids LSA Archives and USBNA, Gayle Woolson Papers. Gayle also explained that this occurred during a period before individuals signed enrolment cards. When these were instituted, Mrs. Beals signed an enrolment card dated 1 March 1941.

13 Letter from Gayle Woolson to Sara Kenny, 20 August 1939, in USBNA, Inter-America Committee Correspondence.

7. 'Costa Rica, the Beautiful'

1 'Abdu'l-Bahá, Tablet to the Western States, in *Tablets of the Divine Plan*, p. 81.

2 See Chapter 4.

3 Shoghi Effendi, *The Advent of Divine Justice,* p. 9.

4 ibid. pp. 41 and 43.

5 Perry et al., *Green Acre on the Piscataqua*, p. 182. The author includes a photograph of Ralph Waldo Trine taken at Green Acre Bahá'í School and states that he wrote *In Tune with the Infinite* while at Green Acre.

6 Trine, *In Tune with the Infinite,* p. 21.

7 *The Bahá'í World,* vol. X, pp. 787–96.

8 Curiously, this first stop happened to be at the birthplace of Gayle's husband, Dr Woolson.

9 See Ginés, 'The story of the Bahá'í Faith in Cuba', in *The Bahá'í World,* vol. IX, pp. 916–17.

10 Gayle added the name of this believer, Esther Le Frank, in ink to a copy of the article.

11 Gayle added these names in pencil to her own copy.

12 Gayle added 'José Joaquim Ullva???' in ink to her own copy.

13 In her papers, Gayle lists the following as the first Bahá'ís of Puntarenas: Jenaro Miranda (the first Bahá'í), Rafael Castillo, Modesto Campos, Señora Dora Arce de Campos, Señora Angela de Zapata, Ernesto Zapata, José Antonio Molina, Tobías Guzman, Jorge Adamson, Miguel Bravo.

14 Quoted from Shoghi Effendi, *The Advent of Divine Justice*, pp. 45–6, 62.

15 Shoghi Effendi, *Afire With the Vision*, p. 144.

16 USBNA, photocopy in Gayle Woolson Papers.

17 Gayle wrote down the following list of Bahá'ís in San José (no specific date): Argelia Contreras de Campos, Raul Contreras, Julieta Contreras, Rosa Quesada, Consuelo Miranda, Margarita Miranda, Felicia Canales, Paulina Barrios, Roberto Castro, Anita Clachar, Guido Contreras, Arnoldo Escalante, Rosario de Escalante, Serapio Hernandez, Bianca Lacayo, Esther Urena de Lefrank, Virginia Paez, Carlos Porras, Isabel Porras, Bolivar Ramirez, Tito Revelo, Gonzalo Solano, Pedro Ujueta, Gerardo Vega.

   Typed on a piece of paper, she listed the first Baha'is of Puntarenas, Costa Rica in 1942: Jenaro Miranda ("el primero de todos), Rafael Castillo M., Modesto Campos, Señora, Dora Arce de Campos, Señora Angela de Zapata, Ernesto Zapata, José Antonio Molina, Tobías Guzman, Jorge Adamson, Miguel Bravo.

18 Mrs Ford (8 February 1881–15 March 1970 per Ancestry. com) was the daughter of Refugio Sanchez and Antonia Mendoza. In 1926 she married George Ellison, but was a widow with one son when she went pioneering. She returned to the Bay Area in California, where she lived until her passing in Berkeley, Alameda, California. Little information is available regarding the details of her subsequent service. Please see the letter from the Guardian to her in Shoghi Effendi, *Afire With the Vision*, p. 158.

19 USBNA, Gayle Woolson Papers.

20 *The Bahá'í World*, vol. XIII, p. 856.

21 USBNA, Gayle Woolson Papers.

8. A World Celebration: Centenary of the Declaration of the Báb

1 Shoghi Effendi, in 'The centenary of a world Faith', in *The Bahá'í World*, vol. X, p. 135.

2 *The Bahá'í World*, vol. X, p. 168. In the same volume, p. 698, Edna True gives the following list of representatives: Dr. Fernando Nova, Brazil; Sr. Esteban Canales Leyton, Chile; Srta. Josephina Rodriguez, Colombia; Sr. Raoul Contreras, Costa Rica; Sr. Eugenio Gines, Cuba; Dr. Edelberto Torres, Guatemala; Mr. William Mitchell, Jamaica; Sr. Carlos Vergara, Mexico; Srta. Blanca V. Mejia, Nicaragua; Mr. Alfred Osborne, Panama; Dr. Manuel Berges, Dominican Republic; Sr. Eduardo Gonzales Lopez, Ecuador.

At the consultation in July, the Latin American representatives were as follows: Sr. Salvador Tormo, Argentina; Srta. Angela OchoaVelasquez, Honduras; Sr. Roque Centurion Miranda, Paraguay; Sra. Isabel Tirado de Barreda, Peru; Srta. Clara Luz Montalvo, El Salvador.

3 True, 'Progress in Latin America', in *The Bahá'í World*, vol. X, pp. 698–9.

4 For a detailed account of the programme, see *The Bahá'í World*, vol. X, pp. 174–9.

5 The Guardian mentions it in conjunction with the achievements of the First Seven Year Plan: 'An International School to provide training for Bahá'í teachers in Central and South America was founded' (Message to the North American Bahá'ís, 15 June 1946, in *This Decisive Hour*, p. 122).

6 Mathews, 'Preface', in USBNA, *US First Four Latin American Sessions Teaching Notes, International School Temerity Ranch, The Bahá'í One Hundredth Anniversary, 1844–1944*.

7 *The Bahá'í World*, vol. X, pp. 170–72.

9. International Travel

1 The War formally ended when Japan signed documents of surrender on 2 September 1945.

2 Spiritual Assembly of the Bahá'ís of Wilmette Archives, Gayle Woolson Papers, 'Datos sobre los actividades'.

3   USBNA, Gayle Woolson Papers, typed document

4   In preparation for writing, Shoghi Effendi had read all
    that was available of the Writings of the Báb, Bahá'u'lláh,
    and 'Abdu'l-Bahá, together with many contemporary
    works – about two hundred books in all. Labouring for
    eight full months, he wrote the manuscript out in long-
    hand on small sheets of paper. He then typed the final
    draft with carbon copies. Together, the Guardian and
    Rúḥíyyih Khánum would sit for hours, entering the dia-
    critical marks for all of the copies. Rúḥíyyih Khánum has
    said that it is a book to be read aloud. While the Guardian
    was composing, she would listen as he chanted phrases
    and sentences until word, rhythm, and sound combined
    perfectly to sing out and illumine the meaning conveyed.

5   Most details in this paragraph are from Rabbani, *The
    Priceless Pearl.*

6   Shoghi Effendi, *God Passes By*, p. 119.

7   USBNA, Gayle Woolson Papers.

8   True, 'Progress in Latin America', in *The Bahá'í World*, vol.
    X, p. 702.

9   Elisabeth Cheney was one of the first pioneers to go to
    South America and the first to go to Paraguay, early in
    1940.

10 True, 'Progress in Latin America', in *The Bahá'í World*, vol.
    X, pp. 702–3.

11 Also in 1945, Gayle states that she had an interview
    with the President of Honduras. In September 1946, a
    door would open for an audience with the President of
    Ecuador.

12 Interview #7389 at the US National Bahá'í Center.

13 USBNA, Gayle Woolson Papers, typed account.

14 True, 'Progress in Latin America', in *The Bahá'í World*, vol.
    X, p. 703.

15 Mr Remey was declared a Covenant-breaker in 1961. The
    resultant tests were particularly severe in Latin America,
    in part because he had visited every centre and had made
    a strong impression on the believers. Later, when he
    sent out his own literature, many would recognize and
    remember his visits.

16 True, 'Progress in Latin America', in *The Bahá'í World*, vol. X, p. 707. There is also an article in *Bahá'í News*, May 1946, describing the conference.

17 *Bahá'í News*, October 1946, p. 7.

18 'Haig' is spelled 'Haik' in some documents. Both spellings may therefore appear in this chapter, depending on the source.

19 Hornby, *Heroes of God*, p. 27.

20 Cornbleth, 'Ilusiones' in *The Bahá'í World*, vol. XI, pp. 753–61. He goes on to describe several towns where he spent time in Ecuador, together with a moving tribute to John Hope Stearns, the first pioneer to Ecuador.

21 USBNA, Gayle Woolson Papers. Typed description of interview by Gayle Woolson.

22 Hornby, *Heroes of God*, p. 29.

10. Colombia, a Call from Home, and a Return Trip through the Islands

1 Spiritual Assembly of the Bahá'ís of Wilmette Archives, Gayle Woolson Papers.

2 The Regional Assemblies are also referred to as National Spiritual Assemblies. While each initially included several countries, by 1961 each country would have its own National Spiritual Assembly.

3 Letter from Shoghi Effendi, 18 August 1950, quoted in *The Bahá'í World*, vol. XI, p. 49

4 Spiritual Assembly of the Bahá'ís of Wilmette Archives, Gayle Woolson Papers.

5 Holley, 'International survey of current Bahá'í activities in the East and West', in *The Bahá'í World*, vol. XI, p. 47.

6 Cornbleth, 'Ilusiones', in *The Bahá'í World*, vol. XI, p. 757.

7 *Bahá'í News*, November 1946, p. 8.

8 *Bahá'í News*, September 1948, p. 8.

9 *Bahá'í News*, November 1948, p. 9.

10 *Bahá'í News*, December 1948, p. 1.

11 *Bahá'í News*, January 1949, p. 5.

12 *Bahá'í News*, March 1949, p. 6.

13 Spiritual Assembly of the Bahá'ís of Wilmette Archives, Gayle Woolson Papers.

14 *Bahá'í News,* July 1949, p. 4. Both Eve Nicklin and Gayle had, through their example, learned the art of empowering others.
15 Spiritual Assembly of the Bahá'ís of Wilmette Archives, Gayle Woolson Papers, letter from Gayle Woolson to Elena Marsella, 1987.

11. The Regional Spiritual Assembly of South America

1 Hornby, *Heroes of God*, p. 44.
2 *The Bahá'í World,* vol. XII, pp. 60–61. Descriptive facts and details stated are also from this article, unless otherwise noted.
3 Handal, *Eve Nicklin: She of the Brave Heart*, pp. 156–7.
4 *The Bahá'í World*, vol. XIII, p. 61.
5 'Abdu'l-Bahá. *Paris Talks,* no. 31, p. 98.
6 The reader will find these qualities substantiated in examples given in Mrs Hornby's book, in the letters from the Guardian written to Gayle, in the chapters below on the Galápagos Islands and other teaching work, and in the communications from Hands of the Cause during her service as an Auxiliary Board Member. These attributes were shared also by many of the constellation of early pioneers in Central and South America.
7 Hornby, *Heroes of God*, pp. 44–5.
8 The new Assemblies in Central and South America are referred to in correspondence both as Regional and as National Spiritual Assemblies.
9 This refers to the National Spiritual Assemblies of Canada, the United States, Central America and the Antilles, and South America.
10 This term, common at the time to refer to indigenous peoples, intended no disrespect or diminishment of their capacity. The Guardian held them in high esteem and affirmed their distinctive destiny in the Age now unfolding.
11 Hornby, *Heroes of God*, pp. 44–5.
12 ibid. pp. 45– 6.
13 To date, no document has been found to corroborate whether these are official Minutes or a transcription of her personal shorthand notes.

14 Salvador Tormo had been a delegate to the 1944 Centenary gathering in Wilmette. His reflections on that experience are printed in *The Bahá'í World*, vol. X, pp. 768–71. He and his wife later became Knights of Bahá'u'lláh for the Island of Chiloé, distinguishing themselves as Latin believers arising to meet the international goals of the Ten Year Crusade. For further information see his In Memoriam, *The Bahá'í World*, vol. XV, pp. 908–9.

15 At this time, Hands of the Cause could also serve on National Spiritual Assemblies.

16 Miessler, *Pioneering in Brazil: Our Glorious Spiritual Adventure*, p. 55. Edmund and Muriel Miessler were pioneers from Lima, Ohio, the home community of Dorothy Baker.

17 The Constitution was printed in *The Bahá'í World*, vol. XII, pp. 423–30, together with other official documents concerning Bahá'í institutions in English, German, Arabic, and Persian.

18 The members were Margot Worley, President; Mercedes Sanchez, Vice-President; Gayle Woolson, Secretary of Correspondence; Edmund Meissler, Recording Secretary; Guillermo Aguilar, Treasurer; Eve Nicklin, Manuel Vera, Bolivar Plaza and Rangvald Taetz.

19 Philip G. Sprague offered a beautiful description of the cemetery in *World Order*, September 1942, pp. 208–9: 'Quilmes is like a small gem. It is the most beautiful cemetery I have ever seen. It stands alone on a plain surrounded by a wall. The wall is a gray and red brick which has been washed by the elements, a lovely gray and terra cotta color. In the cemetery many trees are in bloom, some tropical, some orange and lemon trees, some gardenias. There is a tall gate at the entrance with a bell which rings as the gate is opened, and, as you enter, on the left there stands a small cottage where the keeper of the cemetery lives. Here are sweet peasant people with kind and luminous faces.'

20 These are not necessarily Mrs Baker's exact words. Corroborating documents have not yet been located. Gayle's notes also summarize each of the courses Mrs

Baker offered at the school. They covered Bahá'u'lláh's
messages to the Kings and Rulers, with specific descriptions of the delivery of each message, the response, and
the consequences of this response; individual salvation,
carefully weaving the purpose of life with the gifts of the
next world, the responsibilities of this one, and the role
of sacrifice and suffering in attaining one's destiny in this;
the power and joy of teaching; and finally, the ministries
of Bahá'u'lláh and 'Abdu'l-Bahá, and the initiation of that
of the Guardian.

21 Letter on behalf of Shoghi Effendi, 3 June 1952, in Shoghi
Effendi, *Afire With the Vision*, p. 25.

22 ibid.

12. 'Paradise . . . because reached In time'

1 The four were the National Spiritual Assemblies of the
United States, of Canada, of Central America, and of
South America.

2 The portrait of Bahá'u'lláh is displayed only on special
occasions, due to the injunction not to worship the
physical form but rather to turn towards the spirit of the
Manifestation.

3 Message from Shoghi Effendi, 3 May 1953, in *The Bahá'í
World*, vol. XII, pp. 138–41.

4 Also, for the Guardian's thinking in naming Knights of
Bahá'u'lláh, see Chapman, *Leroy Ioas*, pp. 260–61.

5 Gilstrap, *From Copper to Gold*, pp. 410–11.

6 Message from Shoghi Effendi, 19 June 1953, in Shoghi
Effendi, *Afire With the Vision*, pp. 37–8. The National
Spiritual Assembly of South America was to open the fol-
lowing virgin areas during the first year of the Ten Year
Plan: Chiloé Island, Galápagos Islands, Juan Fernandez
Islands, Leeward Islands, Windward Islands, Cook
Islands.

7 In various publications, both 'Haig Kevorkian' and 'Haik
Kevorkian' appear.

8 Hornby, *Heroes of God*, pp. 57–9.

9 USBNA, Gayle Woolson Papers.

10 USBNA, Gayle Woolson Papers, typed document, 'Taking

the Bahá'í Message to the Galapagos Islands in the Bahá'í
Ten-Year World Crusade, 1953–1963'.

11 Details from Hornby, *Heroes of God,* p. 60.

12 USBNA, Gayle Woolson Papers, typed document, 'Taking
the Bahá'í Message to the Galapagos Islands in the Bahá'í
Ten-Year World Crusade, 1953–1963'.

13 ibid.

14 ibid., note written on back of photograph.

15 ibid.

16 'In Memoriam', *The Bahá'í World,* vol. XV, p. 484.

17 Hornby, *Heroes of God,* p. 60.

18 *The Bahá'í World,* vol. XV, p. 485.

19 Hornby, *Heroes of God,* pp. 64–7.

20 Quoted ibid. p. 65.

13. New Dimensions of Service

1 The Bahá'í Administrative Order consists of an elected
arm (at that time including Local and National or Regional
Spiritual Assemblies) and an appointed arm (including
the Hands of the Cause and their Auxiliary Boards, new
in 1954, and now also the Continental Counsellors.)

2 Shoghi Effendi, cablegram, 8 October 1952, in Shoghi
Effendi, *Messages to the Bahá'í World,* p. 44.

3 Shoghi Effendi, cablegram, 6 April 1954, ibid. pp. 58–9.

4 Mrs Worley had learned of the Faith from the first pioneer
to Brazil, Leonora Holsapple.

5 At this time, Auxiliary Board Members could serve on
both elected and appointed institutions, that is, on both
Spiritual Assemblies and on the Auxiliary Board. Later,
one would have to make a choice to serve on one or the
other.

6 USBNA, Gayle Woolson Papers, letter to the Hands of
the Cause of God for the Americas (Corinne True, Paul
Haney and Horace Holley), 15 June 1954. Copies of the
correspondence cited in this section are all included in
the Gayle Woolson Papers.

7 'At this time we are not making any specific assignment of
countries to you and Mrs Worley. We suggest, however,
that at the next meeting of the National Assembly, you

and Mrs Worley consult together, and then submit to us suggestions concerning a desirable and practical division of countries for assignment to each of you.'

8 At this time, the believers were few and the needs many. Although in the Bahá'í Faith there is no paid equivalent of a clergy, because Gayle and Margot were asked to serve full time as itinerant teachers, essential costs were covered by this budget.

9 Letter from the Hands of the Cause for the Americas to Mrs Gayle Woolson, 27 May 1954.

10 Letter from the Hands of the Cause for the Americas, to the Auxiliary Board, 25 May 1954.

11 Strengthening communities, multiplying groups, assisting groups to attain Assembly status.

12 Letter from the Hands of the Cause for the Americas, signed by Corinne True, Horace Holley, and Paul Haney to the three Board members mentioned above, 12 October 1954.

13 It was not uncommon for the Bahá'ís to be falsely accused of being Communists, despite their complete adherence to the Bahá'í teaching of non-involvement in politics, as had happened in the Galápagos Islands and with Rufino Gualavisi in Ecuador.

14 Hornby, *Heroes of God*, p. 86.

15 Known as Raúl Pavón, his full name was Raúl Pavón Mejia.

16 'In Memoriam', *The Bahá'í World*, vol. XVIII, pp. 671–5.

17 Hornby, *Heroes of God*, pp. 282–3. Other details regarding Otavalo are also taken from this account.

18 For a moving biography of Raúl Pavón, please see the online version under *Raúl Pavón Mejia,* https://sites.google.com/site/raulpavonmejia/. For Radio Bahá'í, see Hein, *Radio Bahá'í Ecuador.*

19 *Bahá'í News,* June 1990, available at Bahá'í Media Resources, blog with biographical sketches, http://bahais-worldwide.blogspot.com/2012/05/blog-post.html.

14. A Pilgrimage Framed by Teaching Trips

1 *Bahá'í News,* May 1956, p. 8.

2 USBNA, Gayle Woolson Papers. Transcribed from an interview with Mrs Janet Marks in Wilmette, Illinois in 1986, at a gathering to honour individuals who had been Bahá'ís for 50 years or more.

3 'Regarding the notes taken by pilgrims at Haifa. The Guardian has stated that he is unwilling to sign the notes of any pilgrim, in order that the literature consulted by the believers shall not be unduly extended . . . This means that the notes of pilgrims do not carry the authority resident in the Guardian's letters written over his own signature. On the other hand, each pilgrim brings back information and suggestions of a most precious cha racter, and it is the privilege of all the friends to share in the spiritual results of these visits' (Letter written on behalf of Shoghi Effendi to the National Spiritual Assembly of the United States, in *Bahá'í News*, no. 281 (July 1954), p. 4; see also *Lights of Guidance*, no. 1432).

4 Bahá'í Library online: Haifa Notes: Gayle Woolson. Available at: https://bahai-library.com/woolson_haifa_notes.

5 USBNA. Gayle Woolson Papers.

6 *Bahá'í News*, May 1956, p. 8.

7 Hornby, *Heroes of God,* pp. 92–3.

8 ibid.

9 Letter from Shoghi Effendi, 3 July 1957, in Shoghi Effendi. *Afire With the Vision*, no. 22, p. 76.

10 This refers to the Plans adopted by the newly-formed Regional NSAs of South America, which would cover the remaining six years of the Ten Year Crusade, and added certain goals for each region to accomplish in addition to the original goals for South America.

11 Shoghi Effendi. *Afire With the Vision,* pp. 79–80.

15. 'What men lose they value much'

1 Chapman, *Leroy Ioas*, pp. 271–2. For further information on the passing of Shoghi Effendi, see *Ministry of the Custodians*.

2 Chapman, *Leroy Ioas*, p. 274. It had been 36 years before, at the Master's passing, that Mrs Collins had read the

following in His Will and Testament: 'It is incumbent upon you to take the greatest care of Shoghi Effendi . . . that no dust of despondency and sorrow may stain his radiant nature, that day by day he may wax greater in happiness, in joy and spirituality . . .' At that time, she dedicated her life to making the Guardian happy. Now, at 84, though bereft of his presence and burdened with painful arthritis, she would continue in that quest.

3 Rabbani, *The Priceless Pearl*. p. 445.
4 ibid. p. 445.
5 As described in *Encyclopedia Britannica*. The following is from an article by Kara Rogers, added online in 2010: 'In the first months of the 1957 Asian flu pandemic, the virus spread throughout China and surrounding regions. By midsummer it had reached the United States, where it appears to have initially infected relatively few people. Several months later, however, numerous cases of infection were reported, especially in young children, the elderly, and pregnant women. This upsurge in cases was the result of a second pandemic wave of illness that struck the Northern Hemisphere in November 1957. At that time, the pandemic was also already widespread in the United Kingdom. By December a total of some 3,550 deaths had been reported in England and Wales. The second wave was particularly devastating, and by March 1958 an estimated 69,800 deaths had occurred in the United States.'
6 *The Bahá'í World*, vol. XVIII, p. 213.
7 Rabbani, *The Priceless Pearl*, pp. 446–7.
8 ibid. p. 447.
9 Rabbani, *Poems of the Passing*, pp. 17–18.
10 Chapman, *Leroy Ioas*, p. 276.
11 Quoted in Hornby, *Heroes of God*, pp. 93–5.
12 USBNA, Gayle Woolson Papers, personal note.
13 Marta Rosales Toromoreno of Ecuador posted a series of reminiscences about Gayle Woolson on her Facebook page, including the following translated in the text above: '*Cuando en 1957 falleció nuestro Amado Guardián, Gayle se había convertido en uno de los soldados más fuertes de la*

Causa de la Bendita Belleza. Recuerdo que la gente se reunía para orar y llorar amargamente la partida del Guardián. Gayle fue un catalizador para que la pequeña comunidad de Quito soporte el dolor y prueba que vivía el mundo Bahai. Después de la ascensión de nuestro Amado Guardian se dejó de realizar las reuniones en el Centro Histórico de Quito. La comunidad atravesó varias pruebas y dificultades, entre otras varios rompedores del Convenio. Todo esto en la década del 50 e inicios de los 60 del siglo pasado.'

16. The Path Forward

1 This would be one of six Conclaves, which would span the period 1957–1963.

2 'where every tree and pebble and flower reminds us that he has ascended to the Paradise of Bahá'u'lláh and been gathered to the glory of his Divine Forebears,' in *Ministry of the Custodians*, p. 76.

3 ibid. pp. 30–39.

4 *The Bahá'í World*, vol. XIII, p. 857.

5 *Ministry of the Custodians*, pp. 35–6.

6 ibid. p. 37.

7 Shoghi Effendi, Message dated 3 July 1957 to the National Spiritual Assembly of the Bahá'ís of Brazil, Peru, Colombia, Ecuador, and Venezuela, in Shoghi Effendi, *Afire With the Vision*, para. 22.13, p. 79.

8 Gayle participated in this election as a member of the National Spiritual Assembly of the northern countries of South America.

9 The remainder of this message may be found in *Ministry of the Custodians*, p. 170.

10 Hornby, *Heroes of God*, p. 104. This book and selected correspondence are the sources of facts for this section.

11 For details of Mr Grossmann's invaluable service, please see the biography *Hermann Grossmann*, by Susanne Pfaff-Grossmann.

12 Marta Rosales Toromoreno, Facebook page responding to requests for her memories of Gayle Woolson.

13 Gayle told of Dorothy Campbell Rougeau in a letter to Dr Robert Henderson on the occasion of Dorothy's passing

on 12 January 1994, in Franklin, Louisiana, where she had lived upon returning from Ecuador.

Dorothy and I were close friends in the pioneering field and served on the same National Spiritual Assemblies of three different jurisdictions in South America. She served the Faith there in Latin America during a period of 23 years, from 1950 to 1973. Those Assemblies were the NSA of South America embracing 10 countries; then when the jurisdiction was reduced to only 5 countries, she was on the NSA of Brazil, Colombia, Ecuador, Peru, and Venezuela, formed in 1957. When in 1961, each Latin American Republic obtained the status of having its own NSA, Dorothy was on the NSA of Ecuador. She served there in that capacity until 1973, when she married James Rougeau and went to reside in Franklin, Louisiana.

The following information was given me in part by Roger Dahl of our National Bahá'í Archives. I added on the names of the Assemblies and years: 'As Dorothy Campbell, she enrolled in the Bahá'í Faith in 1942 in Jackson, Mississippi, where she resided at that time. She started her pioneering career in 1950 when she went to Mexico, Guatemala, Venezuela and Bolivia within the first six months of being in Latin America. She remained in Bolivia from December of 1950 until 1953 when she was elected on the National Spiritual Assembly of South America and transferred to Lima, Peru, the seat of that Assembly, to serve as secretary. Dorothy remained in Peru until 1961, the time when each republic of Latin America was to elect its own NSA. She chose to transfer to Ecuador where she became a member of that NSA and its secretary until 1973 when she married and returned to the United States.

In 1951 while still in Bolivia, Dorothy was appointed secretary of the Bahá'í Publishing Trust of Latin America by the recently established first National Spiritual Assembly of South America. In 1963 she travelled to the Holy Land as a member of the National Spiritual Assembly of Ecuador and one of the electors of the first Universal House of Justice. We went there together.

14 Email message kindly forwarded to the author via Tarasieh Werle Vahdat. Dr Patricia Munoz Naranjo de Dumet is a physician and trainer of adults. She is the Program Coordinator for *Fundación Horizonte*. Her email is undated.

15 See Chapter 8.

16 Hornby, *Heroes of God*, p. 105.

17 USBNA, Gayle Woolson Papers, letter from Mr Faizi to Gayle Woolson, 23 September 1962.

18 ibid., letter from the Hands of the Cause of the Western Hemisphere to local Spiritual Assemblies in Central and South America, February 1961.

19 USNBA, Gayle Woolson Papers.

20 ibid. This correspondence is all included in the Gayle Woolson Papers.

21 The remaining colonies or territories were temporarily represented through the countries governing them. As they gained independence, they would also gain their own NSAs.

22 Hornby, *Heroes of God*, p. 108.

23 Mr Schechter later became a Counsellor.

24 Mrs Mayberry also later became a Counsellor.

25 *Ministry of the Custodians*, pp. 286–7.

26 Rabbání, *The Priceless Pearl*. p. 444.

17. The Election of the Universal House of Justice

1 Amatu'l-Bahá Rúḥíyyih Khánum, speaking in the Youtube video *Election first Universal House of Justice,* Priceless footage.

2 Chapman, *Leroy Ioas,* pp. 330–31.

3 ibid.

4 The Convention sessions took place at this auditorium on Monday and Tuesday, 22 and 23 April 1963.

5 Chapman, *Leroy Ioas,* pp. 331–2.

6 Memories of Fereydoun Jalali, email to the author, 5 April 2020.

7   *The Bahá'í World,* vol. XIV, p. 77.
8   ibid. p. 79.
9   USBNA. Gayle Woolson Papers.

18. 'Steps on New Trails' in Ecuador and El Salvador

1   USBNA, Gayle Woolson Papers, letter to Auxiliary Board Members of the Western Hemisphere, 27 June 1963.
2   USBNA, Gayle Woolson Papers, letter from Gayle Woolson to Hands of the Bahá'í Faith in the Western Hemisphere Messrs. Zikrullah Khadem and Jalal Khazeh, 10 July 1963.
    There were also changes in membership on the Auxiliary Board for the Western Hemisphere. Marc Towers replaced William DeForge, and Hooper Dunbar replaced Masoud Khamsi, who was moved to Persia. Fred Graham replaced Rowland Estall for protection.
3   'Hand' was often used as a brief way of referring to a Hand of the Cause. For the Guardian's expressed wish to have a Hand of the Cause in South America, please see Gayle's pilgrim notes in Chapter 14.
4   USBNA, Gayle Woolson Papers. Both the letter from Mr Faizi and the letter from the Hands in the Holy Land are with her papers.
5   Hornby, *Heroes of God*, p. 166.
6   When used in quotations, terminology of the time is left intact, though modern reference would speak of indigenous people rather than 'Indians'.
7   USBNA, Gayle Woolson Papers, transcript by Gayle Woolson from a tape recording giving 'Highlights of the Talk of Hand of the Cause, Amatu'l-Bahá, Rúhíyyíh Khanum, at the Náw-Rúz Celebration in Quito, Ecuador, March 20, 1968'.
8   Hornby, *Heroes of God,* pp. 167–9, quoting a report to the Universal House of Justice.
9   ibid. p. 170.
10 Cassette tape of interview of Gayle Woolson by Janet Marks in Wilmette, Illinois. Copy given to the author.
11 USBNA, Gayle Woolson Papers, letter from Quentin and Jeanne Ferrand, 7 November 1986.

12 ibid., translation of an item from the Bulletin of the NSA of El Salvador, 27 September 1998.

19. In the Shadow of the Shrines

1 USBNA, Gayle Woolson Papers, copy of letter dated 7 November 1970.
2 USBNA, Gayle Woolson Papers, telegram from NSA of Spain to LSAs of Spain giving itinerary and summary biography.
3 USBNA, Gayle Woolson Papers.
4 USBNA, Gayle Woolson Papers, letter from the Universal House of Justice to Mrs Gayle Woolson, 24 September 1975.

20. Reflections on a Weaving Partway Done

1 USBNA, Gayle Woolson Papers.
2 Quotation included just after the title page of *The Divine Symphony*, quoted from *Abdu'l-Baha on Divine Philosophy*, pp. 77–8.

21. Seeing Both Sides of the Coin

1 Gayle preserved a notice of change of address from 1229 East Third St., Casper, WY 82601 to c/o 1532 West Minnehaha Avenue, St Paul, MN 55104.
2 USBNA, Gayle Woolson Papers.
3 Letter from the Universal House of Justice to all National Spiritual Assemblies, 6 February 1973, in *Messages from the Universal House of Justice 1963–1986*, no. 126, pp. 231–6.
4 In the process of documenting her own and others' service upon her return to the United States, Gayle reread all her Bahá'í books, underlining in red passages that either seem to have been particularly meaningful and/or related specifically to her path of service.
5 Rabbani, *Prescription for Living*. pp. 89–90.

22. '. . . speak forth with wisdom and eloquence'

1 Bahá'u'lláh, Tablet of the Proof: 'O ye loved ones of God! Drink your fill from the wellspring of wisdom, and walk ye in the garden of wisdom, and soar ye in the atmosphere

of wisdom, and speak forth with wisdom and eloquence. Thus biddeth you your Lord, the Almighty, the All-Knowing' (*Tablets of Bahá'u'lláh Revealed After the Kitáb-i-Aqdas*, p. 213).

2 'Abdu'l-Bahá, *Selections from the Writings of 'Abdu'l-Bahá*, no. 108, p. 134.

3 ibid. no. 110, p. 136.

4 ibid. no. 106, p. 133.

5 Bahá'u'lláh, *Tablets of Bahá'u'lláh Revealed After the Kitáb-i-Aqdas*, p. 200.

6 Letter on behalf of Shoghi Effendi, 19 October 1932, in *The Compilation of Compilations*, no. 466, p. 217.

7 USBNA, Gayle Woolson Papers.

8 ibid.

9 ibid.

10 ibid.

11 ibid.

12 ibid.

13 ibid.

23. Desire of the Nations

1 Message from the Universal House of Justice to the Bahá'is of the World, Riḍván 1992, in *A Wider Horizon*, p. 105.

2 USBNA, Gayle Woolson Papers.

24. 'Oneness with this Infinite Life'

1 See Chapter 7.

2 Trine, *In Tune with the Infinite,* p. 21.

3 In hospice care, it is proper practice to allow patients to reduce their intake naturally as the system becomes unable to process fluids and food. This was Gayle's conscious choice and request.

25. Tributes and a Loving Farewell

1 Shoghi Effendi, in *Bahá'í News*, no. 13 (September 1926), p. 1; quoted in many compilations of Bahá'í writings.

Index

About the Author

As a college student, Juliet Gentzkow learned of the Bahá'í Faith. Its teachings became the guiding light and primary motivating factor in her life. Following undergraduate studies in comparative religion and history of art, she completed master's degrees in both education and social work. For thirteen years, she ran a primary school inspired by Bahá'í teachings. Since then, she has worked with students of all ages. After several years of service in Guyana and then in Haiti, she returned to the United States and concentrated on clinical social work. This included coordination of a grassroots project of family empowerment; counselling with individuals and families in hospice and bereavement; and finally a private practice concentrating on fostering resilience during chronic illness and other major life transitions. Turning now to biographical writing, she continues the search to understand how purpose and vision shape motivation in ways that enable individuals to create destinies that far transcend the boundaries of their early lives.